# ROADS, RAILS
# & WATERWAYS

*The Army Engineers
and Early Transportation*

# ROADS, RAILS & WATERWAYS

## The Army Engineers and Early Transportation

## BY FOREST G. HILL

Norman : University of Oklahoma Press

*Library of Congress Catalog Card Number*: 57–11195

Copyright 1957 by the University of Oklahoma Press,
Publishing Division of the University.
Composed and printed at Norman, Oklahoma, U.S.A.,
by the University of Oklahoma Press.
First edition.

# TO HELEN

# *Preface*

THE WESTWARD EXPANSION of the United States, initiated by traders, explorers, pioneer settlers, and, not least of all, by the military, progressed with amazing rapidity in the early years of the nineteenth century.

From the perspective of the twentieth, however, it becomes quite clear that the consolidation of national interest in the West might have been delayed by at least a generation without an early assault on transportation, which was of prime importance then, as it is today, in the settlement and economic exploitation of a vast region.

The work of one agency of the federal government began very early to provide the bases for the required transportation and did it with a service that could have been supplied at the time from no private source—engineering skill. It was the Corps of Engineers, founded for quite different pursuits, namely military defense, that filled this need. These engineers were trained at the United States Military Academy at West Point, long the only school in America offering instruction in this desperately needed technical skill. Applying their knowledge to such projects as road, canal, and railroad surveying, river and harbor improvement, development of technical education, and exploration of the West, these engineers earned a prominent place in the history of American transportation and in the nation's early economic development. In the pages that follow, I have attempted to tell the story of the Army Engineers during a critical period in our history, the half-century between the War of 1812 and the Civil War, when the continental proportions of United States national development were to be asserted.

Professors Carter Goodrich and Joseph Dorfman of Columbia University provided great assistance in my preparation of this work. My research in the National Archives was facilitated by the aid of Miss Elizabeth B. Drewry and Mr. Raymond P. Flynn. At the Office of the Chief of Engineers, I received the kind assistance of Mr. T. S. Bland, Mr. Raleigh B. Buzzaird, Mr. Logan O. Cowgill, and Mr. Harold Kelso. At the publication stage, I was generously assisted by the Bureau of Business and Economic Research at the University of California, and by Professors Frank L. Kidner, Melvin M. Knight, and Paul S. Taylor of that university. My wife's constant help has always been indispensable.

Forest G. Hill

*Berkeley, California*
*April 10, 1957*

# Contents

# *Illustrations*

# ROADS, RAILS & WATERWAYS

## The Army Engineers and Early Transportation

# I: Origins and Early Activities

EVEN BEFORE Horace Greeley gave young men his famous formula for success, the West was fast becoming the magic land of opportunity and adventure in the minds and hearts of young America. The end of the American Revolution saw a fringe of settlement stretched along the Atlantic Coast, with thin strings extended into the backcountry along the great river valleys, and isolated knots of population scattered beyond the mountains in the interior. People were moving steadily, but slowly, westward until the War of 1812, which brought a temporary halt, awoke throughout the country a general feeling of national unity that touched off the first faint glimmering of "Manifest Destiny."

The people were challenged by the vast areas of untouched land lying to the west and were eager to set about the task of exploitation and development. But of what use were vast area, uncounted wealth of resources, and eager markets if there was no way to reach the area and develop the resources, no way to serve the markets? The immediate and pressing need was for adequate transportation facilities—all-weather roads, snag-free rivers, protected harbors, deep canals, and, finally—railroads! But in the first two decades of the nineteenth century it became evident that the transportation facilities of the nation were not being adequately developed. The lack of such improvements was a barrier to political unification, commercial expansion, and military defense. Without government intervention, national development would be obstructed; with proper guidance by the government, it could be accelerated along desired lines. This recognition brought

3

an increasing demand for government planning and execution of transportation improvements.

Of the so-called factors of production needed by early transportation enterprises, labor, capital funds, and entrepreneurial initiative were relatively more plentiful than engineering ability. The government found it advisable to make engineering skill available to meet the needs of the nation; and it came to bear a large share of the social cost of developing the engineering technology of the country. The factor which railroads most needed was that which the government was most able and willing to provide. After examining American transportation improvements in the early 1830's, Michel Chavalier was referring particularly to railroads when he stated: "The greatest difficulty which the Americans encountered in the execution of their public works, was not to procure the necessary capital, but to find men capable of directing operations. . . . To supply the want of men of science, demanded by the spirit of enterprise, the Federal government authorized the officers of the engineer corps and of the topographical engineers to enter into the services of the companies."[1]

The purpose of this account is to relate the story of that invaluable contribution made by the army engineers in the opening of the West and the conquering of a continent.

By the time the General Survey Act was passed in 1824, the Engineering Department was recognized as the appropriate federal agency for promoting internal improvements. The historical preparation of the army engineers for this work must be examined. Their inheritance of a major role in the movement for internal improvements may be explained in terms of the origin and growth of the military engineers, the development of the United States Military Academy, and the early civil functions of the military engineers.

Although the present Corps of Engineers has existed only

[1] *Society, Manners and Politics in the United States*, 272, 274.

since 1802, military engineers served in the Continental Army during the American Revolution. General Washington raised and equipped a corps of engineers. The Continental Congress formally established this corps in 1779 but disbanded it four years later. Since professional engineers were lacking in America, they were sought in Europe. Benjamin Franklin secured several prominent officers of the Royal Corps of Engineers in France.

By 1794 the government's concern over its relations with European powers prompted it to adopt measures for improving its meager coastal defenses. In that year Congress made an appropriation to fortify certain places along the seaboard, and several French engineers were employed under contract to carry on this work. Congress also established the Corps of Artillerists and Engineers to develop a system of seacoast fortifications. In 1798 this mixed corps was increased in size.[2]

An act of March 16, 1802, created the present Corps of Engineers and directed that it be stationed at West Point and constitute a military academy. The new Corps of Engineers devoted its attention almost solely to coastal defenses and its military school prior to the War of 1812. Nearly one million dollars had been spent on fortifications by 1805, but the work increased so rapidly that more than this amount was spent in the year 1808 alone. In 1811 these defenses included twenty-four forts and thirty-two enclosed batteries and masonry works. With the coming of hostilities the following year, the

[2] For the history of the Corps of Engineers before 1802, see Henry L. Abbot, "The Corps of Engineers," *Journal of the Military Service Institution,* Vol. XV (1894), 414; Francis B. Heitman, *Historical Register and Dictionary of the United States Army,* 42–43; W. Stull Holt, *The Office of the Chief of Engineers of the Army,* 1–2; A. A. Humphreys, "Historical Sketch of the Corps of Engineers," 45 Cong., 3 sess., S. *Rept.* 555, 329–30; L. D. Ingersoll, *A History of the War Department of the United States,* 31–32, 264–65; Oliver L. Spaulding, *The United States Army in War and Peace,* 69–70; Raphael P. Thian, *Legislative History of the General Staff of the Army of the United States from 1775 to 1901,* 483–84; and Emory Upton, *The Military Policy of the United States,* 85–87.

Corps of Engineers was increased in size by act of Congress.[3]

The War of 1812 multiplied the demand for coastal defenses. This concern with harbor fortifications was evident in a letter from General Joseph G. Swift, chief engineer, to the Secretary of War on March 21, 1815. Swift reported that after having conferred with James Monroe he had arranged "to send Officers of Engineers to the various important Ports and Harbours between Maine and New Orleans, for the purpose of inspecting and reporting fully upon the present state of Fortifications; and to select, if requisite, judicious sites for new works to protect the principal positions on the sea board and the avenues to them."[4]

Congress and the administration decided to employ a foreign engineer to aid in planning an adequate system of fortifications. A joint resolution of Congress on April 29, 1816, authorized the President to employ a "skillful assistant" for the Corps of Engineers. Upon the recommendation of General Lafayette and Albert Gallatin, American minister to France, the government selected General Simon Bernard, one of Napoleon's best engineers. On November 16, 1816, Madison signed Bernard's commission attaching him to the Corps of Engineers as assistant engineer with the rank of brigadier general.

On the day of Bernard's appointment, the War Department established the Board of Engineers for Fortifications to consist of three officers of the Corps of Engineers and one naval officer. General Bernard, Colonel William McRee, and Lieutenant Colonel Joseph G. Totten were made members. The duties of this board were to select sites and make plans for fortifications. By creating this board the government hoped to

[3] For the growth of this corps from 1802 through the War of 1812, see Abbot, "Corps of Engineers," 2–3; Ingersoll, *War Department*, 29–31, 265–67; and Spaulding, *U. S. Army*, 122.

[4] Engineer Department, Miscellaneous Letters Sent, I, 5–6. (Engineer Department is hereafter abbreviated E.D.)

place Bernard in an influential position without great opposition and conveniently utilize his services without giving him direct command over American military personnel. The board, however, became a permanent part of the Engineer Department of the army.

Objections were nevertheless raised to Bernard's employment. General Swift insisted that the proper place for foreign engineers was as professors at West Point. He stated that army engineers disapproved of the Secretary of War's order of May 8, 1816, suspending all new fortifications until Bernard's arrival from France.[5] Swift was ordered to West Point to supervise the operation of the Military Academy. This action prevented his being able as chief engineer to direct the activities of the Board of Engineers for Fortifications. In January, 1817, Swift persuaded President Madison to relieve him from duty at West Point so that he could supervise the board's operations. President Monroe later assured Swift that he was the board's official head and that Bernard would not exercise command. Since Secretary of War Calhoun often approved Bernard's rather than Swift's plans for fortifications, Swift was irritated by the growth of "an idea that General Bernard had a transcendent genius, and therefore . . . must be consulted upon all public works."[6] Swift resigned in November, 1818;

[5] Swift informed the Secretary of War that "The construction which I am compelled to give the directions for postponement involves disgrace to the Corps of Engineers. Those directions convey the humiliating idea that the Government do not repose sufficient confidence in the talents of the Corps of Engineers to persevere in their plans without the advice of a Foreign Engineer. It is humiliating to find the Corps of Engineers standing thus low in the estimation of the Government who educated and formed it from Native Americans with an express view of avoiding all future recourse to Foreign Military Engineers. A recourse to Foreign Engineers will in my opinion destroy the emulation of the American Corps and finally ruin it." (May 21, 1816, E. D., Misc. Letters Sent, I, 11–12.)

[6] Joseph Gardner Swift, *Memoirs,* 149. For further discussion of relations between Swift and Bernard, see George W. Cullum, *Biographical Sketch of Brigadier-General Joseph G. Swift,* 15–19.

and Colonel McRee, a board member, did the same a year later.

Lieutenant Colonel Totten, a board member and later chief engineer, tended to agree with Swift regarding Bernard's services. Totten wrote Swift in June, 1816, objecting to the placing of a foreign engineer in a position involving knowledge and control of military defense plans. The only proper employment for Bernard was as a professor of military engineering at West Point or as a "practical engineer of roads and canals." Totten predicted, "It can hardly be supposed that this man Bernard can decide in his closet on the fitness of projects to the ground. What journeyings to-and-fro the poor man will have to encounter!"

Totten soon found himself accompanying Bernard on these travels with the Board of Engineers for Fortifications. He felt that the government had acted wisely in creating this board, with Bernard as a member. Bernard had the novel but perhaps satisfactory position of being in the minority and having no command, but of being able to make minority reports and apply his skills. Totten preferred not to be on the board, since he considered this duty exceedingly complex and open to misunderstanding. Although General Bernard did not resign until 1831, Totten felt in 1823 that Bernard's assistance was no longer required. In a private letter to Secretary of War Calhoun, Totten argued that continued employment of the General produced great harm, for he was receiving credit for what the army engineers were accomplishing.[7]

The operations of the Board of Engineers for Fortifications were extensive and important. With the aid of several topographical engineers, it examined the seacoast, approved sites and plans for fortifications, and made frequent reports. Although its activities were primarily along the Atlantic Coast,

[7] (Totten's) Official Letters, I, 1816, 13–16, 81–83; 1817, 11–14, 31–34; 1823, 71–76.

they also extended to Lakes Champlain and Erie, the Ohio and Mississippi rivers, and the Gulf of Mexico.[8]

This board adopted systematic procedures for planning fortifications. It secured many surveys and much topographical data for use in locating and projecting defense works. It distinguished between fortifications in progress and "works remaining to be commenced, according to the plans of the Board of Engineers." It divided the latter into three classes based on "the order of their efficiency to meet the earliest probable emergency."[9] This classification of proposed defense works in terms of their estimated importance became a routine practice in the Engineer Department.

The planning of a scheme of national defense was somewhat comprehensive in another respect. There was a clear recognition that the necessary means of defending the seacoast constituted a general system, including the navy, fortifications, interior communications by land and water, the regular army, and a well organized militia. Inland communications were necessary to expand domestic trade, supply the army and navy, and concentrate troops at points of attack. Commerce, military defense, and inland transportation were closely allied, especially at the great estuaries and harbors where land and water communications met. These facts were emphasized in 1819 by Secretary of War Calhoun in his "Report on Roads and Canals" and in 1821 by General Bernard and Colonel Tot-

[8] The work of Gen. Bernard and the board is discussed in Buell's memorandum (April 21, 1906) on "Service of General Simon Bernard in the United States Army," E.D., Doc. File 1894–1923, Box 1209, File 50734–61; Major Edward Burr, "Memoranda relating to Brevet Brigadier General Simon Bernard, Assistant in the Corps of Engineers, U.S.A., 1816–31" (Sept. 17, 1906), *ibid.,* File 50734–72; and Annual Reports of the Chief Engineer.

[9] Annual Report of the Chief Engineer, Nov. 14, 1822, *American State Papers, Military Affairs,* II, 459. (Henceforth, references to this printed source will be abbreviated *ASP, MA;* and Annual Report and Chief Engineer will appear as A.R. and C/E.) Cf. "Report of the Board of Engineers on the Defence of the Seaboard," Feb. 7, 1821, *ASP, MA,* II, 308, 310–11.

ten in their "Report of the Board of Engineers on the Defence of the Seaboard."[10]

Like the Corps of Engineers, the topographical engineers had small beginnings during the American Revolution. As early as July 25, 1777, a "geographer and surveyor of the roads" was authorized. Robert Erskine was made geographer for the Continental Army in 1777, Simeon DeWitt in 1780, and Thomas Hutchins in 1781.[11] Topographical engineers were not officially used again, however, until the War of 1812. In an act of March 3, 1813, their function was specifically provided for, and eight topographical engineers and eight assistants were commissioned. At the end of the war all except two of these engineers had been mustered out. Majors John Anderson and Isaac Roberdeau were retained to complete surveys along the northern frontier. In a memoir to Secretary of War Crawford, they declared that the nation needed a corps of topographical engineers to explore and map the country, collect topographical information, and make surveys of the coastal and inland frontiers and for military and civil works.[12]

An act of April 24, 1816, provided for topographical engineers with the army general staff. They were placed under the Board of Engineers for Fortifications to make surveys for a system of coastal defenses. In 1818, Secretary of War Calhoun placed them in the newly created Topographical Bureau in the Engineer Department. Major Roberdeau was put in charge of this bureau, whose chief function was to preserve data secured by its engineers. These engineers, ten in number, remained with the Board of Engineers for Fortifications, although by 1824 their operations included civil as well as military works, as is seen later in this chapter.[13]

[10] *ASP, MA*, II, 304–13.
[11] Thian, *General Staff*, 483–84.
[12] Memoir of Anderson and Roberdeau, Jan. 15, 1816, E.D., Bulky File, No. 207.

By the time Calhoun became secretary of war under President Monroe, the Engineer Department included the Corps of Engineers, topographical engineers, and Military Academy. All these engineering functions were controlled by the chief engineer, who reported directly to the secretary of war.

The Military Academy, like the Corps of Engineers and topographical engineers, had its roots in the American Revolution. Although it was not created by Congress until 1802, military schools had operated intermittently at West Point during the previous quarter of a century. In 1777, the Continental Congress provided for a Corps of Invalids "to serve as a military school for young gentlemen previous to their being appointed to marching regiments." This corps of veterans provided for disabled officers and soldiers while functioning as a school of application. In 1778 part of the corps was stationed at West Point, but it also conducted an academy in New Jersey. The entire corps was at West Point by 1782, where it had a military engineering school, laboratory, and library. As early as the Revolutionary War an engineering school was thus in operation at West Point.

Soon after the Revolution many prominent figures advocated a national military academy. Among these were George Washington, Alexander Hamilton, Henry Knox, Benjamin Lincoln, Timothy Pickering, and General du Portail, the French engineer who was wartime chief engineer. A military school was started at West Point in 1794, the year in which the government commenced work on coastal defenses. The law cre-

13 In 1831 the Topographical Bureau was made an independent office in the War Department, and in 1838 Congress established the enlarged Corps of Topographical Engineers. This corps continued as a separate part of the War Department until 1863, when Congress merged it into the Corps of Engineers. Details of the early history of the topographical engineers may be found in Abbot, "Corps of Engineers," 414–15; Henry P. Beers, "A History of the U. S. Topographical Engineers, 1813–63," *The Military Engineer,* Vol. XXXIV (1942), 287–89, 352; Heitman, *Historical Register,* 43; Holt, *Chief of Engineers,* 3; Ingersoll, *War Department,* 281; and Thian, *General Staff,* 483–84.

ating the Corps of Artillerists and Engineers introduced the grade of cadet. The school was open to artillery and engineer officers or cadets and was supervised by Colonel Rochefontaine, another French engineer who was then commandant of the corps. This school was suspended in 1796, when fire destroyed its buildings, books, and equipment.[14]

Such leading officials as Secretaries of War James McHenry and Henry Dearborn and Presidents Adams and Jefferson promptly urged the founding of a military school. A school was again started at West Point, in 1801, by the Corps of Artillerists and Engineers. Its revival was due to the insistence of Jefferson, whose earlier opposition to a military academy had given way to active support. Several engineering and artillery cadets were called to the school; and courses in mathematics, artillery, and engineering were offered by four officers and a civilian. The school as begun in 1801 was small and ineffective.[15]

An act of March 16, 1802, created the Corps of Engineers as a separate service and directed that it be stationed at West Point and "constitute" a military academy. The law, which authorized five engineer officers and ten cadets, indicated that the Corps of Engineers itself was to serve as a military school. This law also provided that the secretary of war procure the necessary books and equipment for the school and that the chief engineer act as its superintendent.[16] The Military Academy was thus instituted to train engineers, a step prompted by the almost complete absence of military and civil engineers in America. Engineering and related subjects were

[14] *The Centennial of the United States Military Academy at West Point, New York, 1802–1902,* I, 1–2, 203–207, 212–14; Humphreys, "Historical Sketch," 329–30.

[15] Gen. Alexander Macomb to Secretary of War Calhoun, March 30, 1822, E.D., Misc. Letters Sent, I, 248; William A. Ganoe, *The History of the United States Army,* 109; Swift, *Memoirs,* 25–26, 34. (Secretary of war is hereafter abbreviated S/W.)

[16] Edward C. Boynton, *History of West Point . . . ,* 207–208.

taught at West Point in a period when there were no other schools of technology or engineering in the nation.[17]

For a decade after 1802, West Point was a military academy more in name than in fact. The number of its officers and cadets was exceedingly small, standards of admission were low, and attendance was irregular. Courses were short, and there were few textbooks in English and few teachers available. In its first ten years, West Point produced only seventy-one graduates, who received only one or two years of irregular instruction. Cadets and instructors frequently resigned or were ordered away to construct coastal defenses. Even though it was introducing in America an early limited curriculum in mathematics, engineering, and the sciences, the Military Academy was as yet contributing little to the material advance of the nation.[18]

[17] That the desired object was an engineering school rather than a strictly military one is suggested in a history of the Military Academy: "In the systematic teaching of the sciences to qualify students for the engineering profession West Point led the way during the first half century of its existence. When the Military Academy was founded . . . our people hesitated at expenditures for purely military purposes, and proposed to employ their officers in time of peace in various useful undertakings. In the beginning, through the personal efforts of President Jefferson, who was 'no great lover of military affairs, but a warm friend of science,' such a teacher as Jared Mansfield was secured, and we know that Mr. Jefferson, when he signed the act establishing the Military Academy, contemplated an institution which would supply the country with engineers for civil as well as military purposes, an institution which would serve as a model for training in the practical sciences." (*Centennial*, I, 835.) See also Gilbert A. Youngberg, "The Civil Activities of the Corps of Engineers," *The Military Engineer*, Vol. XIII (1921), 73–74; F. W. Alstaetter, "The Ohio River," *Professional Memoirs*, Vol. II (1910), 35; J. M. Dickinson, "The Army Engineer and River Improvement," *ibid.*, 77; and Richard S. Kirby, "Some Early American Civil Engineers and Surveyors," Connecticut Society of Civil Engineers, *Papers and Transactions*, XLVI (1930), 27.

[18] Lt. Col. John J. Abert, letter of Jan. 3, 1850, Topographical Bureau, Letters Issued, XII, 155–57; *Centennial*, I, 875–77; George W. Cullum, *Biographical Register of the Officers and Graduates of the U. S. Military Academy*, I, containing a brief biography of each graduate; Ganoe, *Hist. of U. S. Army*, 109; Kirby, "Engineers and Surveyors," 27; Swift, *Memoirs*, 25, 36. (Topographical Bureau is hereafter abbreviated T.B.)

Acts in 1803 and 1808 authorized cadets for artillery, infantry, cavalry, and riflemen. No provision was made to train them at West Point, and few cadet appointments were made. The number of engineering cadets was increased in 1808. In 1812, Congress reorganized the Military Academy, fixed at 250 the maximum number of cadets, and provided that cadets from other services might be sent to West Point. Professorships were authorized in natural and experimental philosophy, mathematics, and "the art of engineering in all its branches." Each professor was allowed an assistant professor, and $25,000 was appropriated for new buildings, a library, and instruments for the school.[19]

The training of cadets was greatly expanded during the War of 1812, but the maximum number of cadets allowed at West Point was not reduced when the army was returned to a peacetime basis. The war thus produced a permanently enlarged Military Academy whose graduates could be commissioned in all branches of the army. The adjustment of the Military Academy to national needs in the decade after the War of 1812 is of focal interest.

The enlarged role of West Point began to take shape rapidly from 1815 onward. In that year President Madison and Secretary of War Monroe decided to send two American engineers to Europe to study the French military establishments. Two brilliant young officers, Colonel William McRee and Major Sylvanus Thayer, were selected for this mission. Monroe provided them with letters of introduction to such figures as Lafayette and Gallatin, American minister to France. In one letter Monroe introduced them as two distinguished officers who "visit France to push researches and improve their knowledge in their profession. The fortifications and schools of France will open to them mines of great wealth in this respect, which they are solicitous to explore and profit of."[20]

[19] Boynton, *West Point*, 209–11; *Centennial*, I, 211.

McRee and Thayer inspected French fortifications, military schools, and military workshops; and they also collected books, maps, and instruments for the Military Academy.

For the last purpose several thousand dollars were made available, with which they bought almost one thousand books and many maps. While studying the operation of the famous École Polytechnique, these American engineers met two noted Polytechnique men. One was Simon Bernard, who was soon serving with McRee on the Board of Engineers for Fortifications. The other was Claude Crozet, who was before long teaching engineering under Thayer at West Point. Thayer personally recommended Crozet for a professorship when the latter emigrated from France in 1816.[21]

Soon after his return from Europe, Thayer was made superintendent of the Military Academy by President Monroe. The date July 17, 1817, on which Thayer took charge of West Point, marked a turning point in its development. Until that time General Swift had taken little interest in the welfare of the school and had practiced favoritism in appointing cadets.[22]

With the support of President Monroe and Secretary of War Calhoun, Thayer effected rapid improvement of the Academy. Thayer's major innovations—largely patterned after the École Polytechnique—were the institution of the four-year system and regular terms of work, organization of the faculty into an academic board, annual examination of the Academy

[20] R. Ernest Dupuy, *Where They Have Trod: The West Point Tradition in American Life*, 81.

[21] Gen. Swift, C/E, to S/W, E.D., Misc. Letters Sent, I, 8; Dupuy, *Where They Have Trod*, 92–93, 97; Boynton, *West Point*, 219.

[22] Swift stated in 1824 that "From an early day I had advocated sending the sons of the most talented men in the country to that institution, as a better plan than selection by congressional districts, that was beginning to have sway at Washington." (Swift, *Memoirs*, 197.) A "Federalist of the Washington school," Swift later declared that he had always used his official position to promote "young men of merit" in the public service. (Charles B. Stuart, *Lives and Works of Civil and Military Engineers of America*, 140. See also Swift, *op. cit.*, 135.)

by an outside Board of Visitors, ranking of cadets according to scholarship, use of the ablest cadets as assistant professors, instruction by the section-room method, extensive use of the blackboard in teaching, greater emphasis on mathematics and engineering, teaching of French, and use of textbooks from France. His improvements resulted in greater scholastic competition, more individualized instruction, and a greatly improved curriculum which made the Military Academy the first engineering and technical school in the nation.[23]

Thayer's insistence on the importance of the French language was significant. He felt that this language was the "sole repository of military science."[24] French was taught at West Point as an essential language; many texts were in French, and several professors were Frenchmen. In the first few years under Thayer, instruction in engineering, French language, and drawing was conducted by Frenchmen. Textbooks in Crozet's engineering courses were studied in the original French. Crozet was at West Point from 1816 to 1823, when he became chief engineer of the state of Virginia. He introduced descriptive geometry and gave a rigorous course in military engineering. In the beginning he taught a few cadets who understood French, and they in turn became the instructors of others.[25]

The greatest advance of the Thayer regime was in the improvement of curriculum. Most important were the gains made in mathematics and engineering. The emphasis of instruction at the Military Academy was indicated by the weights given various subjects in 1820 by the academic board

[23] Boynton, *West Point*, 217–18; *Centennial*, I, 875; Dupuy, *Where They Have Trod*, 137–44, 160–62; Ganoe, *Hist. of U. S. Army*, 151, 163–64; Dirk J. Struik, *Yankee Science in the Making*, 244–45.

[24] Dupuy, *Where They Have Trod*, 138.

[25] Dixon Ryan Fox, "Civilization in Transit," *The American Historical Review*, Vol. XXXII (1927), 757; Roswell Park, *A Sketch of the History and Topography of West Point and the U. S. Military Academy*, 69–70; Dupuy, *Where They Have Trod*, 161; Struik, *Yankee Science*, 245.

in establishing their relative value in the military curriculum. Two points each were given to engineering, natural philosophy, and mathematics; one point was given to drawing and one-half point to French; and three points were distributed among a variety of other subjects.[26] A military historian has stated that by the 1820's "West Point was firmly established as the initial scientific school in the United States."[27]

It may well be asked how the cultivation of technical education by the Military Academy was related to the role of the army engineers in the movement for internal improvements. Both Federalist and Republican leaders favored establishment of this school. In the period before 1824, Presidents Jefferson, Madison, and Monroe consistently supported the progress of West Point. They realized that improved education and transportation were interrelated aspects of public improvement, and they commonly coupled their proposal of a national system of internal improvements with the advocacy of a national university.

Recognizing the need to advance science, Jefferson felt that patriotic Americans paying an import duty on foreign luxuries "would certainly prefer its continuance and application to the great purposes of the public education, roads, rivers, canals, and such other objects of public improvement as it may be thought proper to add to the constitutional enumeration of federal powers. . . . Education is here placed among the articles of public care, not that it would be proposed to take its ordinary branches out of the hands of private enterprise, which manages so much better all the concerns to which it is equal; but a public institution can alone supply those sciences

---

[26] *Centennial,* I, 231–32.

[27] Dupuy, *Where They Have Trod,* 182. Cf. Sidney Forman, "The First School of Engineering," *The Military Engineer,* Vol. XLIV (1952), 109–12. In this section the development of West Point is traced only to 1824. See Chapter V for an analysis of West Point's later contribution to railroading and Chapter VIII for an analysis of its advancement of technical education.

which, though rarely called for, are yet necessary to complete the circle, all the parts of which contribute to the improvement of the country, and some of them to its preservation."[28] Fearing that the public was more interested in federal action for roads and canals than for education, he urged that they be advanced with equal pace. Soon after Gallatin made his "Report on Roads and Canals," Jefferson proposed that the surplus revenue be used to improve "roads, canals, rivers, education, and other great foundations of prosperity and union," even if the Constitution had to be amended.[29]

When the War of 1812 ended, Madison informed Congress of the country's great need for a national seminary of learning and for roads and canals to be executed under federal authority. His last annual message to Congress reiterated the importance of establishing a national university and a comprehensive system of roads and canals.[30]

Monroe also asked that the federal government be given the constitutional power to construct seminaries of learning as well as roads and canals.[31] During his administration it was clearly recognized that national defense, inland transportation, and technical education were interdependent. Much at-

[28] Annual Message, Dec. 2, 1806, *The Writings of Thomas Jefferson,* edited by Paul L. Ford, VIII (1897), 494.

[29] Jefferson to Joel Barlow, Dec. 10, 1807, *ibid.,* IX (1898), 169; Annual Message, Nov. 8, 1808, *ibid.,* IX (1898), 224. Jefferson wrote Du Pont de Nemours in 1811 that the surplus should be used to discharge the public debt and build schools, roads, and canals so that "the farmer will see his government supported, his children educated, and the face of his country made a paradise by the contributions of the rich alone." (*Ibid.,* IX [1898], 321–22.)

[30] Annual Messages, Dec. 5, 1815 and Dec. 3, 1816, *The Writings of James Madison,* edited by Gaillard Hunt, VIII (1908), 342, 379–80. A military historian remarks that before the War of 1812 Madison recognized the importance of "military seminaries," that after the war he urged enlargement of the Military Academy and establishment of other military schools, and that in 1815 as well as afterwards bills for creating additional military academies were introduced in Congress. (Boynton, *West Point,* 198–200.)

[31] Annual Message, Dec. 2, 1817, *The Writings of James Monroe,* edited by Stanislaus M. Hamilton, VI, 40–43.

tention was thus given to fortifications, internal improvements, and the Military Academy. Thayer, who transformed West Point into a technical school, was Monroe's choice for its superintendent; and Calhoun, at this time a great supporter of the army engineers and internal improvements,[32] was his secretary of war. Arguments of the military necessity of technical education and improved transportation were used to secure federal action in these areas.

In 1819, Calhoun advocated an additional military academy. Although West Point annually graduated as many cadets as the army had vacancies, he felt that there should be an additional military academy and a school of practice. The latter could be inexpensively operated by engineer and artillery officers.[33] In 1820, he proposed that West Point be transferred from the Corps of Engineers to the army at large and that a separate school of application and practice be established to cultivate the higher branches of science essential to artillery and engineering. He feared that the nation would neglect military science: "It has become so complicated and extensive as to require for its acquisition extensive means, and much time to be exclusively devoted to it. It can only flourish under the patronage of Government, and without such patronage it must be almost wholly neglected." To overcome this neglect would be both inexpensive and beneficial, for "officers would be trained who would be masters of every branch of knowledge connected with their profession, and who, by their science, would be not only highly useful, but an ornament to their country."[34]

[32] In later years Calhoun was a strong states-rights advocate and opponent of federal internal improvements.

[33] "Letter in Relation to an Additional Military Academy," Jan. 15, 1819, *The Works of John C. Calhoun*, edited by Richard K. Cralle, V, 54–57. General Bernard and Colonel McRee of the Board of Engineers for Fortifications agreed that an adequate system of military education required a school of application and a second basic school similar to West Point. (*ASP, MA*, I, 834–36.)

[34] "Report on the Military Academy at West Point," Feb. 23, 1820, Calhoun, *Works*, V, 79.

The Military Academy undoubtedly benefited from these cumulative demands for federal encouragement of education and military science. It grew rapidly and had to suffice as the only national seminary of learning. West Point became, in effect, a national technical school, and it profited from the continued desire for such an institution. In 1822, President Monroe spoke approvingly of the progress of the Military Academy, at which "the youth are well instructed in every science connected with the great objects of the Institution." Two years later he stated that it was essential to the army and had attained "a high degree of perfection."[35]

Critics of the Military Academy also recognized its evolving role in public improvement. In 1822, the House Committee on Military Affairs objected to the high rate of resignations among cadets, declaring that too few entering cadets became army officers and that half of them left West Point after two years. The committee concluded that "many young men have been sent to the academy for the purpose of receiving a general education, without the intention of engaging in military service. . . ."[36] A critical report on the Military Academy by a House select committee declared in 1837 that the Military Academy had assumed a new and different purpose between

[35] Annual Messages, Dec. 3, 1822, 17 Cong., 1 sess., S. Doc. 1, 6, and Dec. 7, 1824, 18 Cong., 2 sess., S. Doc. 1, 10.

[36] "Report on the Military Academy," March 4, 1822, ASP, MA, II, 349–50. One of these ambitious young men was John H. B. Latrobe, son of Benjamin H. Latrobe (1764–1820), noted architect and civil engineer. He entered West Point in 1818 and resigned while ranking at the head of his class in his senior year, upon the death of his father. He later became a lawyer for the Baltimore and Ohio Railroad. His father had been pleased with his cadet appointment, for it meant a free education with cadet pay under good disciplinary influence. Consequently, "as a preparatory education for a civil department of his preference, he cannot possible have a better. . . . In three years he is entitled to a Second Lieutenancy, and may then stay at West Point or be employed at some fortification. . . . He may then at twenty-one or twenty-two, if I live so long, take my place and continue as an architect or civil engineer." (Letter of Latrobe's father to Isaac Hazlehurst, March 9, 1817, John E. Semmes, *John H. B. Latrobe and His Times, 1803–1891*, 67–69.)

1816 and 1820. Before that time it had been strictly military and "republican" in purpose. Having been expanded by the War of 1812, it was never reduced afterwards. Instead, it started educating persons at public expense, in numbers far exceeding the needs of the public service, without any obligation that its graduates remain in public service.[37]

By 1824 the Military Academy had evolved into the nation's earliest school of technology and engineering. It functioned as part of the Engineer Department to educate military engineers and other army officers needing technical training. Its functions were conceived as intimately related to activities of public improvement in which its graduates were playing an increasingly active part.

It was perhaps inevitable that the army engineers—with their belief that interior communications were an integral part of national defense, their early leadership in engineering education, and their function as the sole engineering agency of the federal government—would give extensive aid to internal improvements. Their participation in civil activities did not become significant, however, until almost two decades after the Corps of Engineers and Military Academy were established in 1802. For the most part, the very limited amount of public improvement before the War of 1812 was made locally. River and harbor works, for instance, were executed by individual cities and states. In this period the Treasury Department had charge of the building of lighthouses and piers, the surveying of the coast, and the making of coastal charts.[38] It was Albert Gallatin who, as secretary of treasury, was called upon by Congress to make his "Report on Roads and Canals" in 1808.

Until this time the Corps of Engineers had been too small

[37] Report of a Select Committee to the House of Representatives, March 1, 1837, *ASP, MA*, VII, 1–18.
[38] Cf. *ASP, Commerce and Navigation*, I, *passim*.

and its officers too busy operating the Military Academy and constructing coastal defenses to permit them to engage in civil duties. In their work on harbor defenses, however, they surveyed estuaries and coastal rivers and were able to give valuable information to seamen and port officials. After the War of 1812, moreover, they were much better able to give such assistance; their number was larger, topographical engineers had been added to the Engineer Department, West Point was training more engineer officers, and General Bernard and the Board of Engineers for Fortifications were examining the coast, surveying harbors, and planning a system of coastal defenses.

With this increase in duties, the Chief Engineer in 1816 asked for more engineers. He explained that thirty officers were needed to inspect fortified places on the coast and that about ten were needed for each of these tasks: supervising the construction of fortifications, examining national frontiers, and surveying the coast. In addition, "should Canals or Bridges upon an extensive scale be commenced, it would be well to attach some, say six at least, Brevet Engineer Officers, to the Director, for the purpose of gaining practical knowledge in that branch of Engineering, thereby laying the foundation to employ Natives of the United States to take charge of the future construction of Canals."[39]

Majors Anderson and Roberdeau proposed a great increase in the number and duties of topographical engineers. Having completed an inspection of the northern frontier of the country, they insisted that these engineers would be useful in exploring, mapping, and collecting topographical data. This knowledge of the nation's resources, geographical features, routes of travel, and economic conditions would have great military and political value. If a corps of topographical engi-

[39] Jan. 8, 1816, E.D., Misc. Letters Sent, I, 9–10.

neers was formed, it could use statistical science in collecting vital information for future use.[40]

After the number of topographical engineers was increased in 1816, they made coastal surveys and also explorations in the interior. Major Stephen H. Long made a reconnaissance between the Ohio and Mississippi rivers and Lake Michigan, upon which he reported in 1817.[41] He paid particular attention to the possibilities of improving river navigation and projecting roads and canals. He described the Ohio, Mississippi, Illinois, and Chicago rivers as important channels of trade and communication.

Long recommended several canal and road routes, the chief of which was a canal to connect the Illinois River with Lake Michigan near Chicago. The Des Plaines River, which flowed into the Illinois and on into the Mississippi, was at one point only nine miles from the Chicago River, an arm of Lake Michigan. Between them was a lake about five miles long which was connected to each river by a washed-out trench or canal, enabling small boats to pass freely between these rivers, except in the dry season when a portage of about three miles was necessary. The mouth of the Chicago River was obstructed by a sand bar which could be removed to provide a good harbor.

Long's other canal proposals involved connections between the Illinois, Wabash, St. Joseph, and Maumee rivers and a canal to unite the Mississippi and Ohio above the obstructions near their junction. The federal government should reserve the right to construct roads while this area was still public domain. The Cumberland Road should be extended through Ohio, Indiana, and Illinois to the Mississippi so as to intercept rivers and permit branch roads along the way. Long concluded

[40] Memoir of John Anderson and Isaac Roberdeau, Jan. 15, 1816, E.D., Bulky File, No. 207.

[41] Report of Major Long to Acting S/W George Graham, March 4, 1817, Corps of Engineers, Reports, 1812–23, 158–65.

that this part of the country exceeded all others in opportunities and inducements for constructing a public system of
roads and canals.

Meanwhile, other topographical engineers were busy with
surveys relating to coastal defenses. In 1817, the Chief Engineer informed officials in North Carolina that no engineer
officer could be spared for surveying the sounds of that state
to obtain plans for improving their navigation "beyond what
may be involved in an examination for military purposes."[42]
A few weeks later the Chief Engineer informed President
Monroe that he and General Bernard would be able to inspect
the site where commissioners of the state of North Carolina
planned to improve the navigation of Albemarle Sound. Since
the proposed improvement was quite important, the engineers
would examine it after studying proposed fortifications on
Chesapeake Bay.[43]

The assistance which the Board of Engineers for Fortifications gave to local sponsors of improvement projects began
to increase at this time. The commissioners of the Albemarle
Sound improvement received additional aid in 1818. Calhoun
instructed General Swift to aid these North Carolina officials
by examining Albemarle Sound and "digesting a plan for the
improvement of its navigation."[44] A few months later Calhoun
approved Major Long's steamboat exploring plan. Long was
authorized to build a small steamboat for exploring the western and southwestern parts of the country.[45] Calhoun's "Report on Roads and Canals" in 1819, proposing that military
engineers survey and construct important roads and canals,

[42] May 6, 1817, E.D., Misc. Letters Sent, I, 20–21.
[43] May 22, 1817, ibid., I, 23–24.
[44] Jan. 6, 1818, E.D., Doc. File B, Misc. Letters, 1813–18, No. 42.
[45] Letter from Calhoun, Sept. 1, 1818, ibid., No. 46. Long reported in 1821
that with the "United States Steam Boat Western Engineer" he had explored
the Ohio, Mississippi, and Missouri rivers. He discussed the navigability of
these rivers and the nature of their obstructions. ("Report of Col. Stephen H.
Long's Western Expedition," Feb. 20, 1821, E.D., Bulky File, No. 107.)

undoubtedly illustrated the usefulness of engineer officers on civil works.

Calhoun in 1820 again directed the Board of Engineers for Fortifications "to furnish any information, or assistance . . . requested by the Commissioners appointed by the State of North Carolina, particularly in relation to the improvement of the navigation of the State by opening or deepening the inlet into Albemarle Sound."[46] The board had the aid of several topographical engineers who executed many surveys and collected useful information dealing with ports, channels, conditions of navigation, and possibilities of their improvement. Instructions given these engineers invariably emphasized the desire for maps and descriptions of rivers, bays, and existing or proposed improvements.

In an act of April 14, 1820, Congress appropriated $5,000 for a survey of the Ohio and Mississippi rivers from Louisville to New Orleans to determine the most practicable means of improving their navigation. General Bernard and Colonel Totten made this examination in 1821. Their report described such obstructions to navigation as shoals and "snags," which were trees embedded in the river. These engineers were primarily concerned with steamboat navigation and proposed ways of removing obstructions. On the Ohio there should be a canal around the falls at Louisville and dikes to deepen the channel over a number of shoals or bars. Experiments with dikes should be made on several bars, accompanied by close study of the

[46] Letter from Calhoun, April 12, 1820, E.D., Letters Received, I, No. R58. The board reported on Dec. 15, 1820, that it had made an examination, checked local plans, and prepared a report for the Board of Public Works of the state of North Carolina. It discussed the practicability of "opening a communication from Albemarle Sound to the Atlantic Ocean" in terms of these queries: "1. Can the project be executed, and if so will the passage remain unaffected, seriously by storms and currents? 2. What will be the expense? 3. Will the advantages resulting to the State be equivalent to the expense? 4. How will the execution of this project effect the interests of the union?" (E.D., Bulky File, No. 146, pp. 138–45.)

behavior of the river. On the Mississippi, snags and rafts should be removed, steamboat pilots should be better trained, and in the long run the banks should be diked to prevent cross currents and flooding.[47]

In 1822 there were increasing demands on the army engineers for civil duties of various kinds. They made surveys of harbors, coastal areas, roads in Michigan, and lead mines on the upper Mississippi.[48] Henry R. Schoolcraft, who acted as mineralogist with an expedition exploring the sources of the Mississippi, reported on the mineral resources of that region. He had found copper, lead, gypsum, coal, salt, and alum; and he desired to publish his report because of its national and scientific importance. These ores would increase manufacturing and raise the value of the public lands; to publish his findings would thus aid science, industry, and the public revenue. He felt a strong obligation "to disseminate throughout the country the knowledge of those varied natural resources, which invite employment."[49]

A few months later, Major Isaac Roberdeau, head of the Topographical Bureau, stressed the potential usefulness of the topographical engineers for public improvement. He noted the military and civil value of engineering surveys and remarked that it had become necessary to assign army line officers to surveying duty, since only ten topographical engineers were authorized. These engineers should be encouraged to share in the profession of the civil engineer, "the want of which is universally admitted."

[47] "Survey of the Ohio and Mississippi Rivers," Dec. 22, 1822, ASP, Commerce and Navigation, II, 740–46. See also Buell's memorandum, E.D., Doc. File 1894–1923, Box 1209, File 50734–61; Isaac Lippincott, "A History of River Improvement," Journal of Political Economy, Vol. XXII (1914), 634; and A.R. of C/E for 1822, ASP, MA, II, 458.

[48] A.R. of C/E, Nov. 14, 1822, ASP, MA, II, 458; Buell's memorandum, E.D., Doc. File 1894–1923, Box 1209, File 50734–61.

[49] Schoolcraft to S/W Calhoun, April 3, 1822, E.D., Bulky File, No. 160. Schoolcraft became a noted American ethnologist.

*. . . there are few well educated practical civil engineers in our country;* the deficiency may be attributed to a variety of causes, but, it is principally, perhaps, because the United States have never yet engaged in public works of a kind requiring talents of this description, and neither the individual States, nor chartered associations, have heretofore, so extensively, or with such success, undertaken them, as to offer suitable encouragement for exclusive devotedness to the profession, and thereby also, no opportunity was afforded of obtaining practical information, without recurring to Europe for the theatre of action.

No country in the world at this time, appears so much to feel the want of professional character of this kind as do the United States, nor is there perhaps a nation whose prosperity, and improvement so much depend upon the establishment of some system by which the deficiency may be supplied. The attention of Congress might be drawn to the subject, as one of superior importance, in the necessity of which every individual impressed with a proper feeling for national advancement must agree, and particularly as from the patronage of Government alone, efficient results can be had.[50]

Training at West Point was not enough for cadets, since they must receive experience on large public works to acquire a practical knowledge of civil engineering. To participate in internal improvements, the topographical engineers should be increased in number, organized as a separate corps, and assigned to civil works.

Roberdeau believed that the government must take an increasingly active part in developing the country, particularly by advancing civil engineering. He saw the lack of civil engineers as the major problem, the point at which the government could do most to promote internal improvement. The practical knowledge and usefulness of the army in peace and war would be increased by adding civil engineering to the regular duties of topographical engineers.

[50] Report on the Topographical Engineers, Dec. 25, 1822, E.D., Bulky File, No. 114, pp. 11–12 (Roberdeau's emphasis).

As Roberdeau had predicted, each passing year witnessed a growing demand for the employment of army engineers on civil works. In 1823, topographical engineers engaged in surveys of rivers, harbors, canals, turnpikes, and lead mines. Their river and harbor surveys along the Atlantic included the Patapsco, Patuxent, and St. Marys rivers and the harbors of Portsmouth and Charleston. There were two surveys for turnpikes, and Major Anderson was employed in locating lead mines on the upper Mississippi.[51] Schoolcraft, then a United States Indian agent, reported to Secretary of War Calhoun that copper ore had been found near Lake Superior. He sent a specimen of the ore and asked permission to publish a scientific article dealing with the discovery.[52] Major Long made a scientific expedition up the Minnesota River to the forty-ninth parallel and back to the Great Lakes.[53]

A significant harbor survey was made on Lake Erie in 1823. Congress ordered a survey of the harbor of Presque Isle in Pennsylvania to secure a plan and estimate for deepening its entrance. Although the act called for a survey by one officer, Calhoun sent the Board of Engineers for Fortifications. Since the people of Pennsylvania had shown great interest in improving this harbor, he felt justified in employing General Bernard and Colonel Totten on this survey.[54] These officers reported that the harbor entrance was obstructed by a sand bar which could be removed by using piers to force the current

[51] A.R. of C/E, Nov. 20, 1823, *ASP, MA*, II, 567–68; Isaac Roberdeau, "Report Respecting the United States Topographical Engineers," Nov. 16, 1825, E.D., Bulky File, No. 114.

[52] Henry R. Schoolcraft to Calhoun, July 28, 1823, E.D., Bulky File, No. 160.

[53] S/W Calhoun to Secretary of State John Quincy Adams, April 28, 1823, E.D., Misc. Letters Sent, I, 391–92; A.R. of C/E for 1823, *ASP, MA*, II, 567–68.

[54] *Laws of the United States Relating to the Improvement of Rivers and Harbors from August 11, 1790, to March 4, 1907*, 58 Cong., 3 sess., *H. Doc. 425*, 26; Calhoun to Patrick Farrelly, May 7, 1823, E.D., Misc. Letters Sent, I, 396; Gen. Macomb, C/E, to Board of Engineers, May 7, 1823, E.D., Letters to Officers of Engineers, I, 419–20.

to deepen the entrance. The harbor of Erie was otherwise satisfactory and had a growing commerce. It was needed as a port of refuge in bad weather, and it possessed both commercial and naval value. They concluded that the proposed improvement was practicable, necessary, and important.[55]

The Engineer Department felt that the rapidly increasing commerce of the Great Lakes necessitated the improvement of lake harbors and the construction of lighthouses. The Chief Engineer argued in 1823 that a lighthouse was essential at the lower entrance to Lake Huron. On several occasions he had reported this need to the government, because "The increase of the trade and navigation on Lakes Huron and Michigan is such as to claim the protection of government; and there is an absolute necessity for a light at or near Fort Gratiot to enable the larger vessels to prosecute their voyage down the lakes with safety."[56]

The army engineers were more interested in the needs of navigation on the Atlantic Coast than on the Great Lakes. In June, 1823, the Engineer Department ordered Bernard and Totten to Philadelphia to formulate plans for a breakwater at the mouth of Delaware Bay, as called for by act of Congress. They were instructed to consult with the Philadelphia Chamber of Commerce.[57] The report of Bernard, Totten, and Commander Bainbridge on a breakwater for Delaware Bay dealt with the utility, practicability, location, size, and cost of the projected Delaware breakwater to protect vessels from tempests and floating ice. It was noted that there was no harbor or safe anchorage near the mouth of the bay and that Philadelphia's commerce and the coasting trade suffered from this de-

---

[55] "Report of the Board of Engineers on the Harbour of Erie in Pennsylvania," Oct. 4, 1823, Corps of Engineers, Reports, 1812–23, 508–18.

[56] Jan. 28, 1823, E.D., Misc. Letters Sent, I, 353.

[57] E.D. to Board of Engineers, June 7, 1823, E.D., Letters to Officers of Engineers, I, 435–36; Calhoun to Robert Ralston, June 7, 1823, E.D., Misc. Letters Sent, I, 409.

ficiency. The proposed artificial harbor would greatly increase the tonnage of the port of Philadelphia.[58]

Army engineers also became involved in the canal craze then sweeping the country, and they aided several canal schemes in 1823. While the Board of Engineers was in Philadelphia to plan the Delaware breakwater, it was also under orders to confer with promoters of the Chesapeake and Delaware Canal. This company had asked that military engineers co-operate with its civil engineers in making a final decision on its canal route. Calhoun agreed to send the board to consult with the company, and the Engineer Department instructed Bernard and Totten to provide full assistance and determine the military worth of each alternative route.[59] They examined the proposed routes and then met with the company's civil engineers, Benjamin Wright and Canvass White, to select the route of the Chesapeake and Delaware Canal.[60]

Maryland next received the aid of army engineers for canal surveys. Its legislature ordered the governor to have surveys made for canals from Baltimore to Conawago Falls on the Susquehanna River and from there to tidewater. The governor's commissioners appointed James Geddes as principal engineer and asked that army engineers make a topographical survey. The Engineer Department sent Captain Hartman Bache and his surveying party to survey the desired canal routes.[61] Cal-

[58] Report of Commission on a Pier or Breakwater in Delaware Bay, July 14, 1823, Corps of Engineers, Reports, 1812–23, 498–508.

[59] June 3, 1823, E.D., Letters to Officers of Engineers, I, 433. Cf. E.D. to these officers, June 7, 1823, ibid., I, 435–36; Calhoun to Meredith, June 3, 1823, E.D., Misc. Letters Sent, I, 406.

[60] Totten to Gen. Macomb, Dec. 6, 1823 and Jan. 20, 1824, (Totten's) Official Letters, I, 1823, 64–65; 1824, 5–6. In requesting this aid, the company had told Calhoun that "the assistance of one or more of the distinguished engineers under the order of your department would be greatly serviceable on this occasion not only in leading the Board to a right conclusion but in attracting to it public confidence and unanimity." (William Meredith to Calhoun, May 19, 1823, E.D., Letters Received, I, No. R458.)

[61] July 8, 1823, E.D., Letters to Officers of Engineers, I, 445–46. Cf. Bland to Calhoun, July 7, 1823, E.D., Letters Received, I, No. R474.

houn told the commissioners that he was willing to provide aid for these important projects, despite the fact that the topographical engineers were very busy with their regular duties. He said that Bache and three qualified assistants would be at their command to perform all the services they required.[62]

New Jersey also obtained the use of army engineers in 1823 for a canal survey. George P. McCulloch, of Morristown, informed Calhoun that the state of New Jersey desired to extend a canal through the section containing its ironworks. Since this canal would make coal and iron more readily available, it would stimulate infant industries and enable fuel to reach New York City. As the elevation to be overcome was too great, common lockage was not practicable; therefore, a new principle of locks was being considered. Since this was a novel idea meeting much opposition, professional opinion of distinguished engineers was essential. McCulloch requested the assistance of General Bernard, who was said to be willing to help.[63]

Calhoun agreed that the proposed canal would produce great advantages for New Jersey, New York, and the nation as well. Consequently, the required aid would be provided by the Board of Engineers, which would confer and co-operate with the canal commissioners.[64] Bernard and Totten reported that the proposed Morris Canal would be financially and tech-

[62] July 8, 1823, E.D., Misc. Letters Sent, I, 414–15.
[63] Aug. 10, 1823, E.D., Letters Received, I, No. R483. Cf. Wheaton J. Lane, *From Indian Trail to Iron Horse; Travel and Transportation in New Jersey, 1620–1860*, 224–26; H. Jerome Cranmer, "Internal Improvement in New Jersey: Planning the Morris Canal" (M.A. thesis, Columbia University, 1949).
[64] Calhoun to McCulloch, Aug. 14, 1823, E.D., Misc. Letters Sent, I, 424. In notifying the board of Calhoun's decision, Chief Engineer Macomb explained that "The Secretary of War, feeling every way disposed to encourage internal improvements, especially those which are in a great measure connected with the defences of the country, by opening communications with the interior resources of the Union, has consented that you should lend your aid. . . ." (Aug. 15, 1823, E.D., Letters to Officers of Engineers, I, 454.)

nically practicable. It would bring coal from the Lehigh Valley and iron from the ironworks in New Jersey to "the flourishing manufacturing village" of Paterson and to New York City. The price of coal, iron, lumber, lime, and farm products would be reduced. Inclined planes would make the canal with its many benefits possible, and its construction would test the value of these devices and promote canal navigation.[65]

The most significant part of this report was a lucid discussion of the general utility of canals:

Of all the means which human ingenuity has devised for facilitating communications between different parts of a country, canals occupy, at the present day, the highest rank, and when well planned and judiciously located, they not only become sources of individual wealth; but they diffuse prosperity over extensive regions, and result in economy and advancement to the nation at large. . . . experience and more precise calculation has taught that it is necessary to reject every useless expense, and that the cost of construction and repair must have a certain ratio to the revenue— being viewed in this respect like all commercial speculations. When viewed, however, with reference to general rather than individual advantage, the condition, that the income must bear a certain proportion to the principal invested, cannot be considered as absolute, for the revenue from a canal may be much less than that on ordinary investments and yet the benefit amount to much more as regards national economy and advantage. On this hypothesis the deficit of revenue is amply compensated, as regards the nation, by the greater facility of speed and transportation, thereby making the articles conveyed less costly, the circulation of capital more rapid, and a larger proportion of the labour of men and animals disposable for the branches of industry; and also by opening extensive regions to a market, which without this cheap mode of conveyance would be inaccessible.[66]

[65] "Report on a Proposed Canal Through the Mining District of New Jersey," by Bernard and Totten, Nov. 5, 1823, Reports of the Board of Internal Improvements, II, 1–27. (This report was printed in a larger report by the New Jersey Commissioners at Morristown in 1823.)

[66] *Ibid.*, II, 1. Bernard and Totten reasoned that "canals, when considered by a comparison of their cost with the revenue derived from them, may be

Bernard and Totten employed physiocratic doctrine to emphasize the economic stimulus of canals. They felt that canals which would produce general benefit, but would not be profitable private ventures, merited public support. Their report illustrated the strong desire of the army engineers to promote internal improvements.

Major Roberdeau in 1823 renewed his demands for a large corps of topographical engineers. He thought their number should be increased from ten to thirty-eight, since demands for their services were growing daily. The great value of their activities had been proved by their recent surveys for internal improvement projects.[67] Roberdeau received the firm support of General Bernard, who described the many services these engineers had performed and the many others they could accomplish if organized into a separate and greatly enlarged corps. In peacetime they could make surveys, maps, and reports of the country's topography, thus enabling other agencies and enterprises to fulfill their own plans more effectively. The topographical engineers could execute surveys of roads, canals, fortifications, seaports, and the coast. All information thus collected should be preserved in a single topographical archive.[68]

President Monroe also recognized the value of the topographical engineers in the field of civil engineering. He recom-

divided into two classes. 1st Those which are made with a view to the general interest of the country—the revenue being a secondary object. And 2nd Those on which the revenue is the principal object. The first can only be undertaken at the charge of the Public Treasury. The other may be either the work of the nation, or particular States, or of private associations." (*Ibid.*, II, 1–2.)

[67] Roberdeau to Gen. Macomb, C/E, Sept. 3, 1823, E.D., Bulky File, No. 114, pp. 18–19.

[68] Bernard to Roberdeau, Dec. 11, 1823, E.D., Letters Received, I, No. E1501. Bernard said that the main purposes of a corps of topographical engineers included "geography, topography, hydrography, critical and military history; and if we reflect on what is yet to be done in this country respecting those branches, a rich harvest of scientific glory will become the share of the American topographical engineers."

mended that they investigate a proposed improvement of great merit, a chain of canals to connect the Potomac with the Ohio and Lake Erie: "Believing as I do that Congress possesses the right to appropriate money for such a national object (the jurisdiction remaining to the States through which the canal would pass), I submit it to your consideration whether it may not be advisable to authorize by an adequate appropriation the employment of a suitable number of the officers of the Corps of Engineers to examine the unexplored ground during the next season and to report their opinion thereon."[69] By this time it was widely realized that the army engineers could be effectively used to promote public improvement. Monroe's proposal that engineer officers execute canal surveys reflected this opinion and foreshadowed their increased participation in such activities.

Before analyzing the work of the army engineers under the General Survey Act of 1824, it is useful to review their qualifications for such civil functions. To account for the place they assumed in the early stages of internal improvement requires an understanding of their military functions. Their chief task was the military defense of the country. The Board of Engineers for Fortifications was organized to plan a system of defense works. The systematic planning of a network of coastal fortifications called for extensive surveying, and topographical engineers examined bays, harbors, and rivers along the coast. These military surveys provided a "school of practice" in civil engineering. Several engineers gained experience in surveying, planning large works, and supervising their construction at a time when major engineering undertakings were few in number. These surveys also produced useful information on navigability of bays and rivers—knowledge highly desired by mariners and promoters of navigation projects.

These systematic efforts to develop a network of defenses

[69] Annual Message, Dec. 2, 1823, *Writings*, VI, 337–38.

sharpened military interest in civil engineering and internal improvements. A theory of national security emerged which emphasized political and commercial as well as military factors. This theory called for balanced development of a small standing army, a well-organized militia, a navy, coastal fortifications, and interior communications as component parts of a unified system. The Engineer Department was made responsible for the correlative needs of this system of defense. Since engineering science was early recognized as a military necessity, the Corps of Engineers was given the task of operating an engineering school. The Military Academy consequently became the first engineering school in the country. Since its graduates received theoretical training in mathematics and engineering, it became the primary source of early trained engineers.

Civil engineering was a critical factor in the movement for internal improvements. Since this profession was a scarce resource over which the government had some control, it was a strategic area in which the government could promote the country's economic development with a minimum of expense and effort. Natural resources were plentiful; labor and capital funds were relatively scarce but not lacking if projects were demonstrably profitable; to combine these resources into practicable, profitable undertakings demanded the efficient application of an expanding technology. Many national leaders recognized this importance of engineering and the need of its public support.

Federal participation in internal improvements through provision of engineering aid had reached a significant level by 1824: an engineering school was in operation; western exploration and mapping were under way; efforts were being made to determine the nation's resources by mineralogical surveys; rivers and harbors were being examined; and roads and canals were being laid out. This work occupied much of the attention of the twenty-two officers of the Corps of Engineers and the ten topographical engineers. Army line officers were also engaged in these civil activities, for the practice of detaching army officers from their regular duties and assigning them to engineering duties had become common.

By this time there had evolved a pattern of fostering public improvement through the army engineers. This emerging system was available as a basis for public promotion of internal improvements under the General Survey Act. Component parts of this pattern consisted of a military justification of aid to inland transportation, an initial monopoly of engineering education at West Point, a growing recognition of the critical importance of civil engineering and its advancement by the federal government, increasing demands for the technical aid of army engineers, and a widening area of their participation in civil works. This pattern gave the army engineers a role in national development which is of central interest in analyzing the application of the General Survey Act.

# II: Setting the Stage

THE GENERAL SURVEY ACT of 1824 may be viewed as an effort to institute national planning of a system of internal improvements. The act specifically provided that the President employ military and civil engineers in securing surveys, plans, and estimates of roads and canals of national importance. He was thus authorized to have a national system of internal improvements studied, examined, and planned.

The first general plan for federal promotion of inland transportation was submitted by Albert Gallatin in 1808 in his "Report on Roads and Canals."[1] Such leaders as Jefferson had previously proposed a national system of internal improvements. In addition, work had begun by 1808 on the Cumberland Road under an act of 1806 appropriating money for its construction. Gallatin's report thus came at a time when there was a growing desire to improve inland transportation, and the report itself had been ordered by the Senate.

Gallatin advocated extensive federal aid to internal improvements, justified the need of this assistance, and proposed the forms it should take. The most essential roads and canals were not being developed by private capital. Obstacles causing improvements to be unprofitable or unattempted were the sparsity of population in many areas and the great demand for scarce capital funds in other, more profitable, activities. The federal government must necessarily overcome these obstacles by participating in the construction of extensive, unprofitable projects which would then make additional improvements profitable for private enterprise.

Gallatin elaborated a "national plan of internal improve-

[1] ASP, Miscellaneous, I, 724–921.

37

ments" which included canals along the Atlantic Coast, canals to connect the Atlantic with the western rivers and the Great Lakes, and roads and canals in the interior to make certain essential local connections. The government could undertake some projects and could promote others by subscribing to stocks of private companies or by making public loans to them. In addition, he proposed that the government make surveys of leading projects to secure a national plan of needed improvements.[2] He recognized that engineering surveys by the government were required for the planning of necessary internal improvements.

All later plans for a national system of roads and canals were patterned after Gallatin's original report. These schemes were commonly similar to their prototype with regard to the argument of military, political, and commercial necessity of publicly sponsored improvements; the selection of major national projects; and the advocacy of federal construction, financial aid, and engineering aid. The Gallatin plan thus became the guiding principle of the movement for internal improvements, particularly for the government's participation in this cause.[3]

The Gallatin plan, however, was delayed in its application, primarily by circumstances involved in the War of 1812. The next general statement of a national plan came in 1819 with the publication of Calhoun's "Report on Roads and Canals."[4] The war had convinced public officials of the pressing need for coastal fortifications and improved inland communication. Intensive efforts to plan a system of coastal defenses had

[2] "As an important basis of the general system, an immediate authority might also be given to take the surveys and levels of the routes of the most important roads and canals which are contemplated: a work always useful, and by which the practicability and expense of the undertaking would be ascertained with much more correctness than in this report." (*Ibid.*, I, 741.)

[3] For an analysis of the Gallatin report and its significance, see Carter Goodrich, "National Planning of Internal Improvements," *Political Science Quarterly*, Vol. LXIII (1948), 16–44.

[4] Calhoun, *Works*, V, 40–54.

brought the Board of Engineers for Fortifications into existence and had emphasized the essential place of improved transportation in any broad plan of national defense.

Despite the admitted need for internal improvements, the movement had continued to lag. In 1816 and 1817, Calhoun urged federal aid for internal improvements through passage of the "bonus bill." This bill, which would have placed the government's bonus and annual dividends from the Second Bank of the United States in a permanent fund for constructing roads and canals, was vetoed by Madison on the ground that Congress lacked the constitutional power to appropriate for the general welfare. In supporting this bill, Calhoun used Gallatin's arguments emphasizing the necessity of government construction of important projects and the military need for such improvements. Since essential major improvements were beyond the resources of individual states and were often blocked by rivalry between states, they would have to be financed by the federal government.[5]

Calhoun at that time felt that the power of Congress to appropriate for the common defense and general welfare involved the power to establish a system of internal improvements. Although Madison believed that Congress possessed no such specific power, he thought it should be delegated by a constitutional amendment. Discussion of the constitutionality and need of these improvements increased; and on April 4, 1818, the House of Representatives instructed Calhoun, by then secretary of war, to submit "a plan for the application of such means as are within the power of Congress, for the purpose of opening and constructing such roads and canals as may deserve and require the aid of Government, with a view to military operations in time of war; the transportation of munitions of war; and also a statement of the nature of the works above mentioned, which have been commenced, the

[5] Speech on the "bonus bill" (Feb. 4, 1817), *ibid.*, II, 186–96.

progress which has been made, and the means and prospects of their completion. . . ."[6]

Calhoun's report constituted a restatement and extension of Gallatin's original plan. Calhoun advocated a broad program of internal improvement involving public construction and extensive use of army engineers in making surveys and plans.[7] His report dealt with the purposes of the proposed system of roads and canals, types of projects included, and means of their execution.

He felt that his scheme would fulfill joint needs in such a way that military and civil benefits would be indistinguishable. After analyzing proposed improvements strictly in terms of the defense needs of the country, he thus concluded that "many of the roads and canals which have been suggested, are no doubt of the first importance to the commerce, the manufactures, the agriculture, and the political prosperity of the country, but are not, for that reason, less useful or necessary for military purposes. . . . whether we regard its internal improvements in relation to military, civil, or political purposes, very nearly the same system, in all its parts, is required."[8]

Calhoun's broad view of the scope and purpose of a system of roads and canals requisite for defense needs was evident in his discussion of the types of works needed. His conception of "roads and canals" included navigable rivers, for he proposed to improve the navigation of inland rivers, as well as to construct intracoastal canals along the Atlantic, a road from Washington to New Orleans, and roads and canals to connect the Atlantic with several western rivers.

More significant than the projects themselves were the

[6] "Report on Roads and Canals," *ibid.*, V, 40–41.
[7] Frederick Jackson Turner, *Rise of the New West*, 230; George Washington Ward, *The Early Development of the Chesapeake and Ohio Canal Project*, 35–36.
[8] Calhoun, *Works*, V, 50.

methods by which Calhoun proposed to complete them. He felt that most road projects and river improvements could be left to the states and cities concerned, but that the federal government would have to develop the chain of canals along the Atlantic. This latter work was very important to national defense and the coasting trade, but no state or group of states would have sufficient interest to complete it. Likewise, roads and canals to connect the Atlantic with western rivers had great military value. Although the large seaports, spurred by their rivalries, would complete these improvements, the federal government should bear its proportional share of their cost of construction. He thus recommended that city rivalry be used as a means of executing his plan. Such rivalry was later to make attempts at comprehensive planning increasingly futile.

Calhoun proposed to use the army as well as public funds in constructing roads and canals. Although the army was small, it could be used on works near the frontiers and in other thinly populated areas. The army could also aid road and canal construction by providing the specialized services of its engineers. Since the cost and routes of proposed improvements could be determined only by able engineers, he proposed "as the basis of the system, and the first measure in the plan for the application of such means as are in the power of Congress, that Congress should direct such a survey and estimate to be made, and the result laid before them as soon as practicable. The expense would be inconsiderable, for, as the army can furnish able military and topographical engineers, it would be primarily confined to the employment of one or more skilful civil engineers, to be associated with them. By their combined skill, an efficient system of military roads and canals would be presented in detail, accompanied with such estimates of expenses as may be relied on. . . ."[9]

[9] *Ibid.*, V, 50–51.

41

Congress could use this information in deciding which undertakings to finance, and the disbursement of funds could be made by the War Department. If a state or incorporated company undertook one of the approved projects, the federal government could subscribe to part of the capital stock. If federal construction was necessary, and if the army could not execute the improvement, it should be constructed by contract under the inspection of engineer officers. This last method had worked well in constructing fortifications and should be an efficient, economical means of executing civil works. The Secretary of War thus proposed systematic use of army engineers in surveying, planning, and supervising the construction of internal improvements.

Certain features of Calhoun's energetic plan took the form in 1822 of a general survey bill, an immediate forerunner of the General Survey Act of 1824. This bill was introduced in the House of Representatives by Joseph Hemphill for the select committee on roads and canals.[10] After considering specific projects referred to it, this committee advocated a general policy of internal improvements. It drew on Gallatin's comprehensive report to form a plan by which the federal government would undertake or aid the construction of designated roads and canals. Proposed improvements should be studied by "scientific men" to ensure their worth in the general system. For this purpose the committee submitted a bill "to procure the necessary surveys, plans, and estimates, on the subject of roads and canals." This bill would have directed the President to examine specifically named improvements and also "such other routes for roads and canals as he may deem of national importance in a commercial or military point of view." He would have been authorized to employ two skilled civil engineers and as many engineer officers as he thought

[10] "Report of the Committee on Roads and Canals on the Subject of Internal Improvements," Jan. 2, 1822, 17 Cong., 1 sess., *H. Rept. 8*, 1–5.

proper. Although the bill was not favorably acted upon, it was debated in 1822 and 1823.

Hemphill made a second report, in which he reiterated the need for surveying proposed routes. Such surveys would produce the relevant data on the practicability and expense of each project needed by Congress in deciding on the wisdom of supporting these projects. These surveys would lay the "foundation of a well-digested and regular system" and could readily and economically be made by the army engineers, a disciplined and capable group of trained men.

The corps of engineers, with the assistance of two civil engineers, and the aid of others who can be detailed to do duty in that corps, are believed . . . to be sufficient. They proceed by a regular system, and report monthly. Young cadets, as they leave the Military Academy, can be employed. It will give them experience, and advance their usefulness to their country. It will render the science appertaining to the engineer department more perfect and extensive, and obviate the necessity of employing foreign engineers. . . . The information, when obtained, would be valuable; for it cannot be otherwise than important to be acquainted with the capabilities of the country for internal improvements. It would be useful to the States who have not the same economical means of acquiring it; and this part of the question cannot be embarrassed by any constitutional question.[11]

With this imposing justification of government surveys, the committee concluded that individual projects should not be authorized by Congress until the system of surveys was in operation.

Influenced by demands for engineering aid and the desire to foster an essential national improvement, President Monroe in 1823 recommended that army engineers be used to survey the proposed Chesapeake and Ohio Canal. He favored

[11] Report on "Roads and Canals" of House Committee on Roads and Canals, April 26, 1822, *ASP, Miscellaneous*, II, 935.

this project because of the great economic, military, and political benefits it would produce. Unlike Madison, he had become convinced that the government could make appropriations to aid such works if individual states retained jurisdiction over them.[12] His proposal came at a time when Congress was already directing army engineers to make surveys for civil works and when Calhoun, his secretary of war, was permitting them to make canal surveys for states and chartered companies. The General Survey Act formalized and systematized practices which had already evolved and gained general acceptance.

This act was passed soon after Monroe proposed government surveys of canals between Chesapeake Bay and Lake Erie. It grew directly out of the survey bill of 1822 and Monroe's survey proposal of 1823 and less directly out of Gallatin's and Calhoun's plans for internal improvements. It was supported by advocates of federal aid to improvement undertakings, particularly by adherents of Henry Clay's "American system."

Such leaders as Clay and John Quincy Adams were the chief proponents of a national system of internal improvements. By changing to the majority view favoring national aid to such improvements, Monroe had a significant effect on the character and application of the General Survey Act.[13] Although Madison had argued in his veto of the "bonus bill" in 1817 that Congress did not possess the specific power to appropriate for internal improvements, Monroe declared in his veto of the Cumberland Road bill in 1822 that Congress could appropriate for projects of a national character but could not assume jurisdiction over their construction and operation.[14]

12 Annual Message, Dec. 2, 1823, Monroe, *Writings*, VI, 337.

13 John W. Burgess, *The Middle Period*, 120–21; Ward, *Early Development*, 70–71.

14 "Message from the President of the United States, with His Objections to the Bill for the Preservation and Repair of the Cumberland Road; Also a

Monroe's view that Congress could finance internal improvements of national value but could not establish control over them was by 1824 the prevailing opinion. The accepted view was that as a result of its power to appropriate, Congress could grant funds to help plan and build improvements. The chief problem was to determine which projects were of such general utility that Congress could finance their construction under the principle laid down by Monroe. This problem of selecting projects was to be met through the General Survey Act by authorizing the President to secure surveys and plans of routes he deemed of national value.[15]

The recognized purpose of this act was to prepare a program of appropriations for nationally important roads and canals, with federal subscription to stocks of enterprises undertaking them.[16] Monroe had in mind the desirability of providing financial assistance to the Chesapeake and Ohio Canal when he proposed that its route be surveyed by army engineers. In the House of Representatives, Hemphill noted Monroe's proposal in his own argument for passage of the Survey Act. Hemphill referred to the failure of a survey bill in 1822 when it had been feared that the President would veto any bill which "looked forward to a system of internal improvements." The President had indicated tacit approval of the principle of the bill by allowing engineer officers to make canal surveys during 1823 and by calling for the Chesapeake and Ohio survey. Hemphill termed his bill "nothing more than an enlargement of the views and objects contained in the Message of the President."[17]

Convinced of the expediency of a system of internal improvements, Hemphill said his bill would accomplish the es-

Paper, Containing His Views on the Subject of Internal Improvements," May 4, 1822, 17 Cong., 1 sess., *H. Doc. 127,* 3–60.

[15] Burgess, *Middle Period,* 121–22.

[16] Turner, *New West,* 232–33.

[17] Speech on Jan. 12, 1824, *Annals of Congress,* XLI, 995.

sential preparatory step of securing basic information needed by states and individuals as well as the federal government. Selection of routes to be surveyed should be left to the President, who would consider the needs of domestic commerce and national defense and would use both military and civil engineers in administering the act. This surveying would supply valuable data at little expense which Congress could use as the basis for designing a regular system of internal improvements.

> Nothing can be more useful than an accurate knowledge of the natural capacities of the country for improvements. . . . Such information, accompanied with plans and estimates of expense, would be of the highest importance; for, whether the improvements of the country are to be made by the individual States, or by the General Government . . . this information would be essentially necessary. All . . . that are in favor of improving the country by any of the means that have been suggested, can, with consistency, vote for the present bill.[18]

Clay, a leader in the debate for passage of the act, felt that two questions of broad principle were involved: the constitutional power of Congress to legislate for internal improvements, and the expediency of exercising this power. He contended that Congress should reach agreement on these major issues before discussing the details of the act. Mercer disagreed with Clay, taking a view similar to Hemphill's. Mercer insisted that topographical engineers could be most profitably employed in surveying for internal improvements without involving the issues of constitutionality and expediency raised by Clay.[19]

In the Senate, Benton took a position favoring both surveys and appropriations for internal improvements. He felt, however, that Congress rather than the President should select

18 *Ibid.*, XLI, 998.
19 *Ibid.*, XLI, 999.

46

projects of national value. This selection was a legislative task which the President, even if wrongly given the duty, could not execute. Those 90 per cent who would be disappointed in their demands for local roads and canals would combine against the President to defeat his program. Quoting Gallatin, Benton asserted that "the National Legislature alone, embracing every local interest, and superior to every local consideration, is competent to the selection of such national objects."[20] He enumerated six canal routes and five roads, typical of those proposed by Calhoun in 1819, which should be surveyed and planned. Ample funds for "this great system" could be derived from increased tariff duties. His effort to amend the act to designate routes to be examined was unsuccessful. In the end he joined Eaton, Hayne, Jackson, and others to pass it by a vote of 24 to 18 in the Senate.[21]

The General Survey Act in its entirety read as follows:

Chap. 46.—An Act to procure the necessary Surveys, Plans, and Estimates, upon the subject of Roads and Canals.

(Sect. 1.)  Be it enacted by the Senate and House of Representatives of the United States of America, in Congress assembled, That the President of the United States is hereby authorized to cause the necessary surveys, plans, and estimates, to be made of the routes of such Roads and Canals as he may deem of national importance, in a commercial or military point of view, or necessary for the transportation of the public mail; designating, in the case of each canal, what parts may be made capable of sloop navigation: the surveys, plans, and estimates, for each, when completed, to be laid before Congress.

(Sect. 2.)  And be it further enacted, That, to carry into effect the objects of this act, the President be, and he is hereby authorized to employ two or more skilful civil engineers, and such officers of the corps of engineers, or who may be detailed to do duty with that corps, as he may think proper; and the sum of thirty thousand

[20] Benton's speech on "Surveys for Roads and Canals," April 21, 1824, *ibid.*, XLI, 536. Cf. Gallatin's "Report on Roads and Canals," *ASP, Misc.*, I, 741.

[21] *Annals of Congress*, XLI, 570–71.

dollars be, and the same is hereby, appropriated, to be paid out of any moneys in the treasury, not otherwise appropriated.[22]

The debate over this act revealed several significant points of view. Sectional feelings were clearly evident,[23] and the main issue concerned the constitutional power of Congress to effect a system of internal improvements. Many congressmen favored federal aid to these improvements, but there was little agreement on the choice and constitutionality of specific methods to be used.

The Survey Act was conceived as an initial step toward the establishment of a system whose nature and content remained to be determined. The surveying and planning of projects would provide the basis for a program of federal grants, and the surveying would in any case provide valuable aid for all concerned. Although there was a question whether the act should be specific or general in regard to designating or leaving to the President's discretion the routes to be examined, there was little opposition to surveying as such. There was widespread agreement that government surveys for internal improvements were necessary and constitutional and that the army engineers should be given this important task in civil engineering.

The act did not authorize construction of a national system of internal improvements.[24] It merely instituted a general

[22] *Acts of the Eighteenth Congress,* 35. The act was approved April 30, 1824.

[23] Turner, *New West,* 233.

[24] One writer states that "the General Survey Act of 1824 could scarcely be taken as an establishment of any system. It was rather the assertion of a willingness to utilize the government engineers in the examination of all projected schemes. To the President was given the impossible task of distributing the new patronage and from the engineers' reports of deciding what measures were of national importance in such a manner as to be pleasing to a permanent majority in Congress." (R. B. Way, "The Mississippi Valley and Internal Improvements, 1824–1840," Mississippi Valley Historical Association, *Proceedings,* Vol. IV [1910–11], 168.)

scheme for the surveying and planning of a series of major improvements.

The President was given wide discretion by the General Survey Act. He was authorized to employ engineer officers, line officers detailed to engineering duty, and two or more civil engineers in surveying and planning improvements of national importance. He was left to his own judgment to determine the meaning of "national importance," the specific roads and canals to be selected, and the administrative procedures to be used. He was no doubt expected to observe the general proposals of the Gallatin and Calhoun plans as well as current opinion in selecting routes. Within these flexible limits, he had to establish the procedures for planning a national scheme of internal improvements to be fostered and presumably financed by the federal government.

To administer the Survey Act, President Monroe created the Board of Engineers for Internal Improvements. On May 31, 1824, Chief Engineer Macomb informed General Bernard, Colonel Totten, and John L. Sullivan, a civil engineer, that the President had appointed them to a "Board of Internal Improvement" to superintend the execution of the act. Three topographical engineers were directly attached to the board, and three surveying parties were put under its orders. The latter consisted of Major Abert and Captain McNeill, each with five officer assistants, and David Shriver, civil engineer, with five civilian surveyors. They were ordered to accompany the board to determine the practicability, best routes, plans, and estimates for canals to connect the Potomac, the Ohio, and Lake Erie.[25]

This board was quite similar to the Board of Engineers for Fortifications, organized eight years earlier when General Bernard was brought to this country as assistant engineer.

[25] T.B., Internal Improvement Letters Issued, A, 3. This board was often called the Board of Internal Improvement.

49

Bernard and Totten were members of both boards. It was evident that the most able and experienced engineer officers were being used to staff the newly created agency. The appointment of Bernard increased the prestige and support of the administration's effort to plan a scheme of improvements worthy of federal backing. The duplication of membership also indicated the close relationship recognized to exist between national defense and internal improvements.

An obvious difference between these boards was the presence of a civilian on the new one. This selection acknowledged the desire of Congress, as expressed in the act, that civil engineers be employed alongside military engineers to investigate and plan improvement projects. The mixed membership may have been designed to secure the confidence and co-operation of the nation's few, but highly respected, civil engineers. Tact and careful administration were needed if military engineers were to work with civil engineers on undertakings primarily civil in character. The need of tact and the role of the Board of Internal Improvement as a civil engineering agency were indicated in a letter from Secretary of War Calhoun to its members on September 11, 1824:

. . . there is nothing in the commission of Mr. Sullivan that was intended to discriminate between his duties and responsibilities and those of the [other] members of the Board. In calling him a Civil Engineer, it was not intended that the term should be considered in contradistinction to that of Military Engineer, as applied to the other members of the Board. As far as their present duties are concerned, all the members of the Board are considered in the light of Civil Engineers, and having equal responsibilities and similar duties to perform.[26]

The great importance of civil engineering in the board's work was revealed by the number of its engineers and extent of their operations. There were initially twenty-four military

[26] E.D., Letters to Officers of Engineers, II, 75.

and civil engineers assigned to the board. Among the former were topographical engineers and army line officers temporarily detailed to topographical duty. As its work commenced, additional officers were assigned to the board; and there were insistent pleas for increasing the number of army engineers.

At the end of 1824, the chief engineer explained that the growing functions of the Engineer Department required many more than the twenty-two officers of the Corps of Engineers and ten topographical engineers. Calhoun insisted that experience had shown that the engineer officers were too few to perform assigned duties which were increasing every year.[27] Monroe described the work already done by the Board of Internal Improvement and emphasized the enormous task yet remaining in surveying and planning civil improvements:

> With a view of these important objects, I submit to the consideration of Congress the propriety of enlarging both the corps of Engineers, the military and the topographical. . . . the more extensively these corps are engaged in the improvement of their country, in the execution of the powers of Congress, and in aid of the states in such improvements as lie beyond that limit, when such aid is desired, the happier the effect will be. . . . By profiting of their science, the works will always be well executed; and, by giving to the officers such employment, our Union will derive all the advantage, in peace as well as in war, from their talents and services, which they can afford. In this mode, also, the military will be incorporated with the civil, and unfounded and injurious distinctions and prejudices, of every kind be done away.[28]

Monroe unmistakably imputed to the army engineers the function of applying civil engineering to the nation's needs for internal improvements. This conception of their role was evident in his plea for more engineers for civil works and in

[27] A.R. of C/E, Nov. 20, 1824, *ASP, MA*, II, 713–14; A.R. of S/W, Dec. 3, 1824, Calhoun, *Works*, V, 147.

[28] Annual Message, Dec. 7, 1824, 18 Cong., 2 sess., *S. Doc. 1*, 11.

his selection of projects to which they devoted their professional services. In the first year of the act, preliminary examinations were made of canal routes between the Allegheny and Susquehanna, the Susquehanna and Schuylkill, the Delaware and Raritan, Barnstable Bay and Buzzards Bay, and Boston harbor and Narragansett Bay, as well as between the Potomac, the Ohio, and Lake Erie.[29]

Canals received predominant attention in the board's first year, for it was created at the peak of the canal craze. Much study went into the selection and comparison of routes deserving examination. Soon after passage of the Survey Act, for instance, a "Board of Engineers" presented "a list of canals in the order of their importance in relation to the defence of the country and to commerce." Twenty-seven canals were rated in terms of their value for defense and "their relative importance as to the interior commerce."[30]

[29] *Ibid.* Cf. A.R.s of S/W and C/E for 1824.

[30] E.D., Letters Received, I, No. E1709. The endorsement shows only the date May, 1824. The Board of Engineers for Fortifications may have prepared this comparison of canals, for the Board of Engineers for Internal Improvements was not officially formed until May 31, 1824. The list rated the proposed canals as follows:

| Routes | Defense | Commerce |
|---|---|---|
| 1. Delaware River to Raritan River | 1 | 3 |
| 2. James River to Ohio River | 2 | 1 |
| 3. Connecticut River to Boston | 3 | 3 |
| 4. Lake Champlain to St. Lawrence River | 4 | 3 |
| 5. Buzzards Bay to Cape Cod Bay, or | 5 | 2 |
| 6. Narragansett Bay to Boston | 5 | 2 |
| 7. Ohio River to Potomac River | 6 | 1 |
| 8. Potomac River to Chesapeake Bay | 6 | 1 |
| 9. Mississippi River to Lake Pontchartrain | 7 | 4 |
| 10. Clearing out pass on Lake Huron | 7 | 4 |
| 11. Mobile Bay to Pensacola Bay | 7 | 4 |
| 12. Delaware River to Susquehanna River | 7 | 2 |
| 13. Schuylkill River to Susquehanna River | 7 | 2 |
| 14. Susquehanna River to Little Lakes of New York | 7 | 2 |
| 15. Connecticut River to New Haven | 7 | 3 |
| 16. Pensacola Bay to Apalachee Bay | 8 | 6 |
| 17. Gulf of Mexico to St. Marys Harbor | 8 | 5 |

The rating of proposed canals by their relative merits and the number of canal routes examined during the first year demonstrated the sweep of the work initially attempted under the Survey Act. In his Annual Report for 1824, Secretary of War Calhoun analyzed the scope and purpose of the surveying activities in progress or being planned. The primary task was to determine which roads and canals were of national importance, for the act had authorized the President to survey only such routes. The government must consider only those major improvements directly affecting the performance of its prescribed duties.

Calhoun then discussed the projects of greatest national value. These were, first, canals to connect the Potomac with the Ohio and Lake Erie, including navigation improvements on the Ohio and Mississippi and canals around the falls at Louisville and Muscle Shoals; second, canals to connect the large navigable estuaries along the Atlantic Coast; and, third, a durable road from Washington to New Orleans. He felt that these major works constituted a system which would provide great benefit for defense, commerce, and the postal service. Other routes, although not essential to this system, were of such commercial and military value that they should be examined by the board. Most of these were routes connecting the "Eastern and Western waters," or the principal rivers flowing into the Atlantic and the Gulf of Mexico. These included connections between the Alabama and Savannah rivers,

| | | |
|---|---|---|
| 18. Western end of Lake Erie to Ohio River | 8 | 3 |
| 19. Susquehanna River to Allegheny River | 8 | 2 |
| 20. Susquehanna River to Baltimore | 8 | 2 |
| 21. Charleston to Cape Fear River | 9 | 5 |
| 22. Cape Fear River to Beaufort, North Carolina | 9 | 5 |
| 23. Upper Lakes to Mississippi River | 9 | 6 |
| 24. Ohio River to Gulf of Mexico | 9 | 3 |
| 25. Ohio River to Lake Erie | 9 | 1 |
| 26. Delaware River to Passaic River | 10 | 3 |
| 27. Delaware River to Hudson River | 11 | 3 |

James and Kanawha rivers, Susquehanna and Allegheny rivers, Lake Champlain and the St. Lawrence, and across Florida at the St. Johns River.

Calhoun suggested that one of these east-west links, a canal between the Susquehanna and Allegheny in Pennsylvania, was a possible alternative to the Chesapeake and Ohio Canal.[31] Proponents of this Pennsylvania canal petitioned the Engineer Department for surveying aid soon after the Survey Act was passed, and Calhoun promised state officials that the board would make a preliminary examination. He stated that if this route showed promise, the government would assist Pennsylvania with surveys, plans, and estimates. The Susquehanna route was an alternative to the Potomac, and the nation should choose between them only after they had been carefully compared.[32]

During 1824, applications were made to the secretary of war for surveys of canal routes in practically every part of the country. Most of these requests were either refused or postponed, since all army engineers were fully employed and the Chesapeake and Ohio Canal survey had been given priority. In some cases surveying aid was promised as soon as engineers were available. One such instance was the proposed canal between Baltimore and the Susquehanna. Another was the proposed canal around Muscle Shoals on the Tennessee River. Calhoun assured Andrew Jackson and other congressmen from Tennessee and Alabama that the latter had first-class priority under the Survey Act and would be surveyed the following year.[33]

Although canal projects at first received primary consideration, some notice was given to roads. Monroe and Calhoun declared in 1824 that henceforth more study would be de-

[31] A.R. of S/W, Dec. 3, 1824, Calhoun, *Works*, V, 147.
[32] June 8, Sept. 10 and 16, 1824, E.D., Misc. Letters Sent, II, 48–49, 105–107, 111.
[33] June 10, 1824, *ibid.*, II, 52–53.

voted to roads, particularly the projected national road from Washington to New Orleans, which Calhoun had rated as the third most important project of his system. The fact that all canal surveys made that year fell north of the Potomac River no doubt prompted them to support this road. The Board of Internal Improvement was informed that in 1825

. . . the first great national object for your consideration will be the route of the contemplated great Southern post road from this City to New Orleans.

Besides the importance of establishing this route as early as possible, in order to facilitate the communication between the Seat of Government and the City of New Orleans, and the intermediate States through which it will pass, it is desirable that the Southern portion of the Union should not only see, but feel some of the immediate benefits which will result from a system of internal improvement. This is the more important at this time, as there seems to be a doubt in the minds of the Southern people as to the support, which they ought to give to the System. Convinced by practical operations affecting their own immediate interests, and demonstrating the advantages which may be expected to result from the System, they would perhaps be earlier induced to consider the subject in its true point of view, and to afford it their countenance and support.[34]

During the first year of the Survey Act, the many demands for surveys began to manifest patterns of city and sectional rivalry. The administration was willing to make a large number of surveys, particularly when they were for nationally important routes and were in great demand. Although the North began to receive the greater engineering aid, definite efforts were made to plan surveys in the South.

Calhoun and the Engineer Department held the conception that they were planning a system of improvements worthy of financial aid from the federal government. They realized that

[34] C/E Macomb, Oct. 2, 1824, E.D., Letters to Officers of Engineers, II, 84–85.

surveying was an integral part of this planning and of the federal aid needed to execute the system, and they were willing to survey all possible routes of any national importance. The Board of Engineers for Internal Improvements was serving as the immediate planning agency, with the support of the President, secretary of war, and Engineer Department.

# III: Getting Down to Work

ALTHOUGH THE General Survey Act was in effect from 1824 to 1838, the Board of Engineers for Internal Improvements existed only until 1831. During its brief life this board operated, as in its initial year, as a planning body to apply the act. The board's policy criteria gradually took clearer form as they evolved under the impact of events. Its surveying operations increased rapidly after 1824. A widening range of projects benefited from surveys, plans, and estimates made by army engineers. Roads and canals receiving this assistance were said to be of national value and thus possibly eligible for federal financial aid. Engineering aid was increasingly provided for undertakings depending primarily or solely on state and private support, and before the end of the board's life, several railroad routes were surveyed by its engineers.

In 1825, canal studies dominated the work of the Board of Internal Improvement. Surveys were made for canal routes to connect the Chesapeake and Ohio, the Ohio and Lake Erie, and Buzzards and Barnstable bays. Examinations were also made of proposed canals along the Connecticut River and of a canal between the Mississippi River and Lake Pontchartrain. An increased interest in roads was marked by efforts to examine routes for the proposed national road from Washington to New Orleans and by the work of commissioners employed by the Engineer Department to extend the Cumberland Road and to lay out roads leading westward from Detroit, St. Louis, and Little Rock.[1]

In 1826 the board was still primarily concerned with the Chesapeake and Ohio Canal and the national road to New

[1] A.R.s of S/W and C/E for 1825, *ASP, MA*, III, 109, 137–39.

Orleans. It also reported on the Dismal Swamp and the Chesapeake and Delaware canals, and its engineers made examinations for canals in Pennsylvania, Maryland, Indiana, and Florida, as well as in New England. A survey to study the practicability of canals or railways or both to connect the Kanawha with the James and Roanoke rivers was the first railroad survey authorized under the General Survey Act.[2] Roads begun earlier were continued, and several additional ones were surveyed. Among these were roads from Washington to Buffalo, Washington to the Cumberland Road, and Baltimore to Philadelphia.[3]

A report early in 1827 indicated that during the first three years, thirty-five examinations and surveys were made under authority of the Survey Act. Nineteen were for canals, two for rivers and canals, one for canals or railways, three for rivers, and ten for roads.[4] Canals obviously exceeded roads in importance, and the river surveys were related to canal projects. Since surveys and improvement of rivers and harbors were specifically authorized by separate acts of Congress, they were not left to the discretion of the President under this act.

In 1827 there was government surveying for canals in every part of the nation, from New England to Florida and from Lake Erie to the Gulf of Mexico. Road works begun earlier were continued, and a new and important "road" survey was started when three topographical brigades were assigned to survey a route for the Baltimore and Ohio Railroad.[5]

A report by the Chief Engineer in 1828 indicated that since 1824 the government had examined, surveyed, or commenced

[2] Lewis Henry Haney, *A Congressional History of the Railways of the United States*, I, 111. Railroad surveys are discussed in the next chapter.

[3] A.R. of C/E, Nov. 18, 1826, *ASP, MA*, III, 358–64.

[4] Report of C/E Macomb, Feb. 5, 1827, 19 Cong., 2 sess., *H. Doc.* 83, 4, and adjoining statement.

[5] A.R.s of S/W and C/E for 1827, *ASP, MA*, III, 616, 628–32.

almost one hundred works of internal improvement. These included thirty-four canal routes, eighteen roads, and forty-four river and harbor projects.[6] In 1828 several new surveys were made by order of the President under authority of the Survey Act. Among them were six surveys involving railroads. Several surveys for roads and canals were in the southern states, but the railroad surveys tended to cluster around New York and Massachusetts. Two of these six surveys were made to determine the practicability of connecting the Tennessee with the Altamaha and Savannah rivers by canals or railways.[7]

During its last three years, the Board of Internal Improvement was engaged principally in preparing instructions for surveys. In 1829 it reported on a Florida canal examination and prepared plans for a canal between Buzzards and Barnstable bays. In the following two years it worked on plans for a canal around Muscle Shoals on the Tennessee River. Army engineers, under its directions, made surveys for a number of canals, several roads, and a few railroads. Four railroads were surveyed during 1829 and three in 1830. In 1831, army engineers surveyed the routes for two railroads and superintended construction of three others. A rapidly growing function of the army engineers was the construction of civil works, consisting primarily of river and harbor improvements and roads. The Engineer Department had about fifty civil works under way each year.[8]

During the eight years of its life, the Board of Internal Improvement examined all major routes proposed by Gallatin and Calhoun, and many more besides. It made more surveys for canals than roads, but with the administration's approval

[6] Report of Gen. Macomb, April 28, 1828, 20 Cong., 1 sess., *H. Doc 261*, 4, and adjoining statement. River and harbor improvements are discussed in Chapter VI.

[7] A.R. of C/E, Nov. 19, 1828, *ASP, MA*, IV, 12–17.

[8] A.R.s of C/E for 1829, 1830, and 1831, *ASP, MA*, IV, 164–69, 593–96, 728–33; A.R. of T.B. for 1831, *ibid.*, IV, 766–68.

it brought railroads within the scope of the General Survey Act. It used civil engineering as the basis on which to plan a comprehensive scheme of roads and canals worthy of federal support. Through this surveying it also gave direct impetus to state and private undertakings. There is thus reason to note how many army engineers the board employed, and how their services were used in planning and encouraging road and canal enterprises.

The order creating the board assigned it twenty-four engineers. Additional civil engineers were later employed, and more army line officers were assigned to topographical duty. During 1824, twenty-six officers were employed in surveying routes for roads and canals, with three surveying brigades in the field. In 1825 and 1826, the number of engineers increased to forty and then to fifty-three, and the number of surveying parties to five and then to eight. There were eleven parties making canal, road, and railroad surveys by 1828 and thirteen by 1830. Of these thirteen brigades, ten were commanded by "military topographical engineers" and three by "civil topographical engineers."[9]

In 1831, the Topographical Bureau, which that year assumed the work of the board, employed twelve civil engineers and thirty line officers on surveys of internal improvements.[10] The ten topographical engineers and a few officers of the Corps of Engineers were also engaged in these activities. Altogether, more than fifty experienced engineers worked for nearly a decade under the board. They were busily engaged in making surveys and plans for transportation routes deemed

[9] "Memorandum of Officers at the disposal of Government for examining and surveying routes for Roads and Canals during the years 1824, 1825, and 1826," E.D., Misc. Papers 1789–1831, File G, No. 158; letter to S/W, June 6, 1828, E.D., Misc. Letters Sent, V, 96–98; letter by Col. Abert, Jan. 2, 1830, T.B., Letters Issued, I, 31–34.

[10] Beers, "Topographical Engineers," 289.

of sufficient national importance to merit consideration in a federally sponsored system of improvements.

Despite their number and active work, these engineers were unable to fulfill the demands for their services. Each year many petitions for surveys and pleas for a larger body of army engineers went unanswered. Monroe and Calhoun noted these growing demands and the lack of engineers in 1824, after the first season of operation under the Survey Act. A year later the *National Journal* and *Niles' Weekly Register* evinced public awareness of this problem.

... the various plans connected with the great scheme of internal improvement, have created a demand for a species of labor hitherto comparatively but little required. . . . Recently . . . the attention of a great proportion of our topographical corps has been called to the practice of civil engineering. . . .  . . . several ineffectual applications have been made to congress to increase the number of a corps the services of which have been thus ramified, and the present force of which is so totally inadequate to the demands of various state governments. It is true, there are some distinguished private engineers in our country, but they are either insufficiently known, or too limited in their numbers for their talents and services to be made available in the greater part of the contemplated projects of canal construction. The advantages of having that part of our engineer corps, which may be detailed for surveys, in connexion with the subject of internal improvement, increased to meet the rising exigencies of the country, require no elucidation. . . . It is well known that the department of war is unable to comply with all the requisitions made for the services of scientific engineers for the purpose of state surveys. Either the spirit of this great system must be checked for want of men of science qualified for these employments, or superficial and incorrect surveys must be made. . . .[11]

President John Quincy Adams and Secretary of War James

[11] "Corps of Engineers," *Niles' Weekly Register,* Oct. 22, 1825, pp. 121–22. Reprinted from the *National Journal,* Oct. 13, 1825.

Barbour in 1825 repeated the proposals of Monroe and Calhoun for additional engineer officers. Insisting that "the spirit of improvement is abroad upon the earth," Adams urged that the number of military and topographical engineers be raised to permit rapid execution of public works. Barbour recognized the importance of civil engineering and noted the inability of the War Department to meet the many calls for engineering aid. He advised Congress of the necessity of increasing the Corps of Engineers and organizing the topographical engineers into a larger corps. The former should be increased by taking the Military Academy's best graduates annually, and the latter enlarged by appointing line officers, themselves West Point graduates, already on topographical duty.[12]

The House asked the Secretary of War to report on the need of military and topographical engineers for strictly military purposes and for civil purposes in the event of federal construction of a system of roads and canals. Barbour repeated the administration's proposal that the Corps of Engineers be gradually enlarged and the topographical engineers converted into a corps of thirty-four officers. Although this number was necessary for purely military surveys, it would be possible for many of these topographical engineers "to be disposable for objects of internal improvement."[13]

Barbour opposed creation of a "corps of civil engineers." His opinion represented the official view that military engineers were preferable to civilian engineers in government surveying. Military tenure and organization produced greater responsibility and fidelity among military engineers than could be expected of civilian engineers. Only graduates of the Military Academy possessed the training required of government

[12] Annual Message, Dec. 6, 1825, 19 Cong., 1 sess., S. *Doc.* 2, 10, 14–15, 19; A.R. of S/W, Dec. 1, 1825, *ASP, MA*, III, 109; Barbour to Chairman of House Committee on Military Affairs, Jan. 10, 1826, *ibid.*, III, 185–86.

[13] "Report on the Subject of an Augmentation of the Corps of Engineers of the Army," April 8, 1826, *ibid.*, III, 278.

engineers. If a corps of civil engineers was later created, it should be staffed by army engineers and other experienced West Pointers. In the meantime, Barbour preferred to carry on government surveying with army engineers and other competent West Point–trained officers borrowed from the line of the army.[14]

In the House, Charles F. Mercer proposed a plan for organizing the army engineers which differed greatly from the views of the War and Engineer departments. He advocated the creation of a federal fund and a set of rules for its application to such canals, roads, and railroads as Congress deemed appropriate. An important part of his program dealt with the system of collecting information needed for selecting projects. He advocated that the army engineers be increased in number and divided into two separate agencies, a corps of military engineers and a corps of civil engineers. The latter would be staffed by West Point graduates and a few experienced civil engineers. One part of this corps, a "Corps of Topographical Civil Engineers," would explore the country at large in order to determine general possibilities of improvement of roads, canals, and railways.[15] The remainder of this corps of civil engineers would be used in

. . . forming estimates of the probable cost of every such work; in supervising, under the orders of the Department of War, the conduct of such works as shall have been begun; in reporting to the Department their gradual progress. . . . That of all those reports, abstracts shall be compiled and transmitted to the Congress. . . . These compilations shall be made under the auspices of the Department of War, by a Board consisting of not less than

[14] *Ibid.*, III, 278–79.
[15] "Mr. Mercer's Resolutions to Provide a Fund for Internal Improvement," April 25, 1826, 19 Cong., 1 sess., *H. Res. 45*, 1–2. Mercer was the author of the Virginia system of state improvement based on mixed enterprise. Cf. Carter Goodrich, "The Virginia System of Mixed Enterprise: A Study of State Planning of Internal Improvements," *Political Science Quarterly*, Vol. LXIV (1949), 355–87.

three Civil Engineers, who shall subjoin to them, a general history of the distribution and operations of the Corps of Civil Engineers during the preceding year, accompanied by such reflections as may serve to detect existing errors in the design or execution of any work; to suggest suitable correctives thereof, and to guard against their recurrence.[16]

Mercer's proposed system would have complemented the General Survey Act in several ways. It would have instituted federal financing and supervision of major transportation improvements. The number of army engineers used to plan and execute this work would have been increased. They would have been recruited from among the country's experienced civilian engineers, as well as from its military engineers trained at West Point. Their work would have been greatly enlarged, for they would have supervised the construction of improvements after having made surveys and project plans. Railroads would also have been eligible for such technical and financial aid.

The organization of these engineers would have been greatly changed. The board would have been established by law as the top co-ordinating agency. A comprehensive system of transportation routes would have been studied and planned in broad outline. This would have been a clearer call for national planning of improvements than that contained in the Survey Act. Government civil engineers would have filled in the general plan by supervising individual projects. Mercer's proposals would have explicitly committed the army engineers to plan a broad scheme of improvements and to encourage individual undertakings by giving them sorely needed engineering aid.

Each year the Engineer Department made insistent pleas for additional engineers. Colonel Abert in 1827 asked that the topographical engineers be increased to a total of forty-two

[16] 19 Cong., 1 sess., *H. Res. 45*, 2.

officers. There were only eight surveying brigades in the field; but if the desired increase was voted by Congress, the number of parties could be raised to fifteen at once and to twenty-one in three years. If this change was made, the two civil brigades would no longer be needed.[17] Chief Engineer Macomb urged in 1828 that twenty-four line officers then engaged in civil engineering be permanently assigned to the Engineer Department for topographical duty. Great loss would result if these trained engineers were removed from important surveys then in progress.[18]

Abert again requested more topographical engineers in 1830. If his proposals were adopted, the Topographical Bureau could immediately put twenty-one surveying parties in the field instead of the present thirteen. All brigades would consist of military engineers, whereas three then consisted of civilians. The "civil topographical engineers" were costly and hard to secure, while "military topographical engineers" were economical and efficient.[19]

Although some fifty army engineers were employed under the General Survey Act, their number was never considered sufficient. The Board of Internal Improvement at no time possessed adequate surveying personnel for the demands made upon it.

From the board's growing activities emerged certain policy criteria which were shaped by the work of the army engineers and which were also crucial in determining the nature of their work. The basic philosophy of the army engineers in their improvement activities may be analyzed in terms of their desire for comprehensive planning, determination to give active encouragement, desire to promote civil engineer-

[17] "Report on the Organization of the Topographical Engineers of the Army" (including Abert's letter of Jan. 2, 1827 and "A communication from the topographical engineers to the Secretary of War"), *ASP, MA,* III, 492–95.
[18] March 24, 1828, E.D., Misc. Letters Sent, V, 1–3.
[19] Jan. 2, 1830, T.B., Letters Issued, I, 31–34.

ing, attitude toward alternative means of transportation, and military considerations. Although these interrelated criteria were of varying importance and were fused in an ever changing philosophical pattern, they were instrumental in shaping the application of the Survey Act.

The administration recognized the need for integrated planning in administering the Survey Act. The Board of Internal Improvement used civil engineering in determining a system of essential improvements to be secured by federal construction or financial aid.[20] Calhoun had outlined the major projects of this proposed national plan in 1824. Promotion of this scheme of roads and canals would guide the economic and political development of the nation along desired lines. This scheme would have great military as well as civil value, for the resulting military, commercial, and political benefits would be mutually advantageous.

The board's planning, however, possessed two divergent aspects, that of determining a general system of transportation routes and that of technical planning and assistance for individual projects. Its planning had both a general and a particular element; it was directed toward fostering a national system of improvements and also toward providing surveys, plans, and estimates for all promising undertakings. The latter aspect took the form of engineering aid to state and private enterprises; it became more a matter of wholesale encouragement than of comprehensive planning.

This board understood that it was to plan a national scheme of improvements which would foster national prosperity and development. It stated in physiocratic terms that the objective was to stimulate the process of circulation by

. . . opening a system of communication to unite all the sections of the Republic by the bonds of commercial intercourse, and rapid

[20] Holt, *Chief of Engineers*, 6–7.

mutual aid in time of danger. This system will contribute essentially to the great end of rendering the means of our Government more efficient; for, by reducing the time necessary for communication, it will reduce, in fact, the great distances which divide the sections of our vast empire from each other, and will enable us easily and promptly to transfer the means and produce of one climate to another; it will give a new value to the agricultural and mineral riches of our soil, and a new life and activity to our manufacturing industry, by facilitating their circulation. Without a free and constant circulation, the political, as well as the human body becomes paralyzed and benumbed in its operations.[21]

The board also explained the careful study and planning required for each proposed route. Its systematic procedure consisted of three steps: reconnaissance and preparatory survey of the project, final location of the route by exact surveys, and preparation of the project plans together with specifications and cost estimates.[22]

In its report on the proposed national road from Washington to New Orleans, the board indicated this need for meticulous investigation in selecting routes. It compared three possible routes with reference to materials, soil, bridges, causeways, grades, population, distance, and expense. It applied certain "considerations of internal policy" bearing on the final selection of a route. These major criteria were summarized as commerce, "accommodation of the population," political benefits, military value, and transportation of the mail.[23] The board manifestly viewed the proposed road in a comprehensive manner.

This conscientious commitment to national planning on the part of the board and its engineers did not alter their determi-

[21] Report of Gen. Bernard and Col. Totten on canal routes examined in 1824, Feb. 2, 1825, 18 Cong., 2 sess., S. *Doc. 32*, 68.

[22] *Ibid.*, 13–14.

[23] Report (by Gen. Bernard) "Upon the Reconnaissance of Three Routes of a Contemplated National Road, from Washington City to New Orleans," April 8, 1826, 19 Cong., 1 sess., *H. Doc. 156*, 21–26.

nation to encourage individual improvements. The planning of transportation projects, in fact, encouraged their construction. The two were somewhat effectively united by the General Survey Act, since surveys, plans, and estimates were essential to each project. Surveying was a strategically effective way of aiding individual undertakings. Faced with a scarcity of civil engineers, states and chartered companies greatly desired the aid of army engineers. The latter felt a duty to supply their technical talents to meet the needs of the country. The Survey Act implemented this desire to foster a more rapid development of roads and canals.

President Adams recognized the ability of the army engineers to stimulate improvement enterprises. Noting that officers trained at West Point provided "the means of multiplying the undertakings of public improvements," he strongly urged an increase in the engineering branches of the War Department.[24] His secretaries of war also favored the principle of encouraging worthy enterprises with surveying aid. In 1825, James Barbour regretted that it was impossible to meet the many demands for surveys. Two years later he again demonstrated his desire to fulfill requests for surveys needed by promoters of useful undertakings:

In selecting among the objects presented for reconnaissance by the State authorities and respectable associations of private citizens, I have endeavored to be governed by their relative importance and a due regard to the fair claims of all parts of the Union. The result of the surveys has, in some instances, reduced the scale of the proposed objects so as to deprive them of the character of national importance; but even in these cases the labors of the corps have not been lost. By their superior science and experience they have given valuable information to those concerned, which, from their limited resources, they would have been unable otherwise to have procured.[25]

[24] Annual Message, Dec. 6, 1825, 19 Cong., 1 sess., S. Doc. 2, 9–10.
[25] A.R. of S/W, Nov. 26, 1827, ASP, MA, III, 616. Cf. A.R. of S/W, Dec. 1, 1825, ASP, MA, III, 109.

*Colonel John J. Abert, Chief of Topographical Bureau, 1829–61.*

Courtesy United States Military Academy.

*Colonel Joseph G. Totten, Chief Engineer, 1838–64.*

In 1828, Peter B. Porter, Barbour's successor, praised the work of scientific military engineers "in developing the capacities of the country for internal improvement, and in building up works which belong exclusively to the department of political economy."[26]

President Jackson's first secretary of war also approved of the civil activities of the army engineers. John H. Eaton in 1829 endorsed the demand for more engineer officers and the principle of their making surveys for enterprises in the various states. He noted that individual states had made many requests for surveys which the War Department had been forced to refuse, despite its strong disposition to provide aid.[27]

The government thus displayed a willingness to make surveys for states and chartered companies applying for such assistance. Applications for engineering aid were commonly presented to the President or War Department by governors and congressmen of the states concerned. A report by the Chief Engineer late in 1826 analyzed the surveys assigned to the Engineer Department that season. Some had been authorized by Congress, but most had been "assigned to the Department, in compliance with the requests of State Executives, members of Congress, and others." In the latter categories were sixteen surveys for canal routes, three for roads, two for river navigation, and one for a canal or railway.[28]

The President authorized the examination of any route he considered nationally important, since the Survey Act gave him this discretion. Once he had approved an application from a state official or group of citizens, he directed that the survey be made and its expenses paid from funds appropriated for executing this act. Although the act named only roads and canals, the government made several railroad surveys. Early

[26] A.R. of S/W, Nov. 24, 1828, *ASP, MA,* IV, 2.
[27] A.R. of S/W, Nov. 30, 1829, *ibid.,* IV, 152.
[28] Gen. Macomb to S/W Barbour, Oct. 3, 1826, E.D., Misc. Letters Sent, III, 397–99.

in 1827, for instance, Governor Peter Little of Maryland notified the government of the proposed Baltimore and Ohio Railroad and the state's desire "to procure the co-operation of the United States in the execution of the said project, and to ascertain to what extent such assistance may be contributed." Secretary of War Barbour replied that surveying aid could be provided, since the President felt that the project was of great importance to those affected by it. Barbour later informed P. E. Thomas, president of the Baltimore and Ohio Railroad Company, that this proposed railroad was of national as well as local importance and that army engineers would make the necessary surveys and charge the expense to public appropriations for surveys of internal improvements.[29]

Other railroad, canal, and road projects were likewise deemed of national importance and given engineering aid under the Survey Act. Army engineers with the Board of Internal Improvement executed these surveys and made frequent reports to company and state officials and to the Engineer Department.

The army engineers realized that they were in a strategic position to encourage internal improvements. The government recognized that civil engineering was a critical national need and an effective means of stimulating transportation enterprises. The advancement of civil engineering was thus an important policy criterion of the army engineers in their work under the Survey Act. The relative scarcity of civilian engineers and the early government monopoly of engineering education gave additional force to this objective. The development of engineering science may be regarded as a social cost which the federal government helped to bear and which produced far-reaching social benefits.

There was widespread recognition of the need for government application of civil engineering. Lack of private engi-

[29] May 2 and June 16, 1827, *ibid.*, IV, 149, 199.

neers and the ability of the War Department to educate and furnish engineers for work on internal improvements soon convinced many people that the government must inevitably make this knowledge more widely available. For this purpose the army needed more "scientific engineers" to make the many surveys being demanded.[30]

President Adams urged greater support of the Military Academy, whose graduates provided "the means of multiplying the undertakings of public improvement, to which their acquirements at that institution are peculiarly adapted."[31] He asked for an increase in the number of army engineers and encouraged Congress to adopt broad measures of public improvement. Feeling that the first instrument for this task was knowledge, he expressed the need, as had his predecessors, for national seminaries of learning. The country possessed a valuable military academy but lacked a national university. He thus emphasized the strategic role of knowledge, particularly engineering, in public improvement.[32] James Barbour, his secretary of war, also believed that the army was nourishing engineering science for the benefit of the country. He termed the Military Academy the nursery of military science and stated that civil engineering, an auxiliary branch of this science, ". . . promises to be among the most beneficial acquisitions in the whole range of science."[33]

The criterion of fostering the growth of civil engineering was clearly evident in the philosophy and actions of the government engineers during the life of the Board of Internal Improvement. This engineering aid benefited canals, roads, railroads, and river and harbor improvements; and the army engineers developed preferences relating to these alternative

[30] Cf. "Corps of Engineers," *Niles' Weekly Register*, Oct. 22, 1825, pp. 121–22.
[31] Annual Message, Dec. 6, 1825, 19 Cong., 1 sess., S. *Doc.* 2, 9.
[32] *Ibid.*, 15.
[33] A.R. of S/W, Dec. 1, 1825, *ASP, MA*, III, 109.

means of transportation. Their activities were guided largely by the pressure of public demands for different modes of communication, but their own preferences were significant. They favored large projects connecting different parts of the country and fitting into a co-ordinated network of improvements. They wanted to determine the most practicable means for each proposed connection and its place in the national scheme. The physical and economic conditions of each project determined which type of improvement would be most suitable in terms of efficiency and cost.

Surveys for canal routes exceeded other surveys in number and extent during the life of the board. Examinations of roads were secondary at first and only gradually increased in importance. Few surveys of rivers or harbors were made under this act, for Congress early adopted the policy of specifying the river and harbor works to be surveyed and executed. Railroads were considered as "roads" under the Survey Act, however, and gained rapidly in prominence after 1827. As a result, army engineers were most interested in canals, with railroads soon becoming a close rival for their engineering assistance.

The first investigation involving railroads took place in 1826 to determine the practicability of uniting the Kanawha with the James and Roanoke rivers by canals or railways or both. In 1827 surveys were started for the Baltimore and Ohio Railroad. For several years there were instances of railway-or-canal investigations, since the period 1826 to 1831 was one in which canals and railroads were recognized as closely competing means of improvement. Although most surveys were for canals, some were to enable a choice between canals and railways, and an increasing number were for railroads alone.[34]

Military considerations were a criterion which the army engineers kept constantly in mind. Like Calhoun, they realized

[34] Haney, *Congressional History*, I, 111–13, 119–20.

that important improvements were beneficial both to national defense and to economic and political welfare. Their defense plans gave a major place to inland transportation. Canals and roads were always examined in terms of both their military and their commercial value, and the military importance of railroads and river and harbor improvements was recognized from the beginning. Engineering science was stimulated by the War Department because it obviously had both military and civil usefulness. Furthermore, national security was an effective argument for promoting internal improvements and employing army engineers in civil engineering. This justification carried much weight as a result of the consensus that national defense and inland transportation were complementary and interdependent.[35]

Surveying for individual civil works was also considered to be of military value. Secretary of War Eaton stated in 1831 that the topographical corps, in its surveys for roads, canals, and river and harbor improvements, gathered information which would be useful in future military operations.[36] Major Abert argued that the work of these topographical engineers had both military and civilian value:

From the character of the duties of such a corps it may be seen with what facility and advantage it may have its attention, when necessary, turned to objects purely civil; and that even while pursuing these purely civil objects, from its military knowledge, its labors will be enriched by all the military considerations which the operations may develop; so that the labors of the corps, if judiciously directed, cannot fail to furnish the government with the most correct knowledge of the resources of the country—civil and military; of its agricultural, commercial, mechanical, and mineralogical advantages, and of its military means of defence; as

[35] Report by Gen. Bernard and Col. Totten, March 24, 1826, on "The Defence of the Seaboard," *ASP, MA,* III, 283–98.

[36] John H. Eaton to Speaker of House, Jan. 20, 1831, *ibid.,* IV, 631.

all these are subjects of the investigations of a topographical engineer.[37]

This emphasis on the military value of internal improvements was clearly one of the criteria of the army engineers. Other policy guides were their commitment to plan and encourage the growth of a national system of transportation and their determination to promote the development of civil engineering. This social philosophy helped determine their place in the movement for internal improvements. Their role was a gradually changing one, even during the life of the Board of Internal Improvement, for they encountered varying forces and tensions which slowly modified their objectives.

The evolution of the board's outlook and function may be examined in terms of certain interrelated aspects. These were a change in emphasis from a few major improvements to many scattered ones, a growing responsiveness to the increasing demands for engineering aid, frictions produced by regional rivalry, and a trend from comprehensive planning to ubiquitous encouragement of improvements.

The government initially proposed an investigation of a system of major national improvements which it might execute or financially support. Surveys of these main roads and canals were completed in the first three or four years of the board's life. Even during this time, routes of a more local character were examined. During ensuing years an increasingly large number of surveys was made; and state and private enterprises, particularly canals and railroads, received a growing volume of engineering aid. The trend towards surveys for smaller and more local undertakings was reinforced by the failure of the government to execute or finance major routes of a national character. As it became evident that the govern-

[37] A.R. of T.B., Nov. 7, 1831, *ASP, MA,* IV, 766–68.

ment would not itself construct a system of roads and canals, engineering aid was directed more and more to projects sponsored by states and chartered companies.[38]

In 1829, Major Abert recommended that his Topographical Bureau be increased in size and status so as to perform its duties more effectively. He proposed that it be made a separate agency within the War Department and that he be placed on the Board of Internal Improvement and made responsible for its performance.[39] He noted that the original intention had been that this board "occupy itself with great and leading questions of national and general interest, and furnish for the judgment of the nation, plans of improving the country in its roads, canals and harbours, of so general and so national a character and so manifestly useful, that feelings of patriotism and of national prosperity would be enlisted in their behalf."[40] This function of the board had declined, however, with the shift of emphasis from this original purpose to less important improvements. The board had come to consist of only General Bernard, and the work of the topographical engineers had become confined to local and secondary projects. Abert explained that this changed emphasis had caused delays, disappointments, and loss of prestige for the army engineers.

The increase in surveys for minor, local undertakings reflected the growing responsiveness of the government to a flood of demands for government surveys. The army engineers were willing to supply engineering services to promising state and private projects. They believed, essentially, that it was their duty to provide necessary technical aid; and they carefully considered all applications for assistance made by congressmen, state officials, or associations of influential citizens.

[38] Turner, *New West*, 286–87, 293–94.
[39] Abert to S/W Porter, Feb. 12, 1829, T.B., Letters Issued, I, 3–7.
[40] Abert to Gratiot, Aug. 11, 1829, *ibid.*, I, 53.

One writer describes the General Survey Act as "the assertion of a willingness to utilize the government engineers in the examination of all projected schemes."[41]

Along with this demand for surveys and the desire of the army engineers to perform them, there developed strong pressures of city and regional rivalry. Each city and section attempted to secure as much government surveying as possible. Governors and congressmen actively sought aid for undertakings in their own states. The Atlantic seaports were jealous commercial rivals for inland trade, and they competed for studies of alternative routes to the West. When one port secured the survey of a canal or railroad route into the interior, other cities quickly demanded equivalent aid for their own projects.

The government attempted to spread its engineering services evenly among the states and satisfy the demands of leading contenders. It tried to provide more surveying in the South and to prevent a concentration of assistance in New England and the central states. The President had the impossible task of trying to distribute the work of the engineers so as to avoid sectional jealousies and charges of favoritism. These conflicts of state and sectional interest increased the demand for aid under the Survey Act. They were also a major cause of the failure to adopt a national system of internal improvements based on investigations authorized by the act.[42]

Such factors as city and regional rivalry, emphasis on smaller, scattered improvements, and desire to fulfill all engineering needs contributed to the trend away from generalized planning and toward more immediate encouragement. The planning actually achieved gradually lost its national character and became a matter of planning individual improvements, and surveying was done on a piecemeal basis.

[41] Way, "Mississippi Valley," 168.
[42] Goodrich, "National Planning," 36–40; Turner, *New West*, 286–87.

A national system for executing and financing major projects was never established; consequently, much of the incentive and justification for national planning disappeared. The government lost its chance to guide, but not its ability to assist the internal improvements movement. Congress remained jealous of the President's broad power under the General Survey Act. There were charges of logrolling and favoritism in the allocation of surveying. After 1825 there were frequent attempts in Congress to reduce appropriations for surveys and to limit future surveys to those specifically authorized by Congress. But congressmen were in an advantageous position to secure surveys for their own sections, and the government was very responsive to their demands. The Survey Act lost its planning purpose but continued to serve as the basis for the ubiquitous encouragement of a growing volume of transportation improvements.[43]

As the planning function of the Board of Internal Improvement declined, the board's usefulness rapidly diminished. Few major works received its immediate attention in its later years. After Major Abert, head of the Topographical Bureau, complained in 1829 that his authority over the operations of the topographical engineers was inadequate, his power was increased. After charging that the board's work was marked by delay and aid to local projects, he was placed on the board to co-ordinate its operations.

In December, 1830, Bernard was granted a six months' furlough, beginning January 1, 1831. In August, 1831, he resigned and returned to France.[44] The Secretary of War issued a regulation separating the Topographical Bureau from the

[43] Haney, *Congressional History,* I, 114–15; Holt, *Chief of Engineers,* 7.

[44] Major Edward Burr, "Memoranda relating to Brevet Brigadier General Simon Bernard, Assistant to the Corps of Engineers, U.S.A., 1816–31," Sept. 17, 1906, Office of the Chief of Engineers, Doc. File 1894–1923, Box 1209, File 50734–72, pp. 22–24.

Engineer Department and making it an independent agency within the War Department. These developments spelled the end of the Board of Internal Improvement, and the Topographical Bureau assumed the surveying duties of the Engineer Department.[45] This bureau subsequently applied the General Survey Act, then at the halfway point of its life.

Although the Board of Engineers for Internal Improvements passed out of existence in 1831, the General Survey Act was not repealed until 1838. During this time the act was administered by the Topographical Bureau, which functioned in many ways as a department of internal improvements. Government surveying continued at a rapid pace, but it took the form of unplanned and diffused encouragement to mushrooming state and private transportation enterprises. The act gradually lost purpose and support, particularly with the failure to use it in guiding national economic development and with the success of influential promoters in securing its benefits for their particular undertakings. The decline of the act may be analyzed in terms of the nature of the work done under its waning authority, the motivation of the army engineers in applying it, and the causes of its eventual repeal in 1838.

Appropriations for applying the Survey Act averaged between $25,000 and $30,000 per year between 1831 and 1838, only slightly less than for the period before 1831. During the life of this act, the sum of $424,000 was appropriated and spent for making surveys, plans, and estimates.[46] The ten topographical engineers had the assistance of ten to fifteen civil engineers and twenty to thirty line officers assigned to topographical duty. Some fifty army engineers were thus continually engaged in surveys for internal improvements during most of the 1830's.

[45] Beers, "Topographical Engineers," 289; Holt, *Chief of Engineers*, 6–8; A.R. of S/W, Nov. 21, 1831, *ASP, MA*, IV, 710.

[46] "Appropriations and Expenditures for Roads and Canals," July 26, 1882, 47 Cong., 1 sess., *S. Ex. Doc. 196*, 332–33.

Within a very few years the work of these engineers changed radically. In 1831 most of their surveys were for canals, with only a few for river improvements, military defenses, roads, and railroads. By 1835, however, the many surveys under the Topographical Bureau included a large number for roads, railroads, and river and harbor works, but very few for canals and fortifications. Mineralogical and geological investigations were also under way by that time.[47]

Surveying activity was reduced in 1836 by failure to enlarge the Topographical Bureau, lateness of appropriations, and withdrawal of line officers and topographical engineers for military field duty. Nevertheless, there were several surveys for railroads, river and harbor improvements, and military defenses. Although there were coast surveys, geological investigations, and supervision of several river and harbor works, only one canal survey was made by army engineers.[48]

In 1837 there were again coastal, military, and geological surveys, in addition to those for river and harbor improvements. No government surveys for canals or railroads were reported. Topographical engineers made military reconnaissances of the national frontiers. Civil and military engineers also supervised the construction of a canal aqueduct, a road, a lighthouse, and several harbor and river works. In 1838, the last year of the Survey Act, the Topographical Bureau reported one railroad survey and seven for rivers and harbors. Its growing construction activities bulked larger than its surveying.[49]

In the last half of its life, the General Survey Act permitted a large amount of surveying. Army engineers became progressively more concerned with railroads, which claimed

[47] A.R.s of T.B., Nov. 7, 1831, *ASP, MA,* IV, 766, and Nov. 2, 1835, *ASP, MA,* V, 711–13.

[48] A.R. of T.B., Nov. 15, 1836, *ASP, MA,* VI, 909–11.

[49] A.R.s of T.B., Nov. 7, 1837, *ASP, MA,* VIII, 723–27, and Nov. 26, 1838, 25 Cong., 3 sess., *S. Doc. 1,* 366–72.

the dominant place previously held by canals. There was also a rapid increase in engineering activities lying outside the scope of the act. Coastal, geological, and military surveys grew in volume, particularly after 1835, and gradually superseded surveying for internal improvements. At the same time the construction of river and harbor works, roads, and lighthouses became an increasing function of the topographical engineers.[50]

With this shift in the character of their work, the outlook of the army engineers changed. In effect, their policy criteria underwent further alteration, and their role in national expansion was gradually modified. Their previous commitment to the comprehensive planning of internal improvements suffered from atrophy, while their willingness to encourage all hopeful improvement ventures remained strong. Although they were still eager to broadcast the services of civil engineering, they found it more difficult to do so. They also tried to have their number increased and reorganized to include only military engineers, thus excluding civil engineers.

Early in 1831, Secretary of War Eaton recommended an increase in the topographical corps and indicated that its primary duty was military surveying. He stated that surveys for civil purposes had unquestioned military worth; but he emphasized the value of exclusively military duties, including surveys for military roads and defenses and examination of the seacoast.[51] Secretary of War Lewis Cass also stressed the need for these surveys, particularly the coast survey: "Labors of this nature have engaged the attention of the most enlightened governments, and the materials become a part of the general stock of public knowledge. . . . Some of the operations require an intimate knowledge of the most abstruse

[50] Beers, "Topographical Engineers," 289. The work of the army engineers extending beyond the scope of the Survey Act is analyzed in the following five chapters.
[51] Eaton to Speaker of House, Jan. 20, 1831, *ASP, MA,* IV, 631.

investigations of the present day in mathematical and physical science, and we shall in vain look for their accomplishment unless the government make provision for the measure."[52]

Colonel Abert likewise expressed the need of a coastal survey by topographical engineers, whose West Point training equipped them for this valuable work.[53] Since topographical engineers possessed military discipline and technical knowledge, they should execute the coast survey, a function with great commercial, scientific, and military value. The work of a body of engineers engaged in such valuable functions would benefit society in many ways and would "eminently qualify its members for operations which might be considered as the peculiar province of the civil engineer."

In 1832, Cass recommended increase of the "engineer corps" and "topographical corps." To enlarge the latter, military engineers should be used exclusively, for they alone had the proper military and technical training. He felt that military engineers were more professional, better disciplined, and more responsible than civil engineers.[54]

Surveying activities of the army engineers began to be restricted in 1832. The practice was adopted of authorizing only surveys ordered by resolution of Congress. In answering an application for a road survey in 1833, Cass stated that if there had been such a resolution, the survey would be readily made. For two years no new surveys had been initiated by the President, who had no intention of doing so until some

[52] A.R. of S/W, Nov. 21, 1831, *ASP, MA*, IV, 710–11.

[53] Abert insisted that "we should be no longer entirely indebted to the imperfect efforts of other nations for information of our own coast, and . . . we should, by our own labors, add something to the general mass of scientific knowledge by, at least, correct determinations of the geography of our own country. The present effort may also be the origin of a school which may hereafter furnish individuals adequate . . . to enter into fair and honorable competition with the distinguished astronomers of Europe, some of whom made their first essays while officers of a similar corps." A.R. of T.B., Nov. 7, 1831, *ASP, MA*, IV, 767.

[54] A.R. of S/W, Nov. 25, 1832, *ASP, MA*, V, 20.

system of internal improvement had been firmly adopted.[55] President Jackson, in effect, had renounced his power under the Survey Act to initiate studies of roads and canals. No longer able to secure surveys by petitioning the President or secretary of war, promoters of improvements had to solicit the Senate or House to order government surveys of their proposed routes.

In 1833, Colonel Abert made his typical plea for more topographical engineers but indicated a special area in which they could encourage economic development. He asked Congressional consent to divert surveying funds

. . . to geological investigations, and to the construction of a geological map of the United States. Few objects connected with the duties of this bureau open so many and so important national advantages, or are adapted to redound more to internal commercial prosperity and to national scientific fame. It is the development of these great resources of wealth and commercial intercourse, which now lie inert and buried in the bowels of the earth, and in which the few partial investigations which have been made exhibit our country as being so extremely rich. The propriety of artificial roads and canals may in many cases be considered as entirely dependent upon them, or as the mere machinery by which they are brought into being and activity.

Already have the results of individual enterprise and scientific devotion brought much of this hidden wealth to our knowledge. But these efforts are but partial, and have their limit in the limited means of individuals. Such extensive resources as we are represented to possess in this respect can be correctly developed only by national encouragement of a regular system of scientific investigation pursued with steadiness and intelligence, and its results fairly exposed to the efforts of our enterprising countrymen.[56]

Abert clearly proposed to use army engineers in this national encouragement of investigations which would stimulate pri-

---

[55] Cass to George Bard, Sept. 21, 1833, T.B., Letters Issued, I, 310–11.
[56] A.R. of T.B., Oct. 19, 1833, *ASP, MA*, V, 219.

vate enterprise and economic progress. Only the government could undergo the social cost of this technical research essential to national development.

In 1834, Abert again urged the reorganization and increase of the topographical engineers. Since 1821 the ten regular topographical engineers had been assisted by officers detailed from the line of the army. These officers had been separated from their line duties for long periods, and the army had objected. A regulation had been issued requiring the withdrawal of line officers after two years of topographical duty. As a result, inexperienced and unsuitable officers were assigned to temporary engineering duties.

Abert also opposed employment of civilian surveyors. A mixed service caused delay, insubordination, increased expenditure, and use of untrained assistants. The only solution was to organize an adequately large corps of topographical engineers. It could then retain expert engineers and increase their speed, skill, and devotion to their profession. It would constitute the country's only school of practice employing complex instruments and higher mathematics for practical purposes. He firmly believed that such a group of engineers "can never be made by the common wants of society—these do not call such talents into activity. It is national objects and national alone which can form and foster them. The experimental operations are of too expensive a character for individual resources, and have in view objects beyond individual interest. Unless therefore a nation takes the necessary preliminary steps for the forming of such a body of officers, it must be subject to the errors of its own inexperienced members or resort to the better educated of other countries."[57] The coast survey was a valuable school of practice which must inevitably be supported by government. On such large undertakings as this, West Point graduates could gain the practical knowledge and

[57] Abert to Cass, April 2, 1834, T.B., Letters Issued, I, 359.

actual field experience which were essential in training a body of expert engineers.

In supporting his plan for enlarging this corps, Abert reviewed the many duties of his bureau, including geological and mineralogical surveys. He stressed the importance of mineralogical researches made by a United States civil agent, George W. Featherstonhaugh, in Arkansas Territory. These activities would add to scientific knowledge, develop new sources of wealth and trade in coal, iron, lead, and the precious metals, and thus encourage industry and the profitable employment of capital.[58] Abert clearly sanctioned the government's efforts to develop and apply the science required in exploiting the natural resources of the nation. He saw this encouragement as a task for which the army engineers were uniquely fitted.

Cass emphasized the need of reorganizing the topographical corps and approved Abert's plan for doing so. If line officers and experienced civil engineers then employed on topographical work were permanently incorporated, the corps would be more efficient and economical. Such a well-trained corps would execute all surveys for civil and military purposes and provide a "fund of experience and information which cannot but be useful to the country."[59]

The House Committee on Military Affairs also saw the need for enlarging the topographical corps and noted that four presidents had made such proposals. The system of short tours of topographical duty by line officers was unsatisfactory. To become proficient in the engineering profession for which West Point initially qualified them, these officers must remain permanently in topographical work.[60]

In 1835, Cass and Abert offered a plan for a larger topo-

[58] A.R. of T.B., Oct. 30, 1834, *ASP, MA,* V, 425.

[59] A.R. of S/W, Nov. 27, 1834, *ibid.,* V, 358–59.

[60] Mr. Johnson's report from the Committee on Military Affairs, Dec. 15, 1834, 23 Cong., 2 sess., *H. Rept. 4,* 1–2.

*Pioneer engineers surveying for the Baltimore and Ohio Railroad, from a painting by H. D. Stitt.*

Courtesy Baltimore and Ohio Railroad.

*United States Mexican Boundary Survey, led by William H. Emory,
at Brownsville, Texas, about 1849 to 1855.*

From Emory's *Report of United States and Mexican Boundary Survey* (1857), I.

*Pacific Railroad Survey Party, led by Lieutenant
R. S. Williamson, at Livermore Pass, California, in July, 1853.*

From Williamson's *Report of Explorations in California
for Railroad Routes* (1855).

graphical body which received President Jackson's explicit approval. Abert carefully demonstrated the need of reorganizing this corps. He first explained the principles on which surveys were authorized. The surveys with highest priority were those ordered by law, for which there were usually special appropriations. Next, there were the surveys ordered by resolution of Congress. The expenses for these were paid from annual appropriations for surveys. Finally, there were the surveys "of a national or highly interesting commercial character applied for by States or incorporated companies." For these the government assigned only the officers and instruments it could spare, and the interested parties paid all additional expenses.[61]

Of the forty-nine engineers then engaged in surveying, ten were topographical engineers, twenty-six were line officers temporarily detailed to this duty, and thirteen were civil engineers. Abert reasoned that the temporary detail of army officers resulted in the use of untrained and disinterested surveyors, loss of line officers with topographical experience, and unpleasant bickering with the army. He was equally opposed to the continued employment of civilian engineers, which resulted in jealousies, confused lines of authority, loss of *esprit de corps,* and injustice to the civilian engineers.[62]

Abert submitted a bill to secure a homogeneous corps of topographical engineers. It would have ended the authority to employ civil engineers and would have created a corps of thirty-six topographical officers by appointing experienced army officers and some of the civil engineers employed under the Survey Act. To gain support for his bill, Abert elaborated the duties of his corps for which its officers were eminently qualified. His impressive list included surveys for coastal defenses, roads, railroads, and canals; surveys of harbors, rivers,

[61] A.R. of T.B., Nov. 2, 1835, *ASP, MA,* V, 713.
[62] *Ibid.,* V, 714.

lakes, coasts, and national frontiers; and superintendence of federal civil construction. In explaining one group of their major duties, he expressed his own point of view concerning the employing of topographical engineers in civil engineering activities:

Surveys for common roads, railroads, and canals. Although these may be considered as purely of a civil character, yet a finer school of practice than they furnish the topographical engineer cannot well be imagined. He obtains on these duties expertness in the use of instruments; the habit of investigating the resources of a country, commercially, morally, and physically; its supplies in provisions, timber, metals, and means of construction; its population, and the best means by which it can be commanded in cases of emergency; its military aspect, hilly, level, or mountainous, and the various roads which intersect the path of his survey. While he is, therefore, apparently engaged on an object ostensibly of mere profit to its undertakers, he is perfecting himself in the practice of his profession . . . and gathering the most valuable information in relation to the capabilities of self-defence of the locality of the survey, and its ability to aid in the defence of other parts of the country.[63]

President Jackson agreed that both engineering corps should be enlarged and approved Abert's plan for reorganizing the topographical corps. This proposal could be adopted without additional cost and with great public benefit, for the work of these engineers "is at all times interesting to the community and the information furnished by them is useful in peace and war."[64]

In 1836, B. F. Butler, interim secretary of war, reiterated the necessity of strengthening both engineering corps. He asserted that the Engineer Department should not employ civil engineers or lend army engineers to states and private companies.[65] It was by then commonly agreed in the War De-

[63] *Ibid.*, V, 715.
[64] Annual Message, Dec. 7, 1835, 24 Cong., 1 sess., S. *Doc. 1*, 22.
[65] A.R. of S/W, Dec. 3, 1836, *ASP, MA*, VI, 810.

partment that government surveying should be done by military engineers without employing civil engineers. This was the first instance, however, of an objection by the War Department to the service of its engineers with state and corporate improvement enterprises.

This objection was alien to the thinking of Colonel Abert and his topographical engineers. When engineering aid to state and private undertakings encountered criticism, Congress decided to investigate. The House Committee on Military Affairs called for information on these questions:

1st. Have officers of the Army been permitted . . . to engage in the service of States, Companies or individuals, and receive compensation. . . .

2d. In case such practice has prevailed, how many officers . . . have been so employed during the last five years, designating the service upon which employed and if with the permission of the Department, the amount of compensation paid to each of them.

3d. The views of the Department as to the effects of the practice upon the public service, and whether it should be prohibited or regulated by law.[66]

In reply to the first query, Abert stated that since 1824 the War Department upon request had ordered officers to assist states, companies, and groups of individuals. These engineers had made reports to the War Department and recipients of the surveys, and their services were considered as authorized by the General Survey Act. Some had been paid for making surveys or superintending construction. Such payment had been voluntarily made by states and companies, for the Topographical Bureau had stipulated only that officers receive from them the equivalent of allowances lost by not being on strictly public duties.

Abert explained in answer to the second question that engi-

[66] Abert to B. F. Butler, interim S/W, Jan. 24, 1837, T.B., Letters Issued, II, 240.

neering aid to states and companies had been limited to such engineers and instruments as could be spared and that the personal allowances of these officers had been curtailed. He named eleven topographical engineers who had served with states, companies, or individuals in the past five years. Several of these officers had used their surveying assistants in this work. Projects receiving this engineering aid included canals and river and harbor improvements, but were commonly railroad projects. Abert emphasized that these projects were of such benefit to national commerce and military defense as to constitute national undertakings meriting all possible aid from the army engineers.[67]

In his answer to the third inquiry, Abert argued that the practice of allowing officers to work with state and private undertakings had not been injurious to the public service. He considered the practice to be within the letter and spirit of the Survey Act. Surveys made on the application of states, companies, or individuals had never been allowed to interfere with those ordered by Congress. Reports on these private surveys contained much geographical, statistical, and military information. Furthermore, prohibition of this practice would drive "some of the most valuable, best informed, and most enterprising officers from the Service."

Abert reasoned, in effect, that the topographical engineers were servants of the people and should be allowed to give occasional aid when the people called.[68] There were not enough civil engineers for all needed improvements, and undertakings of states and companies would be delayed or abandoned if the government did not give them its ready

[67] *Ibid.*, II, 248.
[68] *Ibid.*, II, 251. Abert acknowledged "the right of a state or company or a large body of citizens, to call upon the General Government, for the occasional aid of those officers, whose education has been at their expense, and who are maintained by taxes upon their means, when such aid can be rendered without injury to the duties required by the General Government from such officers."

assistance. Regulation of this engineering aid should be left to the President, for "If such aid should be prohibited by law, it amounts under such circumstances to a prohibition of the improvement of the Country, and divests the Government of its paternal and patronizing character."[69]

Abert later admitted that employment of topographical engineers in "the duties of the Civil Engineer" had caused opposition to an increase of the corps. He told one officer so engaged that this criticism did not come from the corps itself or from the President and urged this officer to stay in the army until it was established that the people of the country could secure the services of army engineers when they could be spared from official duties.[70]

In 1837, Secretary of War Joel R. Poinsett and Colonel Abert again called for a larger topographical corps to meet expanding duties, economize by using military instead of civil engineers, and avoid problems of a mixed corps. Poinsett, however, agreed with Butler that topographical engineers should not be employed by states and companies. When this practice had first begun, there had been so few engineers that works of great public benefit would have been abandoned if the government had withheld assistance. The demand for civil engineers had brought an adequate increase in their number, so that "not only is it no longer necessary to aid States and companies by lending them officers of the army, but, in doing so, an act of injustice is committed towards the civil engineers of the country."[71] Furthermore, the practice interfered with the proper duties of the corps, which were examining and surveying the country for national improvements and defenses and superintending their construction.

In the period from 1831 to 1838, there was thus a change

[69] *Ibid.*, II, 251.
[70] Abert to Major William G. McNeill, Nov. 30, 1837, *ibid.*, II, 429.
[71] A.R. of S/W, Dec. 2, 1837, *ASP, MA*, VII, 574.

in the philosophy of the army engineers engaged in applying the General Survey Act. Their changing outlook reflected modifications of their policy criteria and of their role in the internal improvements movement. Their desire and ability to plan this movement, already weakened before 1831, were further reduced by the President's refusal to authorize examination of roads and canals on his initiative under the Survey Act. They still desired to encourage promising improvement undertakings by providing technical aid. They felt that the Survey Act authorized this promotive assistance; and Colonel Abert expressed the view that the army engineers were public servants who should assist states, companies, and groups of individuals needing surveying aid.

Despite the desire of the Topographical Bureau to provide direct engineering help to state and private enterprises, their power to do so soon diminished. After 1836 the Secretary of War opposed the lending of engineers to these enterprises and insisted that they remain on regular duty. As these official duties increased, army engineers were busily engaged in surveying for and supervising the execution of fortifications, military roads, lighthouses, and river and harbor improvements. An increasing portion of their surveying was for military and geographical purposes, such as coastal, geological, and mineralogical surveys. These activities rapidly increased throughout the 1830's, while surveys for roads, canals, and railroads diminished, particularly after 1835.

The desire to encourage internal improvements as a means of stimulating national expansion was broadened to include exploration and mapping of the country, improvement of navigation on the western rivers and lakes, and discovery of natural resources. Encouragement thus extended far beyond roads and canals, for the engineers desired to apply their skill and experience in many related areas essential to national progress. There was no slackening of their determination to advance civil engineering and make its benefits available to meet national needs. The topographical corps was conceived as a "school of practice" for advancing engineering skills, since only the government could afford to develop and apply these skills in a continuous, extensive manner.

An act of July 5, 1838, provided for organization of the Corps of Topographical Engineers. It repealed the authority contained in the General Survey Act to employ civil engineers and provided that initial vacancies in the new corps be filled by appointments from the line of the army and from among the U. S. civil engineers then employed. It also stated that officers must not be separated from their regiments and corps for use on internal improvements and must not be employed by incorporated companies.[72] This measure constituted repeal of the General Survey Act, which for fifteen years had been the vehicle for surveying many proposed schemes of internal improvement.

The 1838 legislation also ended the mixed topographical corps. The army engineers were no longer to include civil engineers or line officers temporarily on topographical duty. This formal organization of the Corps of Topographical Engineers paved the way for a division of labor between it and the Corps of Engineers. The principle was adopted of assigning civil works to the former and defense projects to the latter.[73] The former corps thus became a construction as well as a surveying agency.

Causes of the decline and repeal of the General Survey Act were complex and varied. Even before the abolition of the Board of Engineers for Internal Improvements in 1831, several causal factors were in evidence. Among these were the atrophy of the planning function, rapid growth of railroads,

[72] Beers, "Topographical Engineers," 291; Haney, *Congressional History,* I, 116; *Acts of the Twenty-fifth Congress,* Chap. 162, pp. 100–106.

[73] Beers, "Topographical Engineers," 348; A.R. of S/W, Nov. 28, 1838, 25 Cong., 3 sess., S. *Doc. 1,* 107.

increase in river and harbor activity, growth of city and sectional rivalry, and jealousy between Congress and the President over distribution of surveying aid. The strength of these factors increased after 1831, and several additional conditions operated to weaken the act. Many forms of encouragement, such as engineering aid to states and companies, became unpopular; civil engineers became less scarce; surveying and construction of works other than roads and canals increased in volume; and panic, debt, and new military needs also caused the activities of the army engineers to be shifted away from the area of internal improvements as originally defined in the Survey Act.

The commitment of the army engineers to the purposeful planning of internal improvements had disappeared by 1838, if not almost a decade earlier. Failure to adopt and execute a national system of improvements and growing dependence on state and private undertakings were responsible for this decline of planning. The doctrine of states' rights, sectional controversy, Jackson's veto of federal aid to non-federal transportation projects, and his refusal to initiate surveys through his authority under the Survey Act contributed to the elimination of the planning initially attempted under this act.

Unpopularity of encouraging state and private improvement enterprises developed rather late in the life of this act. Although the making of surveys for and the lending of engineer officers to these ventures met objection in Congress and the War Department by 1836, the Topographical Bureau defended these practices throughout the entire period. When the 1838 legislation was debated, Senator James Buchanan insisted on a provision "to prevent the employment of [army] engineers by private companies." He argued that civil engineers were no longer scarce and that army engineers employed by canal and railroad companies "had accumulated large fortunes in the service of these companies, while the business of the Government was neglected."[74]

Although direct engineering aid to non-federal improvements gradually became unpopular and diminished, other indirect and diffused forms of encouragement continued. Among these broad aids to national development were geographical explorations and surveys of the coast, lakes, rivers, natural resources, and western territory. Such encouragement provided an impetus to science and industry and contributed to military defense and economic expansion.

The accelerated growth of railroads in the 1830's contributed to the decline of the General Survey Act in several ways. Railways soon displaced roads and canals as the most promising means of transportation. They were built as state and private undertakings without direct federal aid other than engineering. As a result, demands for road and canal surveys and for a national system of roads and canals declined rapidly. Initiative in the development of transportation passed from the federal government to state and private agencies, and the Survey Act became a vehicle for obtaining needed engineering assistance. As rival states, cities, and companies vied for this aid, it increased to such proportions that overpowering opposition arose to this use of government engineering.

At the same time, civil engineers were rapidly increasing in number as a result of the great demand for their skills. Most of these engineers were self-taught, but some had been educated at West Point and trained in the Engineer Department as government engineers. The rate of resignations among engineer officers and other West Point graduates was quite high. Railroad surveys by army engineers consequently encoun-

---

[74] *Congressional Globe*, VI, 133. This 1838 act dealt with the "Increase of the Army," and the few sections affecting the army engineers received scant attention when the act was debated.

tered growing opposition as civil engineers grew in number and resented competing with army engineers for employment. As a result, the Survey Act which allowed this competition became less necessary and more disliked.

There was also a growing demand for greater use of army engineers on work more directly in the public service. Topographical engineers became increasingly engaged in river and harbor improvement and military and geographical exploration. Their surveying for purposes other than roads and canals increased greatly, and their role as the chief federal agency for executing civil works had evolved by 1838. Heavier military duties after 1836 also contributed to their withdrawal from activities encompassed in the Survey Act. Exploration and defense of the West gained military importance relative to coastal defense and inland transportation along the Atlantic seaboard, particularly when railroads rapidly advanced beyond the primitive, experimental stage. In the long period of peace after 1815, during which the country's major transportation problems were being successfully met by private, mixed, and state enterprise, the military justification of federal planning and promotion of internal improvements lost its earlier force and further weakened the Survey Act.

Local and regional rivalry in acquiring surveys and plans for roads and canals made the application of this act increasingly difficult, even for piecemeal encouragement of these undertakings. All demands could not be accommodated, and the influence of state officials and congressmen became crucial in securing engineering aid. Congress was jealous of the President's power under the Survey Act to order whatever surveys he deemed appropriate, although Jackson ceased using this power. As a result, Congress preferred specific to general surveys and often directed that particular surveys be made.

Already obsolescent, this act suffered from growing sectional antagonisms, unsettled constitutional issues relating to internal improvements, and effects of the panic of 1837. This financial collapse brought debt, bankruptcy, and suspension to many improvement projects and caused many states and the federal government to withdraw most of their support from these undertakings. It stalled the national movement for internal improvements and contributed to the forces producing repeal of the General Survey Act in 1838.[75] This repeal removed all vestiges of generalized planning of internal improvements. Although particularized encouragement in this field was modified, it continued to flourish. One of the most important areas of encouragement—an area important enough to compel further analysis—was railroad development.

[75] Haney, *Congressional History*, I, 113–16. For a discussion of the factors which prevented adoption of a national system of internal improvements, see George Rogers Taylor, *The Transportation Revolution, 1815–1860*, 18–22.

# IV: Working With the Railroads

THE DEVELOPMENT of early railroads was a field in which army engineers gave far-reaching encouragement to the internal improvements movement. This engineering aid to railroads was of great importance in their initial growth, for civil engineering was at that time a relatively undeveloped science in the United States. Although the General Survey Act of 1824 empowered the President to authorize surveys only of roads and canals, he was by 1826 and 1827 permitting examinations of railway routes. It has already been seen that much of the surveying done under authority of this act was for the benefit of railroads and that this aid became a major factor leading to the repeal of the act.

In this analysis of the encouragement of early railroads by the army engineers, interest centers on the extent of this aid and the philosophy and policies employed in providing it. This initial railroad assistance included aid to the Baltimore and Ohio Railroad and other pioneer lines between 1827 and 1830. In the last half of the life of the Survey Act, from 1831 to 1838, the railroad work of the army engineers became quite extensive. Repeal of this act reduced this engineering aid to a negligible amount until the Pacific railway surveys in the 1850's. Throughout this entire period, however, the Military Academy and its graduates had a great influence on the progress of railroads. Government engineering aid to railroads before the Civil War was thus substantial and significant.

Several years before the Baltimore and Ohio Railroad received its charter, the subject of railroads had received public attention and some notice from government. At an early period short railways or tramways were built for such purposes

96

as hauling stone from quarries. Such tramways were built in Boston and Philadelphia before 1810 and in several other cities by 1827.[1] In this period several railroad advocates experimented with railways and supported projects to aid their development. Among these proponents of railways were Benjamin H. Latrobe, John Stevens, Oliver Evans, Benjamin Dearborn, William Strickland, and George Armroyd.[2]

The advocacy of railways as a means of public improvement gradually came to the notice of the federal government. With the growing belief that the internal improvements movement required public support, the question of government aid to railroads arose. As early as 1808, railways were discussed in public documents, for Latrobe's letter concerning them was included in Gallatin's "Report on Roads and Canals." Petitions to Congress by Evans in 1816 and Dearborn in 1819 for public support in developing steam carriages called attention to the possibilities of railroad transportation.

By 1825, the year after it passed the Survey Act, Congress showed a direct interest in railroads. At that time it considered a proposal to finance a railway experiment under a patent granted to Stevens the previous year. The House considered a resolution which would have appropriated money for sending four West Point graduates to Great Britain to study roads, canals, and railways. In 1826 the House subscribed to twenty-five copies of Strickland's report on British railroads. Charles F. Mercer proposed that army engineers make surveys of roads, canals, and railways and that the government help

[1] Haney, *Congressional History*, I, 18; Caroline E. MacGill and Balthasar H. Meyer, *History of Transportation in the United States Before 1860*, 308–309; J. L. Ringwalt, *Development of Transportation Systems in the United States*, 69.
[2] For discussions of early advocacy of and experiments with railways, see George Armroyd, *A Connected View of the Whole Internal Navigation of the United States*, 187–88; Seymour Dunbar, *A History of Travel in America*, III, 880–82, 898–99, 943; MacGill and Meyer, *History of Transportation*, 585–86; and Ringwalt, *Transportation Systems*, 64–71.

finance their construction. Such actions as these indicated the growing interest of Congress in the practicability and promotion of railroads.[3]

In view of the concern of Congress with railways, one wonders why they were not included in the General Survey Act of 1824. Although it directed the President to authorize surveys only of roads and canals he considered nationally important, the Executive within two or three years permitted canal-or-railway studies and outright railroad surveys. It may be that railroads were not at this early date thought sufficiently practicable or important to be specifically named, or that they were considered a special kind of road.

The early railed highway was regarded as a public road in England and the United States. Since no other precedent existed, the earliest railways were also treated as public highways on which shippers could move their own vehicles upon payment of tolls. This practice was easily adopted when horsepower was the motive power, and it was the plan first followed in Pennsylvania and Massachusetts. State legislatures did not initially intend to give railroad companies exclusive or preferential rights to operate vehicles upon their tracks, for most early railroad charters specifically provided that shippers using the proper type of cars could use these roads. The traditional principle of the turnpike or common road was thus initially applied to railroads. Acceptance of this principle may have brought railways within the scope of the Survey Act in the beginning or may at least have made their inclusion plausible as railways gained popularity as an alternative to canals and roads.[4]

[3] Concerning early interest of Congress in railways, see Haney, *Congressional History*, I, 16–17, 23–24, 109–11; MacGill and Meyer, *History of Transportation*, 584–86; and "Mr. Mercer's Resolutions to Provide a Fund for Internal Improvement," April 25, 1826, 19 Cong., 1 sess., *H. Res. 45*, 1–2.

[4] Dunbar, *Travel in America*, III, 931–33; MacGill and Meyer, *History of Transportation*, 314–15. One transportation student believes that since early

The railroad craze was superimposed on the canal mania, and by 1826 railways were sometimes considered as competitors of canals for making certain inland connections. When enterprising promoters thought a railway might be a practical alternative to a proposed canal, they felt that the survey, plan, and estimate of their canal project was inadequate without a study of the practicability and cost of a railway. It was thus perhaps inevitable that railroads would be brought within the scope of the surveying operations under the Survey Act. At any rate, the first investigation under this act involving railways was a comparison of canals and railways.

On April 15, 1826, the government was petitioned to make a survey between the Roanoke, James, and Kanawha rivers to determine "the practicability, and if practicable, the cost of uniting them by a navigable Canal, or if that be found physically impossible, the route and estimate of the best rail way which can be constructed between the highest points of their improvable navigation."[5] The sponsors were primarily interested in canals, to be supplemented if necessary by railways at difficult places. On this basis they asked for an engineering study involving railroad surveying. Secretary of War Barbour replied that the project was of great importance but that the War Department was not able immediately to give the desired aid.

The Engineer Department soon assigned Major William G. McNeill, later one of the country's most famous railroad engi-

railroads were conceived as public roads, they would have been subject to federal construction and operation if it had not been for the precedent set by Monroe's veto of the Cumberland Road bill in 1822. As a result, the government was denied the authority and jurisdiction to construct and operate interstate lines of transportation. It thus lost its opportunity to build and run railroads *qua* common roads at the crucial time when railroads were first appearing in America. (Dunbar, *Travel in America*, III, 701–706, 713, 885–86.)

[5] S/W Barbour to James Johnson, C. F. Mercer, J. S. Barbour, Thomas Newton, Alfred H. Powell, William Smith, and B. Estill, May 9, 1826, E.D., Misc. Letters Sent, III, 195–96.

neers, to make the necessary surveys. Acting for the Board of Internal Improvement, General Bernard issued detailed instructions to McNeill for three canal and three railroad surveys between these rivers. He stated that power might be provided by "stationary powers, engines or horses" but felt that horsepower would be most appropriate. He cautioned against surveying railroad routes involving much excavation, embankment, or curvature.[6]

With the aid of four assistants, who later continued in railroad surveying, McNeill completed the necessary surveys and submitted his report early in 1828. He dealt mainly with the proposed canal to connect the James and Kanawha rivers. Canals were practicable between the three rivers, but he indicated briefly that railroads might be just as practicable.[7]

While this canal-or-railway study was being made by army engineers, an important railroad project was set in motion by businessmen and leading citizens of Baltimore. They were motivated by the intense commercial rivalry among the major seaports for more western trade. They wanted to share this prized trade with New York and Philadelphia and to prevent Washington, Georgetown, and Alexandria from gaining an advantage by the Chesapeake and Ohio Canal. They chose the railroad as the means of achieving these objectives, and their action initiated the railroad movement in this country.

Baltimore became interested in the proposal of a railroad in 1826, and early in 1827 several merchants and bankers applied for a charter. On February 28, 1827, an act of incorporation was secured for the Baltimore and Ohio Railroad Company. It became the first railroad company to ask for and

[6] T.B. to McNeill and Bernard, July 21, 1826, T.B., Internal Improvement Letters Issued, Vol. A, 293; Bernard to McNeill, July 29, 1826, Board of Internal Improvement, Board Register, No. 3.

[7] "Report on the James River and Kenhawa Canal Route," March 24, 1828, 20 Cong., 1 sess., *H. Doc. 216*, 6–32. Cf. Haney, *Congressional History*, I, 111, 116.

receive government engineering aid. On April 17, 1827, Peter Little petitioned the government "to procure the co-operation of the United States in the execution of the said project, and to ascertain to what extent such assistance may be contributed." Barbour replied that three surveying brigades would assist the railroad, since the President considered it of great importance and was willing to give all possible aid which did not detract from "objects of primary and national consequence with which this Department is already charged."[8]

The War Department quickly sent the company three engineering parties headed by Dr. William Howard, Colonel Stephen H. Long, and Major McNeill, who had just returned from his canal-or-railway surveys between the Kanawha, James, and Roanoke rivers. Howard was assigned to the company on May 30 and was ordered to consult with its board of directors regarding the services his party would render.[9] McNeill and Long were soon instructed to report to, co-operate with, and take instructions from the company. They were informed that surveying expenses would be paid from Survey Act funds.[10]

Secretary of War Barbour notified P. E. Thomas, president of the Baltimore and Ohio Railroad Company, that since the undertaking was considered to be of national importance, the direct costs of the survey would be "charged to the public appropriation for Internal Improvement."[11] Thomas also asked to use Jonathan Knight "in obtaining intelligence in Europe as to the best mode of locating and constructing Rail-Roads, should the Government be willing to dispense with his services for this purpose." Knight was then employed by the War Department in laying out the Cumberland Road. The

[8] S/W Barbour to Little, May 2, 1827, E.D., Misc. Letters Sent, IV, 149.
[9] Gen. Macomb to Howard, May 30, 1827, *ibid.*, IV, 178.
[10] Macomb to McNeill and Long, June 22 and July 2, 1827, E.D., Letters to Officers of Engineers, III, 84, 87.
[11] Barbour to Thomas, June 16, 1827, E.D., Misc. Letters Sent, IV, 199.

Secretary of War replied that Knight would be made available for this important work, in view of the attitude of the War Department toward railroads:

The successful introduction of Rail-Roads, into this country, is viewed by the Department as of great national importance, and especially any practicable mode of connecting the Atlantic States with the Western; whether by Rail-Roads or Canals, so that the commodities to be found in either can be conveniently and cheaply conveyed to the other, across the barriers which divide them, and which communication, while aiding in the advancement of commercial enterprise, offer the most sure and economical means to the Government to convey, to the different parts of the Union, the means of defence, in the transportation of men and munitions to the seat of war, wherever it shall exist.[12]

Barbour placed railroads alongside canals as alternative means of improvement which the government should assist under the Survey Act. He later declared that even though the proposed Baltimore and Ohio Railroad was to be developed by private enterprise, its national importance "justified the department in applying its means to ascertain its practicability."[13] His position illustrated the desire of the government and army engineers to utilize the act in applying civil engineering to aid state and private projects as well as federal improvements.

Preliminary surveying for this railroad was begun in 1827 by army engineers, and the company continued to receive their engineering services until 1830. During the first two years of surveying, three brigades were employed. These parties, each including about three assistants, were headed by Long, McNeill, and Howard. During 1828, however, the Engineer Department notified the company that it would have to bear the total cost of Howard's civil brigade if the company

[12] Barbour to Thomas, June 25, 1827, *ibid.*, IV, 224.
[13] A.R. of S/W, Nov. 26, 1827, *ASP, MA*, III, 616.

wished to retain it. Limited appropriations made it necessary to withdraw some surveying aid originally afforded the company. Howard and his party were later ordered to South Carolina to survey a proposed railroad route from Charleston to Hamburg.[14]

Lack of funds imposed an additional limitation giving rise to an established rule for government surveying. The government ceased bearing the total cost of surveys and agreed to pay only the personal remuneration of its engineers who made surveys for improvement enterprises. The government would provide trained engineers, but the companies had to bear all incidental surveying costs.[15]

As the work of the army engineers progressed, the route was located and construction started for the Baltimore and Ohio Railroad. On July 4, 1828, the first stone was laid by Charles Carroll of Carrollton, who considered this act as important as his signing of the Declaration of Independence. With the location of the road determined, Long and Knight, who were in charge of engineering operations, advertised for bids for constructing the first few miles of the road. There were then twelve army engineers in the service of the Baltimore and Ohio.[16]

About this time the company decided to send engineers to England to examine railroad construction there. For this task it chose Major McNeill, Lieutenant George W. Whistler, and Knight, who had resigned from his job on the Cumberland Road. They left Baltimore late in 1828 and spent several

[14] E.D. to Thomas, June 13, 1828, E.D., Misc. Letters Sent, V, 105; Col. Gratiot to Howard, Dec. 2, 1828, *ibid.*, V, 342–43.

[15] Macomb to Thomas, May 20, 1828, *ibid.*, V, 69.

[16] Robert G. Albion, *The Rise of New York Port, 1815–1860*, 379; Edward Hungerford, *The Story of the Baltimore And Ohio Railroad*, 51; Stephen H. Long and William G. McNeill, *Narrative of the Proceedings of the Board of Engineers of the Baltimore and Ohio Rail Road Company*, 9–18; Milton Reizenstein, *The Economic History of the Baltimore and Ohio Railroad, 1827–1853*, 20.

months investigating methods of construction and locomotive power of the two British railroads then in operation. The fact that the company sent two army engineers demonstrated their technical competence and strategic importance in early railroad development. These two officers were to become the most famous railroad engineers of their day.[17]

Upon their return from England, McNeill and Knight served with Long as the company's board of engineers, with Whistler as superintending engineer. In October, 1829, the laying of track was started under Whistler's supervision. An army engineer was thus in charge of laying the first railroad track for passenger cars in this country. Construction continued under Whistler's immediate supervision until the railroad was completed from Baltimore to Ellicott's Mills in 1830.

The engineers who had examined British railways preferred heavy, solid construction, including stout masonry bridges and a stone foundation under the rails. Their preferences were followed in the early work on the Baltimore and Ohio Railroad. Colonel Long, however, favored lighter and more economical construction, including wooden bridges. One such bridge was constructed, found to be practicable, and patented by Long. He also aided the progress of railroading by writing a technical, pocket-size *Rail Road Manual*, dedicated "To the President and Directors of the Baltimore & Ohio Rail Road Company."[18]

[17] Carlisle Allan, "George W. Whistler, Military Engineer," *The Military Engineer*, Vol. XXIX (1937), 179; *Centennial*, I, 843–47; Cullum, *Biographical Register*, I, 161–66, 214–22; Hungerford, *B. and O.*, 31, 69, 91–93; Long and McNeill, *Narrative*, 76, *passim;* George L. Vose, *A Sketch of the Life and Works of George W. Whistler, Civil Engineer*, 16.

[18] Allan, "George W. Whistler," 179; Cullum, *Biographical Register*, I, 161–66, 214–22; Hungerford, *B. and O.*, 62–63, 69, 91–93; Vose, *Sketch of Whistler*, 17; Stephen H. Long, *Rail Road Manual, or a Brief Exposition of Principles and Deductions Applicable in Tracing the Route of a Rail Road*. The advertisement in Long's book stated that its purpose was "to place in the pocket of the Engineer, a brief and perspicacious compend of easy rules, that may serve as a Directory, to guide him in tracing the route of a Rail Road." Long acknowl-

Between 1827 and 1830 the army engineers serving with this company functioned as an effective school of practice for railroad engineers. The training they acquired was undoubtedly as important to the growth of railroads as the pioneer engineering on the Erie Canal had been to the progress of canals and training of canal engineers. In the first two years, Long, McNeill, and Howard, all government engineers, were in charge of engineering operations; and during the last two years Long, McNeill, and Whistler managed these activities. The first two were on the company's board of engineers, and Whistler superintended track-laying operations. Each year ten to twelve army engineers were in the company's service. At one time or another in this period some fourteen army engineers took part in the survey, location, and initial construction of the road. All of these officers were later engaged in railroad engineering.[19]

edged the assistance of "the Engineers, military and civil, employed in conducting the surveys made in behalf of the Baltimore and Ohio Rail Road Company. . . ."

[19] Cf. Edward C. Kirkland, *Men, Cities, and Transportation*, I, 121 for a statement of the importance of the Baltimore and Ohio Railroad survey as a "training ground for engineers."

Among the army engineers who participated in this "school of practice" were the following:

1. Col. Stephen H. Long, member of company's board of engineers
2. Major William G. McNeill, member of board of engineers
3. Lieut. George W. Whistler, superintending engineer
4. Dr. William Howard, U. S. civil engineer
5. William B. Guion, U. S. assistant civil engineer
6. William Harrison, U. S. assistant civil engineer
7. Lieut. Joshua Barney, on topographical duty
8. Lieut. William Cook, on topographical duty
9. Lieut. John N. Dillahunty, on topographical duty
10. Lieut. Walter Gwynn, on topographical duty
11. Lieut. John M. Fessenden, on topographical duty
12. Lieut. Richard E. Hazzard, on topographical duty
13. Lieut. W. B. Thompson, on topographical duty
14. Lieut. Isaac Trimble, on topographical duty

Jonathan Knight, permanent company employee and member of board of engineers, was previously a commissioner on the Cumberland Road. Casper

In 1830 there was a disagreement about construction and disbursement procedures within the company's board of engineers, which was dissolved. Colonel Long was withdrawn in March, and Captain McNeill and his assistants were ordered away to other duties in June.[20] Work of the army engineers with the Baltimore and Ohio Railroad thus came to an end, but not before its route had been surveyed and located and its first section constructed. The company had received valuable engineering services which otherwise would have been very difficult and expensive to secure. These army engineers had become experienced railroad engineers and had demonstrated their ability to encourage transportation.

While its engineers were assisting the Baltimore and Ohio, the government received demands for other railway surveys and started granting engineering aid to new railroad projects. In June, 1827, Governor Levi Lincoln of Massachusetts asked for the survey of a railroad route from Boston to the Hudson River. The Secretary of War replied that the War Department was impressed with the importance of the proposed railroad but had no officers readily available.[21] A few months later an inquiry reached Barbour concerning the possibility of securing a railroad survey in North Carolina. He replied that he wished to aid all states with their important improvements. The proposed railroad promised such great advantages that the War Department would willingly provide engineers for a survey, if the state legislature would pass a resolution requesting the survey.[22]

During 1828, army engineers made surveys for five railroads

W. Wever, permanent company employee and superintendent of construction, previously superintended construction on the Cumberland Road. (Cullum, *Biographical Register*, I, *passim*; Hungerford, *B. and O.*, *passim*; Long and McNeill, *Narrative*, 11, 18, 76, *passim*; and Vose, *Sketch of Whistler*, 16.)

[20] Cf. E.D. correspondence for 1830; Long and McNeill, *Narrative, passim*.
[21] Barbour to Lincoln, July 5, 1827, E.D., Misc. Letters Sent, IV, 235.
[22] Barbour to Dr. Joseph Caldwell, Chapel Hill, N. C., Dec. 1, 1827, *ibid.*, IV, 371.

in addition to the Baltimore and Ohio. In June, Colonel P. H. Perrault, topographical engineer, was ordered to survey a railroad route from Hudson, New York, to Berkshire County, Massachusetts. He was assigned three assistants, one of whom had participated in the Baltimore and Ohio survey. Sponsors of the project were informed that expenses of the survey, other than personal compensation of army engineers, must be borne by the company, as in the case of the Baltimore and Ohio.[23]

Perrault reported that this railroad would be part of a line from Boston to the Hudson River and that horsepower would probably be used on it. He noted the possibility of using locomotive engines and suggested that "Should they be adopted for the present intended rail road, and should they perform as they are represented to do, every and all difficulties in the way of transportation would disappear at once."[24]

Lieutenant William H. Swift was ordered to make the necessary surveys for railroads between Ithaca and Owego and between Catskill and Ithaca in New York. The Ithaca and Owego Railroad Company applied through a congressman for the survey of a route to connect Lake Cayuga and the Susquehanna River. The Secretary of War acted favorably on the request, and Chief Engineer Macomb instructed Swift to secure needed instruments in New York City and proceed to Ithaca.[25] In his report Swift stated that it might be necessary

[23] E.D. to Hudson Railroad Committee, June 27, 1828, *ibid.*, V, 129; E.D. to Perrault, June 13 and 27, 1828, E.D., Letters to Officers of Engineers, III, 213, 223. This rule that the company must pay all costs of surveying other than the regular salaries of army engineers was applied in all later cases of direct government surveying for railroads.

[24] Report on the Hudson and Berkshire Railroad, Jan. 14, 1829, 20 Cong., 2 sess., *H. Doc.* 89, 10.

[25] Macomb to Swift, April 22, 1828, E.D., Letters to Officers of Engineers, III, 186. Macomb told Swift that "There is a young Gentleman at Ithaca, a Mr. Hughes, who was formerly at the Military Academy, who will be a very able assistant to you and I desire that you employ him in order that he may be useful to the Company after you have completed the location of the road. . . ."

to use inclined planes and stationary power at certain points, but he mentioned the possibility of using locomotive engines instead of horsepower.[26] After completing this survey, Swift proceeded to locate a railroad route from Ithaca to Catskill on the Hudson River. This survey had been granted by the Secretary of War at the request of several congressmen.[27]

The other two surveys in 1828 relating to railroads were designed to permit choice between canals or railways. Army engineers made surveys between the Savannah and Tennessee and between the Tennessee and Altamaha rivers to determine the practicability of connecting them by canals or railroads. William Jerome, U. S. civil engineer, made the latter investigation after consulting with the governor of Georgia. He reported that hilly terrain made canals or railroads difficult but that both could be used. A short railway could be used at one place as an inclined plane to supplement a canal project.[28]

During 1829, army engineers continued their engineering aid to the Baltimore and Ohio and the railroad from Ithaca to Catskill. They initiated surveys for a railroad from Catskill to Canajoharie in New York and for the Charleston and Hamburg Railroad. Lieutenant Swift had been instructed the year before to survey a route from Catskill to Canajoharie on the Erie Canal after completing his survey between Catskill and Ithaca. During 1829, he and two assistants were engaged in surveying these two routes.[29] Swift reported that the railroad between Catskill and Ithaca would provide a year-round con-

[26] "Report in relation to a communication between Cayuga Lake and the Susquehanna River," July 31, 1828, Reports of the Board of Internal Improvements, III, 232–51.

[27] Gen. Macomb, May 6, 22, and 23, 1828, E.D., Misc. Letters Sent, V, 45, 70, 76.

[28] "Report on the Canal or Rail Route to connect the Rivers Tennessee and Altamaha" (no date), Reports of the Board of Internal Improvements, III, 74. Cf. A.R. of C/E, Nov. 19, 1828, ASP, MA, IV, 16–17.

[29] C/E to Swift, Aug. 6, 1828, May 13, 1829, and May 14, 1830, E.D., Misc. Letters Sent, V, 188, VI, 47, and VII, 103–104.

nection between the Great Lakes and the Hudson River. He discussed the general merits of canals and railways and touched on British experience, locomotives, and stationary power for inclined planes. He felt that such inclined planes were practicable and that railroads were preferable to canal navigation.[30]

In October, 1828, the Engineer Department informed Dr. William Howard and the South Carolina Canal and Railroad Company that Howard's brigade would survey a railroad route from Charleston to Hamburg, in compliance with an earlier promise by the Secretary of War. Two months later he and his assistants were ordered to Charleston to arrange with the company for the survey.[31] In his report to the company in August, 1829, Howard acknowledged the aid of five U. S. assistant civil engineers. He advised that the road be constructed so as to permit use of either horsepower or locomotives, whichever would be found best by experience. A year later this railroad ran the first practical locomotive in the United States. Howard felt that it would later be profitably extended to the Tennessee River and thus tap the great inland trade which needed an outlet such as Charleston. His optimism was undoubtedly well received by Charleston railroad promoters facing the commercial rivalry of Savannah. He also noted that the military value of the projected railroad would increase the prosperity of the state by "adding to the security of its commercial capital."[32]

In 1830, army engineers continued their railroad surveying and received demands for additional aid of this kind. Besides

[30] "Report on the Catskill and Ithaca Rail Road," March 31, 1830, Reports of the Board of Internal Improvements, III, 252–72.

[31] Oct. 4 and 15 and Dec. 2, 1828, E.D., Misc. Letters Sent, V, 249, 259–60, 342–43.

[32] "Report on the Charleston and Hamburg Rail Road," Aug. 27, 1829, 21 Cong., 1 sess., *H. Doc.* 7, 34. Cf. Haney, *Congressional History*, I, 26–27, and U. B. Phillips, *A History of Transportation in the Eastern Cotton Belt to 1860*, 116–18, 143–46.

working part of the year with the Baltimore and Ohio and continuing the location of a railroad from Catskill to Canajoharie, they began a survey for the Baltimore and Susquehanna Railroad. Among the demands for government surveying which could not be satisfied were calls to locate railroads between Boston and Ogdensburg, New York, and between the latter and Port Kent on Lake Champlain, and to aid the Lexington and Ohio Railroad Company.[33]

Surveying for the railroad from Catskill on the Hudson to Canajoharie on the Erie Canal was resumed by Lieutenant John Pickell, artillery officer on topographical duty, and George W. Hughes, U. S. assistant civil engineer. Both had previously been assistants on this survey. Pickell reported that this railroad would provide a more direct and rapid connection and would be open a greater part of the year than the Erie Canal. It would diverge from the Erie Canal as far to the west as practicable and lead directly to the Hudson, providing a link which would "not only be certain and uninterrupted, but facilitated and improved."[34]

The Baltimore and Susquehanna Railroad received the aid of Major McNeill and Lieutenant Whistler, the two army engineers who had gained prominence with the Baltimore and Ohio and had been sent to Great Britain to study railway construction and locomotion. Colonel Charles Gratiot informed George Winchester, president of the Baltimore and Susquehanna Railroad Company, that the Secretary of War realized the importance of this project but felt that the War Department's official engineering duties were too great to permit it "to dispose of any of its officers in aid of private enterprizes."

33 E.D. letters of May 8 and 14, and June 10, 1830, E.D., Misc. Letters Sent, VII, 96–97, 105, 158.
34 "Report on the Survey from Canajoharie on the Erie Canal to Catskill on the Hudson River in the State of New-York, in relation to a communication connecting those points, by means of a Rail-way," Nov. 3, 1830, Reports of the Board of Internal Improvements, III, 282–94.

A month later, however, when the army engineers were withdrawn from the Baltimore and Ohio Railroad, McNeill, Whistler, and another officer were directed to consult with the new company in locating its route. Although he remained an army officer, McNeill was made chief engineer of the road, a position he held until 1836.[35]

By 1830 another form of engineering aid to railroads was in evidence. Army officers were being given furloughs to enable them to work for railroads. The New Jersey Railroad Company, for instance, asked to obtain the services of Lieutenant William Cook, who had until then worked on the Baltimore and Ohio. The Chief Engineer replied that if the company applied directly to the secretary of war, he would undoubtedly grant the officer a furlough for six months and would later extend it if necessary.[36]

Railroad development started with surprising rapidity in the period 1827–1830, and army engineers were quickly introduced into railroad engineering. Spurred on by commercial rivalries, several cities and regions hastened to promote railroads or canal-and-railway projects to share in the growing inland trade. Promoters of these improvements commonly looked to the government for engineering assistance, and congressmen and governors actively sought the desired surveys. The government willingly provided surveying for these undertakings through its authority in the General Survey Act, and upon occasion it furloughed officers to work with railroad

[35] E.D. to Winchester, May 5, June 10 and 30, 1830, E.D., Misc. Letters Sent, VII, 91–92, 161–62, 194; E.D. to McNeill, June 10, 1830, E.D., Letters to Officers of Engineers, III, 524; Allan, "George W. Whistler," 179; Cullum, *Biographical Register*, I, 164, 216; Vose, *Sketch of Whistler*, 17.

[36] Gen. Gratiot to "The Hon. Sam. Southard, Trenton, N. Jersey," June 10, 1830, E.D., Misc. Letters Sent, VII, 155. Lieut. Cook entered the service of this company in June, 1830, and resigned from the Army in January, 1832. From 1831 until his death in 1865, he was chief engineer of the Camden and Amboy Railroad. (Cullum, *Biographical Register*, I, 280.) During 1830 an army officer, Major John Wilson, directed surveys for the Camden and Amboy Railroad. (Lane, *Indian Trail*, 286.)

companies. If it considered a proposed railroad to be of national importance, it instructed government engineers to make the desired surveys, plans, and estimates. It initially attempted to pay the total cost of such studies, but by 1828 lack of funds and engineers to meet growing demands for surveys forced the War Department to change its rules. It thereafter provided only engineers and instruments when it consented to make surveys for states and companies. It paid the personal compensation due the officers, but recipients of their aid had to pay all other expenses.

This restriction on the dispensing of engineering aid came in the last year of the Adams administration. Although Adams was quite favorably disposed toward government assistance to railroads, the practice continued through Jackson's administration. New railroad surveys made by army engineers were initiated each year after 1827. Government engineering aid to railroads later reached its highest level in Jackson's second term of office.

Abolition of the Board of Engineers for Internal Improvements in 1831 marked the end of systematic efforts at national planning of internal improvements. In the last eight years of its life, the General Survey Act served as both the rationale and the instrument for extensive piecemeal encouragement of transportation ventures. Since state, private, and mixed enterprises executed these improvements, they received much specialized aid from the army engineers. Although canals and roads also received government surveying, most of this technical aid went to railroads.

In 1831 there was a great increase both in demands for railroad surveys by army engineers and in their work of this kind. The government acted favorably on several applications for engineering assistance for both locating and supervising the construction of railroads. The sudden popularity of railroads, willingness of the government to give technical aid, and cessation of assistance to the Baltimore and Ohio enabled army engineers in 1831 to aid five railroads, three of which had not received help previously.

Major McNeill superintended construction of the Catskill and Canajoharie, Baltimore and Susquehanna, and Paterson and Hudson River railroads. The first two had previously received government surveying, and the latter two had retained McNeill as their chief engineer with the approval of the War Department. He had the able assistance of Lieutenant Whistler as associate engineer, particularly on the Paterson and Hudson River Railroad.[37]

Surveys were also granted during 1831 for railroads from Winchester to Harpers Ferry in Virginia and from the portage summit of the Ohio Canal at Akron to the Hudson River at Jersey City. Captain James D. Graham and two assistants were assigned to the former survey and DeWitt Clinton, Jr., U. S. civil engineer, to the latter. The company had specifically asked for Clinton, and the Secretary of War had granted the request.[38]

Lieutenant William Cook, an artillery officer furloughed to the Camden and Amboy Railroad the year before, continued to aid this company. On November 11, 1831, however,

[37] A.R. of T.B., Nov. 7, 1831, *ASP, MA*, IV, 766; Gen. Gratiot to McNeill, May 9, 1831, E.D., Letters to Officers of Engineers, IV, 134; Allan, "George W. Whistler," 179; Cullum, *Biographical Register*, I, 164, 216; Vose, *Sketch of Whistler*, 17. McNeill was chief engineer of the Paterson and Hudson River Railroad from 1831 to 1834. Its first two locomotives were named the *McNeill* and *Whistler*. (Lane, *Indian Trail*, 375.)

[38] A.R. of T.B. for 1831, *ASP, MA*, IV, 766; Abert to C. A. Clinton and DeWitt Clinton, Jr., Aug. 5, 1831, and to President of Winchester Railroad Company and Capt. Graham, Aug. 16, 1831, T.B., Letters Issued, I, 95, 98, 99. In his report on this survey, Clinton spoke of the many national, state, and local benefits of railroads. He considered it fortunate that this road would start at Paterson, near New York City. He felt it would not hurt the Erie Canal and proposed that it have a double track and be built for locomotives. (Clinton's "Report on a reconnaissance of a railroad route between the Hudson river, at Jersey City, and the portage summit of the Ohio canal at Akron," Jan. 26, 1832, 22 Cong., 1 sess., *H. Doc. 133*, 4–19.)

the War Department issued a regulation withdrawing all army officers not employed under its jurisdiction. The many detachments were reducing army discipline and efficiency and were causing limited appropriations for surveying to be spent in hiring civil engineers.

Colonel Abert explained that the War Department was pleased that its officers could be employed advantageously on such projects of civil engineering as railroads. This beneficial work was a tribute to their useful technical education. Although the War Department desired to encourage these projects and give officers the opportunity to demonstrate their ability as civil engineers, they had to choose ultimately between resigning to adopt this profession and returning to army duties.[39] Although the War Department stopped lending or furloughing line officers to railroad companies, it was sometimes still willing to lend or assign topographical engineers to them. Aid of this sort was in addition to the regular government surveys made by army engineers under the General Survey Act.

Demands for engineering aid to railroads and efforts of the army engineers to fulfill them were greater in 1832 than previously. McNeill continued to supervise the construction of the Baltimore and Susquehanna and the Paterson and Hudson River railroads. He also became chief engineer of the Boston and Providence and the Providence and Stonington railroads. He took charge of the construction of the former and started a survey of the latter. Further, the Topographical Bureau instructed him to survey routes for railroads from New London, Connecticut to Providence, Rhode Island, and from New London to Worcester, Massachusetts. He made the latter survey during 1832.

[39] Abert to Governor of New Jersey, Nov. 30, 1831, T.B., Letters Issued, I, 136–37. Cook resigned from the Army a few months later and continued as chief engineer of this railroad until his death in 1865. (Cullum, *Biographical Register,* I, 280.)

McNeill's new duties were so extensive that the Baltimore and Susquehanna Railroad, for which he was chief engineer, complained of delays in its own necessary surveying. Colonel Abert replied that the War Department was willing for Mc-Neill to remain with the company for general superintendence but that the company must employ its own engineers for detailed operations. His bureau could not provide additional assistants for this routine work. He explained that the regulation of November 11, 1831, withdrawing army officers from work outside the jurisdiction of the War Department, had been relaxed "only with Capt. McNeill, whose connexion with several private companies has been long and with the express sanction of the War Department, as still to permit him to give his personal attention to these private objects, when the same could be spared from his public duties, but it has not been in contemplation to furnish him with Assistants for such purposes. . . .

"Also . . . under this regulation, several officers who were on furlough and in the employ of private companies, and who could not or preferred not, to break off from these connexions, have had to resign their commissions."[40]

Abert felt that the principle of the regulation should be preserved, for to do otherwise would be an injustice to officers who had been forced to resign and would "lead to demands upon the army which it could not well endure, as the demands now made under present limitations are considered pernicious to its discipline and propriety."[41] He concluded that McNeill should have assistants necessary only for his strictly public duties but should be permitted to use them for other purposes during periods of leisure. McNeill was then given two more assistants who, together with Lieutenant

---

[40] Col. Abert to S/W Cass, April 27, 1832, T.B., Letters Issued, I, 175.
[41] *Ibid.* (A penciled notation in the letter book substitutes *prosperity* for *propriety* in this passage.)

Whistler, were considered sufficient for his public duties. Abert then left McNeill to his own judgment in determining when these assistants could be spared for "duties not directly ordered by this Bureau."[42]

There was surveying during 1832 for the Winchester and Potomac Railroad, which Captain Graham's party had begun the year before. With the aid of three assistants, Graham then made a survey and reported favorably upon the practicability and probable cost of a railroad from Winchester to Harpers Ferry. He said that this road was well adapted to locomotive power and would be valuable in war and peace. Since it would terminate on the Chesapeake and Ohio Canal and the Baltimore and Ohio Railroad, it would connect the interior with Washington and Baltimore, to the great benefit of agriculture, commerce, and national defense.[43] Two U. S. civil engineers and an engineer officer also examined a railroad route from Potomac Creek to Fredericksburg. In their report they discussed horses, stationary engines, and locomotives as motive power. They concluded that horsepower would be used, and presented a proposed plan for the railroad.[44]

In 1832, DeWitt Clinton, Jr., continued his survey between the Hudson River and the portage summit of the Ohio Canal for a railroad to connect New York and Lake Erie. He was allowed four U. S. civil engineers and later an additional surveyor. From these he formed two surveying parties whose contingent expenses the government paid under the provisions of the Survey Act.[45]

[42] Abert to McNeill, April 27, 1832, *ibid.*, I, 176. For further discussion of McNeill's railroad activities during 1832, see Abert to Cass, May 29, 1832, and to McNeill, July 9, 1832, *ibid.*, I, 188–90, 204; A.R. of T.B., Nov. 9, 1832, *ASP, MA*, V, 63; and Cullum, *Biographical Register*, I, 164.

[43] Reports on the Winchester and Potomac Railroad, March 31 and Sept. 22, 1832, 25 Cong., 2 sess., *H. Doc. 465*, 1–29.

[44] "Report on the Survey of the Fredericksburg and Potomac Creek Rail Road," by George W. Hughes, May 1, 1832, E.D., Bulky File, No. 81; Abert to Hughes and Wilson Allen of Bowling Green, Va., March 23, 1832, T.B., Letters Issued, I, 162–63.

One officer made a railroad survey as far west as the Mississippi River in 1832. Captain William Turnbull made two reports on a railroad route from St. Francisville, Louisiana, to Woodville, Mississippi. He prepared plans, profiles, and estimates for the West Feliciana Railroad Company of a route from the Mississippi to the plantation of Walter Turnbull and terminating at Woodville.[46]

Two other railroad surveys were begun during 1832. Major Hartman Bache and three officers were assigned to investigate a railroad route from Williamsport, Pennsylvania, to Elmira, New York. It was intended to link the Pennsylvania Canal with the Chemung Canal at Elmira on the proposed railroad from New York to Lake Erie then being surveyed by Clinton. Dr. William Howard, who had surveyed the Baltimore and Ohio and the Charleston and Hamburg railroads, was directed to make a railroad survey in Ohio. He and three assistants were instructed to examine a route between the Mad River and Lake Erie, to connect the latter with the Ohio River.[47]

In 1833 railroad activities of the army engineers continued at a high level. McNeill superintended construction of four railroads for which he was serving as chief engineer. These were the Baltimore and Susquehanna, Paterson and Hudson, Boston and Providence, and Providence and Stonington railroads. He completed reports and drawings on the survey of this last road and on a route from New London to Worcester. Lieutenant Whistler, his capable associate engineer, resigned late in 1833. He became chief engineer for the Proprietors of

[45] A.R. of T.B. for 1832, *ASP, MA*, V, 63; Abert to Clinton, July 5 and 9, 1832, T.B., Letters Issued, I, 199, 203.

[46] Reports on the West Feliciana Railroad, May 3 and July 14, 1832, E.D., Bulky File, No. 82. Turnbull engaged in this survey in 1831 as well as 1832. (Cullum, *Biographical Register*, I, 211–12.)

[47] T.B. correspondence for 1832, T.B., Letters Issued, I, *passim*; report by Bache on a survey of the Williamsport and Elmira Railroad, 23 Cong., 1 sess., *H. Doc. 69*, 2–24.

Locks and Canals on the Merrimack River and designed and built steam locomotives in their machine shops at Lowell.[48]

Army engineers also made surveys for railroad routes from the portage summit of the Ohio Canal to the Hudson River, from Williamsport to Elmira, and from the Mad River to Lake Erie. Surveys were also made for a railroad across southern Vermont and for a canal or railroad between the Pearl and Yazoo rivers in Mississippi.[49]

The President's refusal to initiate new investigations through his authority under the General Survey Act limited the railroad surveying of the army engineers. He viewed it as improper to authorize surveys for internal improvements until a "general system of operation" was adopted. No exceptions had been made during 1832 or 1833 other than to complete surveys already in progress. A resolution of one or both houses of Congress was consequently necessary to obtain army engineers for locating railroad routes.[50]

Railroad work of the army engineers declined somewhat during 1834 but included surveys of two additional routes. McNeill supervised construction of the four railroads with which he was employed as chief engineer. Surveys were completed and reports submitted for a railroad from the Mad River to Lake Erie and for a railroad or canal between the Pearl and Yazoo rivers. Reports and drawings were completed for a railroad between Williamsport and Elmira. An army engineer also surveyed a proposed right of way over public land at Harpers Ferry for the Winchester and Harpers Ferry Railroad. The two new railroad surveys were for routes across

---

[48] A.R. of T.B., Oct. 19, 1833, ASP, MA, V, 218; Allan, "George W. Whistler," 179; Cullum, Biographical Register, I, 164, 216; Vose, Sketch of Whistler, 17–18.

[49] A.R. of T.B. for 1833, ASP, MA, V, 218.

[50] S/W Cass, Sept. 21, 1833, T.B., Letters Issued, I, 310–11. A further limitation of this surveying was imposed by the perennial shortage of army engineers during the life of the Survey Act, as discussed in the previous chapter.

the isthmus of Michigan and from Memphis to the Atlantic.[51]
Colonel Stephen H. Long was ordered to examine a railroad route from Memphis to Augusta. He made this investigation for Joseph Camack of Athens and General Edmund P.
Gaines of Memphis. Camack desired that the road terminate
at Charleston, but Gaines wanted it to end at Baltimore. Both
Gaines and Long believed that the latter route was important
and feasible, for it would connect with the Winchester and
Harpers Ferry and the Baltimore and Ohio railroads. Long
later submitted a detailed comparison of alternative routes.
These included, first, a line from Memphis to Augusta, connecting with the Charleston and Hamburg Railroad; second,
a route eastward through Tennessee to join the Baltimore and
Ohio; and, third, a route through Montgomery into Georgia,
where it might end at Savannah or run up to Norfolk. Long
and his one assistant examined these routes during the years
1834 and 1835.[52]

There were other applications for railroad surveys in 1834,
but the army engineers were too few in number and too busy
to permit further engineering aid to railroad companies.
Colonel Abert explained the inability of his bureau to survey
a railroad from Montgomery, Alabama, to West Point, Georgia; but he sent the Montgomery promoters a copy of Long's
*Rail Road Manual* to show them how routes were surveyed
and located.[53] Abert also rejected an application for an engi-

[51] A.R. of T.B., Oct. 30, 1834, *ASP, MA,* V, 425; Cullum, *Biographical Register,* I, 164.
[52] Cass to Camack, May 10, 1834, and Abert to Long, June 12, 1834, T.B., Letters Issued, I, 371, 375; Gaines to Cass, Sept. 10, 1834, E.D., Bulky File, No. 94; "Report . . . on a reconnaissance for railroads from Augusta, Georgia, to Memphis, Tennessee; from Memphis to the eastern base of Cumberland mountain, East Tennessee, and from Memphis to Savannah, Georgia," by Stephen H. Long, Feb. 10, 1835, 23 Cong., 2 sess., *H. Doc.* 177, 2–88. Late in 1834, Long was ordered to Virginia to survey a railroad route from Fredericksburg to the Ohio River. (Abert to Long, Nov. 29, 1834, and to Cass, Dec. 9, 1834, T.B., Letters Issued, I, 439.)
[53] Sept. 1, 1834, T.B., Letters Issued, I, 407–408.

neer to superintend the survey of a railroad from New Orleans to Nashville. He suggested that if Congress were to pass a pending bill for an increase of the topographical corps he would be able to provide engineers for this survey.[54]

During 1835 insistent demands for government surveys of railroads were rewarded by a sudden increase in this surveying by army engineers. McNeill was still chief engineer for the Baltimore and Susquehanna, Boston and Providence, and Providence and Stonington railroads. He also became chief engineer of the Taunton and New Bedford Railroad in Massachusetts and the Long Island Railroad in New York. He supervised the surveying, planning, and construction of these roads.[55]

There were further examinations in 1835 to determine railroad routes from Memphis to the Atlantic and across the Michigan isthmus from Detroit to St. Joseph. Most surveying, however, was for several new railroad projects. In addition to the two new roads to which McNeill gave his attention, projected routes receiving surveys included railroads from Portland, Maine, to Quebec, from Boston to Whitehall, New York, from Detroit to Pontiac, Michigan, and from Pensacola, Florida, to Columbus, Georgia. One or two other railroad surveys were made in New England and four in Indiana. At least fifteen railroads thus received engineering aid from army engineers in surveying or supervision of construction.[56]

The government also permitted army engineers to do off-duty or part-time work with railroad companies. Promoters of a railroad from Detroit to St. Joseph in Michigan Territory

[54] Abert to Cass, Dec. 24, 1834, *ibid.*, I, 442. Abert strongly advocated reorganizing and increasing the topographical engineers. Their participation in civil activities benefited civil works and also increased their military usefulness. These "apparently civil occupations" were an essential "school of practice" for training military engineers. (Abert to Cass, April 2, 1834, *ibid.*, I, 355–64.)

[55] Cullum, *Biographical Register*, I, 162, 164.

[56] A.R. of T.B., Nov. 2, 1835, *ASP, MA*, V, 711–13.

asked to be assigned an officer to supervise the building of the first section of their line between Lakes Erie and Michigan. The Topographical Bureau explained that such aid was feasible, but not by the direct loan of an engineer: "It is not at present the practice of the Department to detail officers of the Army to superintend the construction of rail roads. Whenever they are thus employed, they are engaged upon their own responsibility, and they must be either on furlough, or they must devote to the business such portion of their time, as does not interfere with their public duties."[57] The bureau then informed Lieutenant John M. Berrien that he was free to superintend the construction of this railroad in his spare time.[58]

In his annual report for 1835, Colonel Abert noted that many surveys made that year had not been ordered by Congress. According to prescribed rules, surveys ordered by acts containing specific appropriations were executed first. Next came surveys called for by resolutions of either house of Congress, the cost of these being paid from general appropriations for surveys. Finally there were those surveys of a "national or highly interesting commercial character" requested by states and private companies. Only such officers and instruments as could be spared were allowed for this type of survey.[59] Abert included the surveying of railroads as well as roads and canals among the major duties of the topographical engineers. Their work on these civil undertakings was profitable to such enterprises and also had military value by increasing professional training and knowledge of the country and its terrain.

[57] Nov. 17, 1835, T.B., Letters Issued, II, 34.

[58] *Ibid.* Berrien was told that the Secretary of War had decided that "there is no objection to your taking charge of the work if ( as he supposes ) it will not interfere with the performance of your present duties—and that, probably no other services will be required of you until after the next appropriation for surveys."

[59] A.R. of T.B. for 1835, *ASP, MA,* V, 713.

In 1836 railroad aid by army engineers slackened somewhat but remained extensive. Many of the surveys begun the previous year were continued, and a few new ones were started. This work was limited by the withdrawal of all line officers from topographical duty and the detail of most topographical engineers to field duty with troops. Nevertheless, army engineers gave railroad aid in Maine, Massachusetts, Rhode Island, Connecticut, New York, Maryland, North Carolina, and Missouri. They also completed a survey for a railroad from Pensacola to Columbus and started examining a route between Charleston and Cincinnati.[60]

Reports by Colonel Abert indicated that six topographical engineers were engaged in railroad work before being withdrawn for military duty. Colonel Long and two assistants surveyed a railroad route from Belfast, Maine, to Quebec; Major Kearney and one assistant made a survey and estimate for the Eastern Shore Railroad in Maryland; Major McNeill superintended construction of railroads in New York, Connecticut, Rhode Island, and Massachusetts; Major Graham and two assistants made the survey, plan, and estimate for the route between Pensacola and Columbus; Captain Swift unofficially directed construction of a railroad in Massachusetts while officially on the coast survey; and Captain Williams with three assistants made the survey, plan, and estimates for the railroad route from Charleston to Cincinnati.[61]

Late in 1836, Major McNeill was ordered to lay out a military road in the west. Abert consulted with Secretary of War Cass to see if McNeill's orders could be withdrawn. He urged McNeill to comply rather than resign but stated that the Secretary of War had no objection to his resigning if he so desired.[62] An application was made for Major McNeill to

---

[60] A.R. of T.B., Nov. 15, 1836, *ASP, MA*, VI, 909–10.

[61] Abert to Cass, June 21, 1836, *ibid.*, VI, 795–96, and July 6, 1836, T.B., Letters Issued, II, 102–104.

supervise a railroad survey in North Carolina. Abert strongly recommended to Secretary of War Cass that McNeill be given this assignment. He described McNeill's useful engineering career with public and private undertakings and noted that McNeill "has now under his charge, several Rail Roads, involving extensive interests of the States of Massachusetts, Connecticut, Rhode Island, New York and Maryland. And the application now before you is to extend his service, practical acquirements, promptness and integrity of action, upon similar employ in the State of North Carolina. Where so extensive a mass of population, and so vast an amount of enterprize and Capital, call for the services of a public officer, it comes in the aspect of the people of the U. S. asking for the services of one of their own servants, on duties of a public and very general character, although the result of individual or State enterprize."[63] Abert's forceful recommendation was successful, for he shortly ordered McNeill to North Carolina to superintend the survey of a railroad route. Abert notified a sponsor of the railroad that this was the decision of the Secretary of War.[64]

A few months later, however, B. F. Butler, interim secretary of war, took a position opposing the loan of engineers to railroads. He declared that inconveniences caused by this practice outweighed the military value of information secured by these officers.[65] In 1837 the succeeding secretary of war again strongly criticized the employment of army engineers by states and private companies. Joel R. Poinsett explained:

[62] Aug. 19, 1836, T.B., Letters Issued, II, 141–42. McNeill's orders were withdrawn when other arrangements were made for laying out this military road.

[63] Sept. 11, 1836, *ibid.*, II, 160. Abert added that to force McNeill's resignation would separate the War Department "from operations so acceptable to the people and diffusing so extensively the elements of general prosperity and wealth."

[64] Abert to McNeill and C. L. Winslow, Sept. 15, 1836, *ibid.*, II, 162–63.

[65] A.R. of S/W, Dec. 3, 1836, *ASP, MA*, VI, 810.

At a period when it became a practice of the government to permit these officers to aid in the construction of public works in the several States, the description of talent and knowledge which they possessed was uncommon in our country, and works of great public utility would have been suspended or abandoned altogether if this permission had been withheld. A different state of things now exists. The demand for civil engineers has created them; and not only is it no longer necessary to aid States and companies by lending them officers of the army, but, in doing so, an act of injustice is committed towards the civil engineers of the country. There can be no doubt that the practice impairs, very sensibly, the surveys and the erection and superintendence of works of national utility.[66]

Despite opposition of two successive secretaries of war to this practice, Colonel Abert attempted to keep Major McNeill in the army doing railroad work. McNeill resigned late in 1837, however, when he was given military duties in Florida. Abert admitted that some of the opposition to enlarging the topographical corps was due to the fact that several of its officers were engaged in civil engineering activities. He said this opposition did not come from the President or the corps itself and noted that a committee of Congress had recently given some support to this practice.[67]

In his report for the investigating committee, Abert discussed the practice of lending army engineers to state and private enterprises in terms of its nature, extent, and effects.[68] As to its nature, the War Department had adopted the custom of acting favorably on requests of states, companies, and groups of individuals for surveys. Reports on these investigations were submitted to the parties concerned and to the War Department. The practice had been in effect since about 1824 and was considered as authorized by the General Survey Act. Several officers had received compensation from states or

[66] A.R. of S/W, Dec. 2, 1837, *ibid.*, VII, 573-74.
[67] Nov. 30, 1837, T.B., Letters Issued, II, 429.
[68] Abert to B. F. Butler, interim S/W, Jan. 24, 1837, *ibid.*, II, 240-52.

companies, but such payment had commonly been made voluntarily. After 1835 these enterprises were required to pay the extraordinary expenses of officers and the personal allowances they lost by not being on public duties. Earlier than this, however, the Baltimore and Ohio Railroad had voluntarily paid the allowances and extra expenses of officers in its employment. Under the Survey Act the government at first not only furnished engineers for surveys, but also paid all surveying expenses from annual appropriations for surveys. Later, however, it adopted the more restricted practice of providing only the engineers who could be spared and of curtailing their personal allowances. Only when Congress by law or resolution ordered particular surveys did the government pay the entire cost.

Abert explained in considerable detail the extent of this lending of army engineers to private and state enterprises. He summarized the activities of eleven topographical engineers still under his jurisdiction who had served with such undertakings during the past five years. Eight of these eleven had worked for railroad companies. At least three of the eight had received direct compensation from the railroads, in addition to the personal allowances and extra expenses which they had all received. At least four of the eight had used their officer assistants when not engaged on public duties. This aid was in addition to official government surveys for railroads made upon the direct call of Congress and falling specifically under the General Survey Act.

These eight topographical engineers had been in the private employment of twenty-one different railroads during the past five years. Colonel Kearney had made the survey, plan, and estimate for the Eastern Shore Railroad in Maryland. Colonel Long had surveyed for five railroads, including three in New England, one in Virginia and one between the Mississippi and Atlantic. Major Bache had completed the survey, plan, and estimate for a railroad route between Williamsport and Elmira. Major McNeill had supervised the survey and construction of six railroads: the Boston and Lowell, Boston and Providence, Paterson and Hudson, Baltimore and Susquehanna, Long Island, and a railroad in North Carolina. Major Graham had made surveys, plans, and estimates for railroads from Winchester to Harpers Ferry and from Pensacola to Columbus. Captain Swift had surveyed for railroads from New London to Worcester and from Stonington to Providence and had superintended construction of a third railroad. Captain Williams had surveyed a railroad from Charleston to Cincinnati, upon the application of Senator Calhoun. Finally, Lieutenant Berrien had surveyed for two railroads in Michigan leading from Detroit to Pontiac and St. Joseph.

Abert explained that these surveys had been made at the expense of interested parties, despite the fact that the projects surveyed could be termed national undertakings in view of their great value to commerce and defense. Since they were of such national importance, they deserved "all the aid, which . . . can be derived from the science, general intelligence, and practical knowledge, of the officers of the nation."[69]

Abert categorically denied that the lending of engineers to state and private enterprises had an injurious effect upon the public service. Quite the contrary, for this professional work increased the military value and experience of the officers involved. The practice was completely within the letter and spirit of the Survey Act. Surveys made solely upon the application of states and companies were not permitted to interfere with those ordered by Congress, for private surveys were made at the close of the surveying season, during off-duty time, or in some other part-time manner which did not delay the public functions of these officers. Valuable reports and

[69] *Ibid.*, II, 248.

greater knowledge of the country resulted from this engineering aid to states and companies.

If this practice was regulated by law, it could not be administered as beneficially or co-ordinated as efficiently with public duties as was being done through the discretion of the President and War Department. Its prohibition by law would result in "driving some of the most valuable, best informed, and most enterprising officers from the Service." Capable engineers could not then be retained, and the public service would suffer.

Furthermore, states, companies, or groups of citizens possessed the right to call for the occasional aid of officers educated and supported by public taxes when this aid could be given without harm to their regular duties. These engineer officers were servants of the people and should give professional service when the people demanded it. Since states and companies spent large sums for improvements, engineering demands were greater than the civil engineers could handle. The government must give aid if these projects were not to be delayed or abandoned. "If such aid should be prohibited by law, it amounts under such circumstances to a prohibition of the improvement of the Country."[70]

During 1837 there was no government surveying of railroads upon the call of Congress. Lack of army engineers, concern with military and other public needs, the panic of 1837, and changing attitudes toward the propriety of engineering aid to railroads contributed to this result. The only assistance given to railroads was of the type defended by Abert. Several officers, including Long, Swift, Williams, and McNeill, were employed by railroads, although McNeill resigned during the year. Colonel Long was employed by the state of Georgia as chief engineer on the Western and Atlantic Railroad. He obtained a leave of absence from the War Department and

[70] *Ibid.,* II, 251.

drew a yearly salary of five thousand dollars plus expenses from the state of Georgia.[71] While serving on the coast survey, Captain Swift acted as resident superintending engineer on the Western Railroad in Massachusetts.[72] Major McNeill and Captain Williams surveyed for the Charleston and Cincinnati Railroad.[73]

During 1838 the Corps of Topographical Engineers was reorganized, enlarged, and assigned most of the civil works handled by the War Department. The act of July 5, 1838, which reorganized this corps, also repealed the provision in the General Survey Act authorizing employment of civil engineers. It stated in addition that army officers could not be removed from their regiments or corps for work on internal improvements and that they could not be employed by private companies.[74]

This act specified that officers already employed with private enterprises need not be withdrawn for one year if their immediate recall involved inconvenience to these enterprises. Colonel Abert immediately instructed the four officers to whom the prohibition then applied, Colonels Kearney and Long and Captains Swift and Hughes, to end their service with states and companies as soon as convenient, preferably before the time limit of one year had expired. He wanted them to return to public duties by the following spring, so that he could report that their private connections had ceased before the deadline.[75]

[71] James H. Johnston, *Western and Atlantic Railroad of the State of Georgia*, 19–21; Long's "Report on a reconnaissance and survey of the Western and Atlantic railroad of the State of Georgia," Nov. 7, 1837, 25 Cong., 2 sess., S. *Doc. 57*, 3–17. Long was chief engineer of this road until 1840.

[72] Cullum, *Biographical Register*, I, 236–44. The War Department allowed Swift to hold this position unofficially from 1836 to 1840.

[73] "Joint report of the chief and associate engineers of the Louisville, Cincinnati, and Charleston railroad" by McNeill and Williams, Oct. 7, 1837, 25 Cong., 2 sess., S. *Doc. 157*, 2–35.

[74] Beers, "Topographical Engineers," 291; Haney, *Congressional History*, I, 116; *Acts of the Twenty-fifth Congress*, Chap. 162, pp. 100–106.

At the end of 1838, Abert explained the nature of this prohibition and the work of the officers to whom it applied. Although the new law specifically barred their employment by private companies, it did not clearly prohibit their service with state-owned civil works. The War Department's interpretation, however, was that the law applied equally in both cases.[76] Abert felt that the practice being barred was greatly misunderstood and was not the evil that had been supposed. At any rate, it applied to only four officers at the time the corrective law was passed. Only two of these engineers, Colonel Long with the Atlantic and Western Railroad of the state of Georgia and Colonel Kearney with the Cincinnati and Charleston Railroad, were officially assigned to railroad work; but both had other public duties at the same time. The other two officers, Captains Swift and Hughes, had only unofficial connections with railroads and were concurrently on assigned public duties.

The years 1839 and 1840 marked the end of employment of army engineers by railroad companies. Lieutenant William H. Emory became the chief engineer of the Eastern Shore Railroad in Maryland early in 1839, but he was informed that this connection would have to end by July, the legal deadline.[77] The state of Georgia attempted in 1839 and 1840 to secure an extension of Colonel Long's service with its Western and Atlantic Railroad, in the interest of rapid and efficient

[75] Aug. 25 and Sept. 10, 1838, T.B., Letters Issued, II, 572–73, 598.

[76] A.R. of T.B., Nov. 26, 1838, 25 Cong., 3 sess., S. *Doc. 1*, 371. Specifically, the act declared that "the officers of the army shall not be separated from their regiments and corps for employment on civil works of internal improvement or be allowed to engage in the service of incorporated companies. . . ." (*Acts of the Twenty-fifth Congress*, 105.) In an earlier debate (Jan. 24, 1838), Senator James Buchanan had called for a provision to prevent the employment of army engineers by private companies. He stated that army officers had neglected public business and had "accumulated large fortunes" while employed by railroad and canal companies. (*Congressional Globe*, VI, 133.)

[77] Abert to Emory, Feb. 25 and May 11, 1839, T.B., Letters Issued, III, 90, 197–98.

construction. Abert stated that the act of July 5, 1838, prohibiting the service of officers with incorporated companies, by inference barred them from the employ of states. This had been the original interpretation of the War Department and should be considered binding.[78] He granted that the national importance of this railroad might justify an exception even though the law did not. Although the official deadline was July 5, 1839, Long and Swift served until 1840 with railroad companies, the former as chief engineer of the Western and Atlantic of Georgia and the latter as resident engineer for the Western in Massachusetts.[79]

Although government surveys of railroad routes came to a stop by 1838, and the loan of engineer officers to railroad companies ceased by 1840, the army engineers continued to be interested in the progress of railroads. This interest was later displayed in the Pacific railroad surveys of the 1850's, but there was evidence in the intervening period of their favorable attitude toward railroads. In 1839, for instance, Colonel Joseph G. Totten, chief engineer, expressed his belief in the great military value of railways. He felt that the military importance of a railroad from the interior to a naval base at Pensacola, Florida justified government support of its development: "Under this view, the Government seems imperatively called on to patronize and accelerate all works of interior communication, leading thither, that may be objects of private speculation; and in a special manner to encourage and foster such projects, not less important to the welfare of the establishment, as are not likely, without such assistance, to be thrown into the hands of private enterprise."[80]

In 1840, the Secretary of War referred a plan by General Edmund P. Gaines for an extensive system of railroads useful

[78] Abert to S/W, Oct. 22, 1839, *ibid.*, III, 355.
[79] Abert to S/W Poinsett, May 28, 1840, *ibid.*, IV, 151–52; Cullum, *Biographical Register*, I, 236–44; Johnston, *Western and Atlantic*, 20–21.
[80] Feb. 15, 1839, 25 Cong., 3 sess., *H. Doc. 198*, 1–2.

in national defense to Colonel Abert for an estimate of its probable cost. Abert reported that the total length would be over six thousand miles but that states and private companies had constructed or were building one thousand miles of this network. The remaining mileage with double track would cost $106,200,000, plus the cost of locomotives and cars which the government must own in order to guarantee the full military usefulness of the proposed system of railroads.[81] Abert insisted that accurate surveys alone would produce sound estimates and determine the practicability of each proposed route.

Attention was later drawn to a project for a railroad across Florida, and a government survey by the Corps of Topographical Engineers was recommended. Abert favored such a railroad, which would connect the Atlantic with the Gulf of Mexico, avoid the physical dangers of the voyage around Florida, and aid national defense in case of war with a maritime power. He thought that this road, which might be built by soldiers, would have a large traffic. He proposed that a survey be made, and Congress in 1844 appropriated $3,000 for this purpose. Although this grant was inadequate, a topographical engineer surveyed a route from Cedar Key to Jacksonville and the St. Johns River.[82]

A decision by the government in 1847 illustrated the continued desire of the army engineers to stimulate railroad development. Colonel Long was informed that he was "permitted to give your attention to the contemplated Rail Road from Alton to Springfield, Illinois, to the extent proposed in your letter, being careful that your absence from your post, shall be at such periods, and for such length of time, as shall

---

[81] Abert to S/W Poinsett, April 24, 1840, 26 Cong., 1 sess., *H. Doc. 206,* 145.

[82] Abert to Porter, Jan. 20, 1844, T.B., Letters Issued to S/W, I, 43–45; Abert to Lieut. J. E. Blake, July 2, 1844, T.B., Letters Issued, VII, 294–96; A.R.s of T.B., Nov. 15, 1844, 28 Cong., 2 sess, S. *Doc. 1,* 216, and Nov. 6, 1845, 29 Cong., 1 sess., S. *Doc. 1,* 378–80.

in no wise interfere with your duties under this Bureau."[83] Although Long was allowed to devote his off-duty service to this railroad, he could not lend it any government instruments. The practice of lending instruments to companies or individuals had resulted in damage, lack of repair, and delay in their return. Long was told that he could avoid delay in assisting this company by selling it at a fair value such instruments as he had on hand.

Government surveying for railroads and the outright loan of engineer officers to them had ceased by the 1840's. Engineering aid to railroads on the scale achieved between 1827 and 1838 had disappeared, and comparable aid to railway progress was not again given until the Pacific railroad surveys in the decade before the Civil War.[84]

[83] Abert to Long, May 14, 1847, T.B., Letters Issued, X, 104.

[84] It has been estimated that the aggregate cost of government railroad surveys under the General Survey Act was about $75,000. (U.S. Office of Federal Coordinator of Transportation, *Public Aids to Transportation*, Vol. II, *Aids to Railroads and Related Subjects*, Part I, "Aids to Railroads," 5.) This estimate is based on fragmentary data and on the assumptions that thirty, or half, of the routes surveyed became railroad lines not later abandoned and that each survey cost $2,500. This estimate is probably much too low. The sum of $424,000 was appropriated and spent for surveys under this act, and easily half of this sum may have been spent on railroad surveys. Furthermore, this figure completely omits the cost to the government of loaning engineers to railroads and the public compensation of military engineers engaged in both government surveying and private railroad work, to say nothing of the cost of educating and training these engineers and operating the engineering agencies of the War Department. If such costs as these could be allocated to government engineering aid to railroads, the figure of $75,000 would be insignificant in comparison.

# V: Railroad Progress

THE RAPID westward movement and the California gold rush drew attention to the Pacific Coast, and in 1849 Congress made an appropriation for military and geographical surveys west of the Mississippi. Topographical engineers rapidly explored the West and located wagon roads and military posts. As interest in good routes to the Pacific grew, attention turned to projects for ship canals and railroads across Central America. President Zachary Taylor in 1849 expressed the need of a railroad or canal across the Isthmus of Panama.[1]

Colonel Abert was among those who believed that the best route to the Pacific would be a transcontinental railroad across the southern part of the country. He said that the ignorance of proposed railroad routes across Central America was due not to the Corps of Topographical Engineers, which had wanted to make the needed surveys, but to the government's refusal to allow officers to make these surveys. He argued that railroads across Panama might be expensive and might involve the United States in legal and military difficulties or even war with a European power.

The best transportation route to the Pacific—one avoiding the danger of war while binding the country together politically and commercially—must necessarily lie on United States soil. These considerations, plus those of economy and speed, favored "a direct and continuous railroad from the Missis-

[1] Annual Message, Dec. 4, 1849, 31 Cong., 1 sess., S. Ex. Doc. 1, 8–9; A.R. of S/W, Nov. 30, 1849, ibid., 95; A.R. of T.B., Nov. 20, 1849, ibid., 294–96. Cf. Robert R. Russel, *Improvement of Communication with the Pacific Coast as an Issue in American Politics, 1783–1864.* This section is intended only as a cursory treatment of the Pacific railroad surveys; for further details, see Russel, *Improvement of Communication,* and George L. Albright, *Official Explorations for Pacific Railroads.*

sippi, through about the middle of Texas, and by the valley of the Gila to San Diego on the Pacific."[2] Such a railroad would be a military and commercial route and would increase the political and moral unity of the nation. It should be as short as possible, provide year-round service, pass through habitable country with good soil and climate, permit branch lines to the northeast and southeast, and connect with existing railroads. This road could branch out to Little Rock and St. Louis leading to the northeast and Vicksburg leading to the southeast. At the Mississippi it could connect with private railroads leading to Pittsburgh, Washington, and other eastern cities.

This railroad to the Pacific could be built by chartered companies which the federal government could aid by stock subscriptions made on prescribed conditions. Abert felt that the government could grant a charter for a railroad through territories where no organized states existed. As an alternative to this, it could build this railroad on the legal precedent of constructing military roads in the territories. Private railroads would then quickly complete the connecting links between the public road and private lines already reaching toward the Mississippi. Government surveying of possible routes need not be delayed, since "there are no conflicting opinions in reference to the right of the U. S. to authorize the survey and to meet its expenses."[3]

During 1850, military and geographical surveys west of the Mississippi were continued by topographical engineers. Although much of this exploration was to locate wagon routes, it was in part to determine possible railroad routes. Colonel

[2] Abert to Francis Markoe, May 18, 1849, 30 Cong., 2 sess., *H. Rept. 145*, 645.

[3] *Ibid.*, 649. For further views of Abert on the military, commercial, and political value of a Pacific railroad, see his letters to John A. Rockwell, June 30, 1849, *ibid.*, 639–41, and to J. Loughborough (who had invited Abert to a Pacific railroad convention at St. Louis), Sept. 24, 1849, T.B., Letters Issued, XII, 11–26.

Abert was particularly interested in planning a railroad from the Mississippi to the Pacific. Secretary of War C. M. Conrad directed Abert to report on surveys reputedly being made for such a route. This order was prompted by a letter from a congressman to the Senate Committee on Roads and Canals which stated: "I find on enquiry that an exploration and survey are in progress, preparatory to the location of a rail road to the Pacific, under the direction of Col. Abert, Chief of the Topographical Bureau, who is well disposed to the general object, tho I do not know his particular plan or whether he has formed any. He informs me he will be able to present a map and report to the Committee in a short time, which will contain much valuable information."[4]

Abert replied that surveys had not been made specifically to determine the actual cost or location of such a railroad. No plan or route for a Pacific railroad had been adopted. He admitted that he had made public his unofficial opinion on a proposed route. Although outright railroad surveys had not been made, surveys for western roads were producing data relevant to the problem of selecting the route of a Pacific railroad.[5] He was unable to submit a proposed route and plan, since other examinations and surveys were needed. Surveys were already in progress between the Mississippi and the Río Grande, and an examination was being made west of the Río Grande.

A report from one surveying party in 1850 indicated that it was examining the route for a common road and a railroad from the lower Mississippi to the Great Bend of the Red River. The report was made by a United States agent employed by the Topographical Bureau. He stated that this survey was made under an appropriation for geographical surveys west

[4] Abert to Conrad, Aug. 26, 1850, T.B., Letters Issued to S/W, IV, 202.
[5] *Ibid.*, IV, 203.

of the Mississippi, and he submitted estimates for a railroad and a road.[6]

Another United States agent surveyed a railroad route from St. Louis to the Great Bend of the Red River. His report was entitled "Survey of route for a Railroad from the Valley of the Mississippi to the Pacific Ocean, commencing at St. Louis, Missouri." He clearly stated that the purpose was "to determine the elements of a railroad from some point near . . . St. Louis, to the Arkansas river, intersecting the same not lower than Little Rock."[7]

Western explorations and surveys continued in 1851. Abert noted a survey for a road from St. Louis to the Great Bend of the Red River, but the United States agent in charge stated that this road survey was made "to determine also the elements of a Rail Road on the route indicated."[8]

Abert maintained active support of the Pacific railroad proposal. On one occasion he presented estimates of the probable cost and annual revenue of a railroad from the Mississippi to Southern California, suggesting that it could earn a 6 per cent return on its stock. The total cost of this road by El Paso to San Diego might be about $85,000,000.[9] He was quite forceful and appealing in his advocacy of this transcontinental railroad: "The subject is a vast one. It fills the imagination, and unless I am much mistaken, it would also fill the pockets of our people."[10] Such a road would complete the chain of connections formed by western rivers and lakes and would make

[6] Report on "Red and Mississippi Rivers Rail-Road," by W. H. Sidell, "Civil Engineer in charge, and United States Agent," Nov. 30, 1850, *DeBow's Review,* Vol. XII (1852), 409–20.

[7] Report by Joshua Barney, May 25, 1850, 32 Cong., 1 sess., *S. Ex. Doc.* 49, 2.

[8] Report by Barney, Nov. 1, 1851, *ibid.,* 17; A.R. of T.B., Nov. 18, 1851, 32 Cong., 1 sess., *S. Ex. Doc. 1,* 386. Barney's manuscript report was titled "Report on Survey of a Route for a Railroad from Fulton, Ark. to St. Louis." (E.D., Bulky File, No. 99.)

[9] Abert to V. E. Howard, House of Representatives, Jan. 25, 1851, T.B., Letters Issued, XIII, 241–46.

New Orleans "the great emporium for the Pacific trade." It would greatly exceed the proposed isthmus routes in safety, speed, and permanent commercial usefulness.

Abert still believed that army engineers should be allowed to work temporarily for railroads when their public duties were not impeded. Since 1838, officers had been prohibited from serving with incorporated companies. Leaves of absence allowing officers to enter such employment had been refused. An officer on leave, however, had superintended a survey for the Panama Railroad Company. Secretary of War Crawford had initially objected to this officer's action but had not withdrawn the leave since the officer was outside the country. This objection had been modified, for John G. Barnard of the Corps of Engineers had been granted a leave in order to work for the Tehuantepec Railroad Company. Feeling that this new principle might be applied to the temporary service of officers on undertakings within the United States, Abert argued that the purposes of the 1838 legislation were "to prohibit details of officers for such duties, which would give to companies a right to object when the officers were withdrawn; and to appease an ill founded apprehension on the part of the Civil Engineers of the Country, that these employments injured their expectations. These objects can be accomplished by the clear understanding that the officer can be ordered on such duties only temporarily, and at the pleasure of the War Department, so as to obstruct or embarrass no public duty; and secondly these orders could be limited to cases of application from the executive of a State."[11]

[10] Abert to Glendy Burke of New Orleans, Dec. 17, 1851, *ibid.*, XIV, 146. (Also in *DeBow's Review*, Vol. XII [1852], 402–406.)

[11] Abert to S/W Conrad, April 11, 1851, T.B., Letters Issued to S/W, V, 58. Abert said it would be all right for Col. Long to correspond with a state governor "and to give his attention to any general directions or instructions in reference to the location of this road." (*Ibid.*, V, 59.) There was no indication whether this "road" was a railroad or whether the secretary of war consented.

In 1852 there was further evidence of a renewed desire to give occasional aid to railroads. The House of Delegates of the state of Maryland asked that an engineer examine the proposed site of a railroad bridge across the Susquehanna at Havre de Grace. Upon Abert's recommendation, the secretary of war granted the request; and a topographical engineer was sent to make the desired study.[12]

Abert was eager to secure permission for topographical engineers to survey transcontinental railroad routes. When a congressman asked in 1852 about the practicability of a railroad from Lake Superior to Puget Sound, Abert replied that his bureau lacked the necessary information. He thought this route was too far north. Lake Superior was closed by ice much of the time, and this railroad might give service only half the year. He said that if Congress so authorized, a surveying party could examine the route to secure detailed information.[13]

On March 3, 1853, Congress appropriated $150,000 to the War Department for the Pacific railroad surveys. This was the first explicit authorization for government surveying of railroad routes in the West. It came at a time when railways were reaching as far westward as the Mississippi and when it was evident that the government would have to aid their extension to the Pacific. Colonels Abert and Long drew up plans for the necessary surveys. Four routes were to be examined, three under the direction of topographical engineers and one under Isaac I. Stevens, governor of Washington Territory and formerly an engineer officer.[14]

Secretary of War Davis recognized that these surveys to determine the best route for a Pacific railroad were an enor-

12 Abert to Col. William Turnbull, April 27, 1852, T.B., Letters Issued, XIV, 339.
13 *Ibid.*, XIV, 342–43.
14 Abert to S/W Jefferson Davis, March 26, 1853, T.B., Letters Issued to S/W, VI, 71–73. Abert favored a southern route from El Paso to San Diego, falling into Mexican territory part of the way. ( *Ibid.*, 93–96.)

mous undertaking. He said they would greatly increase the limited information then available but would require more time and funds than had been expected. Accurate instrumental surveys and greater knowledge of the productive character and general resources of the country along the routes were essential. Decision on the desirability of a railway and its proper route called for data on the meteorology, geology, mineralogy, zoology, and botany of the West. In assessing the potential value of a Pacific railroad, he noted its commercial and agricultural benefits and emphasized its political and military necessity.[15]

Davis reported in 1854 that six engineering parties had made explorations and surveys to determine the best railroad route from the Mississippi to the Pacific. Since a second appropriation had been made to continue investigations, parties were being organized for field operations the coming year.[16] At the end of 1855, he stated that surveys and reports had been completed and that a route along the thirty-second parallel was most practicable and economical. His attitude toward these engineering investigations was clear:

> The prosecution of instrumental surveys, accompanied by investigations into many branches of physical science simultaneously over lines of such length . . . is a work of greater magnitude than any of the kind hitherto undertaken by any nation; and its results . . . possess a value peculiar to the scale on which it has been conducted, as affording a basis for the determination of some questions of science which no number of smaller and detached explorations could have furnished. Should means be granted . . . for continuing these explorations, I have every confidence that the expenditure will be well repaid by these contributions to our knowledge of the interior of the country.[17]

Davis felt that the government was effectively utilizing its

15 A.R. of S/W, Dec. 1, 1853, 33 Cong., 1 sess., S. Ex. Doc. 1, 16–25.
16 A.R. of S/W, Dec. 4, 1854, 33 Cong., 2 sess., S. Ex. Doc. 1, 23–24.
17 A.R. of S/W, Dec. 3, 1855, 34 Cong., 1 sess., S. Ex. Doc. 1, 14–15.

engineering personnel to advance science and national development.[18] He argued that these explorations had produced a railroad route of great military value and that railroad transportation to the Pacific was an integral part of the nation's plan of military defense. He urged the study of means for building this railroad, including possible federal aid.

Colonel Abert of the Topographical Bureau and Colonel Totten of the Corps of Engineers also recognized the military value of railroads. Strictly military surveys were made with attention devoted in part to locating railroad routes. Abert instructed a topographical engineer surveying a route in Texas during 1853 and 1854 to "report upon its military peculiarities, and upon its adaptation for a Rail Road."[19]

Colonel Totten was directed by Secretary of War Davis to report on "the relative value, for military defensive purposes, of the Western rivers, canals, and railroads, as now severally provided with the means of transportation." Totten replied that railroads were superior to canals for travel and for transportation of commercial and military freight. The greater speed and certainty of transit added to the military value of railroads as compared to canals and rivers. If time was not important, however, rivers would provide cheaper transportation for military supplies than railroads. Railroads had the further advantage, however, that accidents did not impede transportation to anything like the extent that ice and low water obstructed and impeded river and canal navigation.[20]

Activities of the army engineers in determining routes for

[18] The total cost of the official Pacific railroad surveys finally amounted to $455,000, and about twice this amount was spent on publishing the extensive reports. (Russel, *Improvement of Communication,* 186.)

[19] Abert to Capt. John Pope, June 19, 1854, T.B., Letters Issued, XVII, 408. Abert stated that although the survey was being made through use of funds appropriated for military surveying, "the rail road peculiarities of the road should also be prominently set forth, as an interesting and important episode to the work."

[20] Dec. 13, 1856, E.D., Communications to S/W, IX, 21–29.

a Pacific railroad undoubtedly contributed to the growing demand for transcontinental railroads. The survey of four routes from the Mississippi to the Pacific between 1853 and 1855 has been called the most notable railroad work of the army engineers. At this time they still possessed much of their earlier leadership in engineering knowledge and skill.[21]

About twenty experienced military engineers participated in these surveying expeditions, and other army officers accompanied them as escort officers. Several of these Pacific railroad explorers who gained this topographical experience and knowledge of transportation problems over vast stretches of territory became famous field officers during the Civil War. Among those who later earned wartime fame were Henry L. Abbot, John B. Hood, Andrew A. Humphreys, George B. McClellan, John G. Parke, John Pope, Philip H. Sheridan, and G. K. Warren.[22]

The large role of the U. S. Military Academy in the early growth of railroads has been implicit in the preceding analysis of the engineering aid given to railroads by the army engineers. As shown in Chapter I, West Point by 1824 had become the first school of engineering in the nation. It stimulated railroad development through its pioneering advancement of engineering science and the work of its graduates who became civil engineers, as well as the government surveying of army engineers. The role of West Point may be better understood by examining the contribution of its curriculum to railroad engineering, the railroad work of some of its leading gradu-

[21] Beers, "Topographical Engineers," 351; *Centennial*, I, 838; Dupuy, *Where They Have Trod*, 378–79; Ingersoll, *War Department*, 291.

[22] *Centennial*, I, 838–39; Dupuy, *Where They Have Trod*, 378–79; Ingersoll, *War Department*, 284–85, 291; Thomas W. Symons, "The Army and the Exploration of the West," *Journal of the Military Service Institution of the United States*, Vol. IV (1883), 229–36. About forty military engineers became general officers during the Civil War. (*Centennial*, I, 874; Ingersoll, *War Department*, 284–85.)

ates, the process of resignation by which its graduates became civil engineers, and the extent to which these West Pointers followed railroad careers in civil life.

There is ample evidence that War Department officials recognized and sanctioned the place West Point assumed in the first few decades of railroad progress. They saw military and civil engineering as integrally related and considered the scarcity of civil engineers a major barrier to improved transportation. They wanted to utilize the engineering potential of the government to stimulate this improvement, and the General Survey Act implemented their basic desire.

In 1828, when several government surveys of railroads were already in progress, Secretary of War Porter declared that the Military Academy as a national school was "scattering the fruits of its science." Its graduates were carrying theoretical training to the civil engineers of the nation and were furnishing "every part of the country with the most accomplished professors in every branch of civil engineering."[23] Secretary of War Eaton stated in 1831 that the Military Academy was one of the most valuable institutions in the nation, that the number of cadets was not excessive, and that the many graduates not needed by the Army should be allowed to enter civilian callings of their own choice.[24]

The Board of Visitors in 1831 concluded that the curriculum was very good in military and civil engineering, particularly with regard to land and water transportation, including railroads. Speaking at a time when government surveying of railroads was increasing, this board declared that civil engineering as taught at West Point was a fundamentally important branch of education.[25] A year later the board was equally well pleased with the teaching of "the science of engineering,

[23] A.R. of S/W, Nov. 24, 1828, *ASP, MA*, IV, 2.
[24] Report "On the Subject of a Change in the Organization of the Military Academy at West Point," by John H. Eaton, Jan. 28, 1831, *ASP, MA*, IV, 676.
[25] Report of Board of Visitors, June 21, 1831, *ASP, MA*, IV, 737.

with all its auxiliary branches" at West Point. This instruction was helping all parts of the country in "the successful prosecution of those great internal improvements which, in this enlightened age, the States are planning and executing."[26]

The growing importance of West Point in the internal improvements movement was criticized in the 1830's as a perversion of its original purpose. In reply to such criticism, the House Committee on Military Affairs reported that the army and the nation had benefited from West Point's progress. It approved of the training of engineers "competent to superintend the construction of those chains of internal improvement which are to be the eternal bonds of our national Union." In this category were the Baltimore and Ohio, Charleston and Hamburg, and Baltimore and Susquehanna railroads, as well as railroads in New England—all of which had been aided by army engineers.[27]

Military historians have noted the strategic part which West Point played in the early decades of railroad engineering. Through the railroad activities of its graduates, West Point initially dominated this area of civil engineering. Until 1840 or 1850 it was practically the only school in America offering systematic instruction in any branch of engineering. It was thus the primary source of academically trained engineers for planning and building railroads in the first three decades of their development. During the first half-century of railroad progress, engineers trained at West Point took a leading responsibility in the construction of railroads.[28]

[26] Report of Board of Visitors, June 16, 1832, *ASP, MA,* V, 60. The advancement of technical education by West Point is discussed further in Chapter VIII.

[27] "Statement of the History and Importance of the Military Academy at West Point, New York, and Reasons Why It Should Not Be Abolished," May 17, 1834, *ASP, MA,* V, 354–55.

[28] *Centennial,* I, 289, 375, 376, 835, 843, 876, 878; Dickinson, "River Improvement," 77–79; Dupuy, *Where They Have Trod,* 368, 369, 382; Humphreys, "Historical Sketch," 45 Cong., 3 sess., *S. Rept.* 555, 348; Ingersoll, *War*

Although most railroad engineers trained at West Point made their professional reputation after resigning, many of them started their railroad careers while still in the army. Practically all officers who made government railroad surveys or were loaned to railroad companies were West Point graduates, and so were many of the U. S. civil engineers engaged in these activities as employees of the Engineer Department.[29] The first railroad survey made in this country by army engineers, that in 1826 for canals or railways to connect the Kanawha, James, and Roanoke rivers, was made by five West Point officers with later careers in railroading. Of the fourteen army engineers who surveyed and directed the building of the Baltimore and Ohio Railroad between 1827 and 1830, ten were West Pointers with later railroad experience. The three army engineers with the most famous railroad careers were Colonel Long, Major McNeill, and Lieutenant Whistler. All except Long were graduates of the Military Academy, and all three worked on the Baltimore and Ohio. Although Whistler resigned in 1833 and McNeill in 1837, these three officers were instrumental in establishing the national reputation of army engineers as railroad builders.

Department, 289–90; Struik, Yankee Science, 244–47; E. D. J. Waugh, West Point, 51, 95–97. One military historian states the contribution of the Military Academy to railroads as follows: "Railroading in the United States, to put it bluntly, owes more to West Point than to any other institution in the country. Graduates not only surveyed and constructed the early rights of way, but also took active part in the building and improving of rolling stock. . . . Outside of the Army there were but few men with technical education sufficient to accomplish the task. The Government accordingly lent officers, and these men, together with their brethren resigned and resigning from the service, did the work. West Pointers predominated. Railroad systems now existing, and hundreds of others long since amalgamated or abandoned . . . owe their foundation to West Point." (Dupuy, Where They Have Trod, 382.)

[29] Engineer Department records show that more than fifty army engineers participated in railroad work at some time during the period 1826–40. Over two-thirds of these were army officers, and the remainder U. S. civil engineers. The latter were commonly West Point graduates or assistants to such graduates.

Before resigning, McNeill was connected with some twelve railroad companies, usually as chief engineer. He supervised construction of railroads in several states and earned a reputation as the leading railroad builder of the nation. After his resignation in 1837, he was chief or consulting engineer for several railroads until his death in 1853. In his early railroad work, McNeill was assisted by Whistler in the capacity of associate engineer. Known for his technical competence, Whistler directed the construction of several railroads before he resigned in 1833. He then became chief engineer for the Proprietors of Locks and Canals on the Merrimack River and directed their machine shops at Lowell. Here he designed and built steam locomotives which were rated among the finest in his day. He was later consulting and chief engineer of the Western Railroad of Massachusetts. In 1842, he went to Russia to build the St. Petersburg and Moscow Railroad, where he died in 1849.[30]

Other railroad engineers also began their careers as army engineers. McNeill was asked in 1835 to name engineers quali-

[30] Cf. Allan, "George W. Whistler," 177–80; Cullum, *Biographical Register*, I, 161–66, 214–22; Kirkland, *Men, Cities*, I, 121–22, 131, 246; Ringwalt, *Transportation Systems*, 95; Struik, *Yankee Science*, 246; Vose, *Sketch of Whistler*, 16–36; Waugh, *West Point*, 96–101.

Long worked with at least ten railroads between 1827 and 1847. He surveyed for railroads in New England and in the South and West. From 1837 to 1840, he was chief engineer of the Western and Atlantic Railroad built by the state of Georgia. He also wrote a technical manual on locating railroad routes, made improvements in railroad bridges, built locomotives, and helped plan the Pacific railroad surveys. (Johnston, *Western and Atlantic*, 19–21; Kirkland, *Men, Cities*, I, 163, 290–91; Ringwalt, *Transportation Systems*, 95; and Robert H. Thurston, *A History of the Growth of the Steam Engine*, 218.)

Lieutenant William H. Swift was another West Pointer and colleague of McNeill and Whistler who became known as a railroad builder. Although he did not resign until 1849, he served with six railroads in New York and New England between 1828 and 1840. He was resident superintending engineer between 1836 and 1840 on the Western Railroad in Massachusetts, of which he was later president. In later life he held executive positions with several railroad companies and was president of the Illinois and Michigan Canal from 1846 to 1871. (Cullum, *Biographical Register*, I, 236–44; Kirkland, *Men, Cities*, I, 131; Struik, *Yankee Science*, 246; Vose, *Sketch of Whistler*, 20–21.)

fied to direct railroad construction in Cuba. He recommended four engineers who were then engaged in railroad work as civilians, but all were West Pointers who had started their railroad careers as army engineers on the Baltimore and Ohio.[31] Colonel Abert reported in 1837 that during the past five years eight topographical engineers, sometimes with their assistants, had been lent to or employed by railroad companies.[32] The extensive service of West Point officers with railroads has been emphasized by military historians, who have noted the early prevalence of loaning engineer officers to railroad companies.[33]

West Point probably contributed more to railroad progress through its graduates who became civil engineers than those who remained military engineers. A high rate of resignations among army engineers and other officers with West Point engineering training continually increased the supply of civil engineers available for railroading. This process of resignation enabled West Point to serve as a national school for educating civil as well as military engineers. The Engineer Department operated the Military Academy as a technical school,

[31] McNeill to Gen. Gratiot, March 10, 1835, E.D., Misc. Letters Sent, X, 490–91. McNeill named Isaac Trimble, William Cook, Joshua Barney, and Whistler.

[32] Abert to S/W Butler, Jan. 24, 1837, T.B., Letters Issued, II, 240–52.

[33] Abbot, "Corps of Engineers," 423; Alstaetter, "Ohio River," 36; Centennial, I, 843; Cullum, Biographical Register, I, 163, 216, 238; Dupuy, Where They Have Trod, 382; and other works cited in this chapter. One writer says that "Up to 1855 there was scarcely a railroad in this country that had not been projected, built and in most cases managed by officers of the Corps." (Henry C. Jewett, "History of the Corps of Engineers to 1915," The Military Engineer, Vol. XXXVIII [1946], 344.) Another states that "Almost without exception, the engineers chosen to conduct the surveys for these early railroads were graduates of the Military Academy. The War Department at once adopted a very liberal policy of lending its officers to the newly organized companies, and, if the phenomenal growth of the United States during the first half of the last century may be ascribed in a large measure to the building of railroads, then the nation owes a great debt to the skill and diligence of those young graduates of West Point, who, alone, could plan and construct them." (Allan, "George W. Whistler," 178.)

and the War Department did not object when young West Pointers resigned to follow civil professions. Since promotion in the army was very slow and the Military Academy graduated more cadets each year than the army had vacancies, resignations were freely tolerated, if not encouraged.

Of the ten West Point engineers employed on the Baltimore and Ohio Railroad between 1827 and 1830, eight had resigned by 1832 and all ten by 1837. The number of resignations was very great in 1832, partly because of a War Department regulation late in 1831 withdrawing line officers from duties not directly under its command. This rule ended the furloughing or lending of line officers to railroad companies, with the result that many resigned to accept positions with these companies.[34]

In 1836, Colonel Abert assured Major McNeill that it was McNeill's own decision whether he should resign. This seems to have been the typical attitude of the War Department, for in this case McNeill was informed that the Secretary of War saw no impropriety in his resigning if he desired to do so.[35] Resignations in 1836 were very large as a result of low pay and lack of promotion in the army and expanding opportunities in civil life. It is reported that 117 officers left the army that year.[36] The Secretary of War decided that West Point graduates were resigning too soon. Cadets at that time were required to serve five years—only one year beyond graduation. Although he said early resignations had not become a serious problem, he recommended that the term of required service be increased. A year later President Van Buren proposed that the term of prescribed service be seven instead of five years.[37]

[34] Cullum, *Biographical Register*, I, *passim;* Col. Abert to Governor of New Jersey, Nov. 30, 1831, T.B., Letters Issued, I, 136–37.

[35] Aug. 19, 1836, T.B., Letters Issued, II, 142.

[36] Ganoe, *Hist. of U. S. Army*, 179.

[37] A.R. of S/W for 1836, *ASP, MA,* VI, 813; Annual Message, Dec. 5, 1837, 25 Cong., 2 sess., *S. Doc. 1*, 18. Van Buren was pleased, however, that the Academy diffused civil engineers throughout the country.

Army officers continued to be attracted to promising careers in civil engineering, for which their West Point training qualified them. Secretary of War William Wilkins stated in 1844 that it was proper to encourage resignations, since graduates of the Military Academy were useful in private as well as public life.[38] In 1848, the Board of Visitors reviewed the civil professions of graduates and indicated the extent to which they had entered railroading and other branches of civil engineering. By that time 3 graduates had become presidents and 29 had become chief engineers of railroads or canals. It is presumed that railroads predominated and that many of the additional 103 graduates who had become civil engineers were also with railroads.[39]

The significant inference is that West Point produced many engineers who adopted railroading as a profession. In 1868 a study of the civilian occupations of all 2,218 West Point graduates between 1802 and 1867 showed 35 presidents of railroads and other corporations, 48 chief engineers and 41 superintendents of railroads and other public works, and 7 treasurers of railroads and other companies. Presumably railroads were dominant in these overlapping categories. Many of the additional 155 civil engineers probably worked for railroads.[40]

[38] A.R. of S/W, Nov. 30, 1844, 28 Cong., 2 sess., S. *Doc. 1*, 116, 118.

[39] Report of Board of Visitors, June, 1848, 30 Cong., 2 sess., *H. Ex. Doc. 1*, 282–95.

[40] Cullum, *Biographical Register* (1868 edition), I, 7. A similar analysis of the civil careers of West Pointers graduating before 1903 may be compared to those for graduates up to 1848 and 1867. (Cf. *Centennial*, I, 483–84 for figures covering graduates to 1903.)

| | *Graduates for the Period:* | | |
| Civil Occupation | 1802–48 | 1802–67 | 1802–1903 |
| --- | --- | --- | --- |
| Presidents of railroads and other corporations | 3 | 35 | 87 |
| Chief engineers of railroads and other public works | 29 | 48 | 63 |

United States Snag-Boat.

*Sketch of a snag-boat.*

From J. L. Ringwalt's *Development of Transportation Systems
in the United States* (1888).

*Snags in the Missouri River in the early 1830's.*

From a lithograph after Carl Bodmer, in the atlas accompanying Maximilian,
Prince of Wied, *Travels in the Interior of North America.*

*Cleveland lighthouse on Lake Erie.*

From a lithograph after Carl Bodmer, in the atlas accompanying Maximilian, Prince of Wied, *Travels in the Interior of North America.*

*Passenger packet boat on the Erie Canal, 1830.*

Courtesy New York Central System.

To assess the exact contribution of West Point to early railroad progress would be admittedly difficult. This school developed the engineering skill which was necessary in locating routes and constructing railroads and their equipment. West Point produced engineers with the technical ability required to survey and build the early railroads and to train and supervise practical civil engineers needed in detailed operations. West Pointers engineered the construction of many early railroads either as army engineers or as civil engineers who resigned to work for railroads. It is quite likely that the Military Academy contributed much more to the growth of railroads through its graduates who became civil engineers than through those who remained army officers.

West Point's contribution to railroading was only one element in the relationship between the federal government and railroads. Although the government developed West Point into an effective school of engineering and approved of the early resignation of its graduates to become railroad engineers, this was a somewhat indirect form of engineering aid.

The effects of this engineering assistance were quite large and important in the first two or three decades of railroads. The government gave them no financial aid, although for several years it granted tariff remissions on imported railway iron. There were no federal land grants until 1850, and these benefited western rather than eastern railroads. In terms of engineering knowledge and skills, however, the government gave much aid and encouragement from the beginning.[41]

| | | | |
|---|---|---|---|
| Superintendents of railroads and other public works | | 41 | 62 |
| Treasurers of railroads and other companies | | 7 | 24 |
| Civil engineers (many presumably with railroads) | 103 | 155 | 228 |

[41] For a brief description of these forms of federal aid to railroads prior to 1860, see George Rogers Taylor, *The Transportation Revolution, 1815–1860*, 94–96.

When several large railroads asked for the continued service of Major McNeill, Colonel Abert unequivocally stated that "Where so extensive a mass of population, and so vast an amount of enterprize and Capital, call for the services of a public officer, it comes in the aspect of the people of the U. S. asking for the services of one of their own servants, on duties of a public and very general character, although the result of individual or State enterprize."[42]

The impetus of government engineering to infant railroads may perhaps be suggested by a comparison of the annual increase in railway mileage and the number of railroads annually receiving government surveying or the loan of army engineers.[43]

| Year | Railroad Miles Added | Approx. No. of Railroads Receiving Engineering Aid |
|------|------|------|
| 1829 | —— | 4 |
| 1830 | 39.80 | 4 |
| 1831 | 98.70 | 7 |
| 1832 | 191.30 | 12 |
| 1833 | 115.91 | 10 |
| 1834 | 213.92 | 10 |
| 1835 | 137.82 | 20 |
| 1836 | 280.00 | 14 |
| 1837 | 348.38 | 5 |
| 1838 | 452.88 | 5 |

[42] Abert to S/W Cass, Sept. 11, 1836, T.B., Letters Issued, II, 160.

[43] For railroads receiving government engineering aid each year, see annual reports and correspondence of the engineering agencies; for railroad miles added annually, see Armin E. Shuman, "Statistical Report of the Railroads of the United States," U. S. Department of the Interior, Census Office, *Report of the Agencies of Transportation of the United States,* 289. Approximate figures for railroads receiving engineering aid each year may be too low; sources are fragmentary and incomplete, particularly for the work of army officers with railroads while off duty or on furlough.

By 1830 there had been ten railroad or canal-and-railway surveys, while only forty miles of railroads had been built. By 1838, when 1,879 miles had been constructed, at least sixty railroad companies had received government surveys or other engineering aid.

The War Department attempted to divide this surveying so that all parts of the country benefited. Illinois and Delaware, however, received no surveys; and New Hampshire, North Carolina, and Florida saw very few surveys. Massachusetts and Alabama shared heavily in this railroad aid; and New York, Georgia, New Jersey, Maryland, and Virginia fared well. Although most surveys fell north of the Potomac River, the South received a large share of the more important ones. Some of the surveying was also distributed in the Ohio and Mississippi valleys, and many examinations were for east-west routes to link seacoast cities with western rivers and trade.

Opposition to this railroad aid gradually arose in Congress, which in 1836 made an investigation into the employment of engineer officers by railroad companies. The secretary of war decided that this practice was injurious to the public service. Congress grew increasingly critical of the service of army engineers with states or companies and in 1838 prohibited it by law.

Military historians sometimes appear to suggest that engineer officers and other West Point graduates located and built the early railways almost singlehandedly. This claim is of course an exaggeration. It must not be forgotten that much of the work was done by practical engineers, largely self-taught, such as those who had accomplished some of the most notable works of the canal era and had found in them their own school of practice. But in the early railroad era the great majority of engineers who had received systematic schooling were or had been army men; and they brought to American railroading a major contribution in the initial, experimental stages of its development.[44]

[44] For this writer's evaluation of the railroad work of the army engineers, see "Government Engineering Aid to Railroads Before the Civil War," *The Journal of Economic History*, Vol. XI (1951), 235–46.

# VI: Early River and Harbor Work

THE ENGINEER DEPARTMENT has been the only federal agency to make river and harbor improvements. Army engineers had become involved in this work by the time the General Survey Act was passed in 1824, and within a few years it became one of their major duties. The way in which these river and harbor projects were executed established precedents for what later became the most important civil function of the Engineer Department.

River and harbor works were extensive during the life of the Survey Act as well as after its repeal. They became important when the army engineers were devoting most attention to roads, canals, and railroads; and they remained a major duty after the engineers had been withdrawn from other types of improvements.

The early civil activities of the army engineers were discussed in Chapter I. These engineers possessed the best technical training to be had in this country, and they believed that military and civil engineering were interdependent and that national defense necessitated internal improvements. While surveying for coastal defenses, they became familiar with the navigability of rivers, bays, and harbors. In making topographical examinations of the country, they became aware of the transportation needs of the nation. Their chief task was to plan a system of fortifications to defend the major ports whose ultimate protection depended on interior communications for troops and supplies in the event of attack. Greater trade, better transportation, and increased military defense were thus integral elements of a general plan for improving national security.

After the War of 1812, the Board of Engineers for Fortifications was created to execute this military planning. This board employed topographical engineers in surveying the coast, particularly in the vicinity of inlets and harbors, and used officers of the Corps of Engineers in supervising the construction of defenses. The board had a wide reputation, trained engineers, and intimate knowledge of the sites of proposed improvements; consequently, its advice and engineering services were in great demand.

Before 1824, river and harbor improvements had commonly been executed by local or state agencies. During the first two or three decades of its existence, the federal government had never appropriated funds to remove obstructions to navigation. It had been customary for the Treasury Department to render navigation safer by making harbor surveys and coastal charts and by erecting lighthouses, public piers, beacons, and buoys. Cities benefiting from them usually executed local harbor improvements. Congress frequently passed enabling acts permitting individual states and ports to levy tonnage duties on local shipping to help pay for their river or harbor improvements.

Army engineers provided occasional engineering aid after 1816 to states, localities, and chartered companies making navigation improvements. In that year Major James Kearney, a topographical engineer, reported on his examination of the routes for two coastal canals between Virginia and North Carolina. Charters had been granted for these undertakings by these two states, and Kearney inspected and reported on the routes and operations under way for their improvement.[1]

In the following years topographical engineers assisted the commissioners in charge of improving the navigation of Albemarle Sound. In 1817, Chief Engineer Swift informed President Monroe that he and General Bernard would examine the

[1] Nov. 5, 1816, Corps of Engineers, Reports, 1812–23, 142–48.

proposed improvements and provide the commissioners with information.[2] The Board of Engineers for Fortifications annually examined these projects in Albemarle Sound and advised these state officials regarding plans for their execution. In 1820, for instance, Secretary of War Calhoun stated that the board's members "have been instructed to furnish any information, or assistance, in their power, and which may be requested by the Commissioners appointed by the State of North Carolina, particularly in relation to the improvement of the navigation of the State by opening or deepening the inlet into Albemarle Sound."[3]

Between 1820 and 1823 the board's engineers made further examinations of harbors and bays on the Atlantic and Gulf coasts. These were primarily military surveys, but the engineers were particularly interested in the navigability of these waters and of rivers flowing into them and projects for their improvement. Since they possessed the requisite engineering ability and knowledge of the coastal areas, these engineers were called upon to make surveys of several canal routes along the Atlantic Coast. In 1823 they made studies of the Chesapeake and Delaware Canal, the Morris Canal in New Jersey, and two proposed canals in Maryland. The board itself examined the former two canals and a surveying party under Captain Hartman Bache inspected the latter two.[4]

Military engineers also became involved officially in other activities relating to river and harbor improvements in 1823. One of these was the making of surveys and plans for a breakwater at the entrance to Delaware Bay. A grant of $22,700 in

[2] May 22, 1817, E.D., Misc. Letters Sent, I, 23–24.

[3] Calhoun to John Branch, April 12, 1820, E.D., Letters Received, I, No. R58. Cf. other E.D. files between 1817 and 1820 regarding continued correspondence about federal engineering aid to North Carolina.

[4] Cf. A.R. of C/E, Nov. 20, 1823, *ASP, MA,* II, 567–68, and other E.D. correspondence for that year in Misc. Letters Sent, I, Letters to Officers of Engineers, I, and Letters Received, I.

1822 for constructing this artificial harbor was the first appropriation made by the federal government for improving harbors or rivers. The purpose of this breakwater near Cape Henlopen was to protect vessels from tempests and floating ice. In reporting on their survey and plan, the Board of Engineers for Fortifications stressed the need for a harbor of refuge and safe anchorage at the mouth of Delaware Bay and the potential benefits for the coastal trade and the port of Philadelphia.[5]

By 1823 military engineers had also become concerned with rivers and harbors in the interior. Topographical engineers began to explore the "western waters" soon after the War of 1812; Major Stephen H. Long made such explorations in 1817, 1819, and 1823. He first made a reconnaissance of the area between the Ohio, Mississippi, and Lake Michigan. He described the major rivers, discussed their value for future trade and travel, and showed how they could be supplemented by roads and canals. Such rivers as the Mississippi, Ohio, Illinois, and Chicago were the channels of future commerce between all parts of the country, "the cords which will unite the northern interests of the country, and will eventually become the most important links in the grand chain that surrounds the whole."[6] He indicated the need for an improved harbor at Chicago and for a canal between the Chicago and Illinois rivers to connect Lake Michigan with the Mississippi.

[5] "Report of the Board of Commissioners on the utility, the practicability, the situation, the magnitude, and the cost of a projected Pier or Breakwater near the Capes of the Delaware, for the Protection of Vessels against Ice, and against Tempests," July 14, 1823, Corps of Engineers, Reports, 1812–23, 498–508. Concerning the significance of this appropriation, see Albert B. Hart, *National Ideals Historically Traced, 1607–1907*, 291; Emory R. Johnson, *Inland Waterways, Their Relation to Transportation*, supplement to *The Annals of the American Academy of Political and Social Science*, Sept. 1893, 111; Emory R. Johnson, "River and Harbor Bills," *The Annals*, II (1892), 786–87; and I. Y. Schermerhorn, "The Rise and Progress of River and Harbor Improvement in the United States," *Journal of the Franklin Institute*, Vol. 139 (1895), 258.

[6] Report of March 4, 1817, Corps of Engineers, Reports, 1812–23, 159.

Long explored western rivers in 1819 and 1820 with the "United States Steam Boat *Western Engineer*," for which Congress had appropriated $6,500. Long examined the Ohio, Mississippi, and Missouri rivers and reported on the condition of their navigation and the extent to which snags, sand bars, and rapids obstructed their use. Authorization of this survey showed the interest of Congress in the western rivers, and Long's report suggested the improvements needed on these rivers.[7] His third exploring expedition in 1823 carried him up the Minnesota River to the forty-ninth parallel and back to the Great Lakes. Calhoun called this a purely scientific expedition and indicated that Long was to gather information about the western lakes.[8]

Soon after it authorized Long's second river exploration, Congress appropriated $5,000 for a detailed study of western rivers. On April 14, 1820, it authorized the survey and mapping of the Ohio below Louisville and the lower Mississippi to determine practicable means of improving their navigation. The Board of Engineers for Fortifications was removed from its work on coastal defenses to make this study in 1821. In their report General Bernard and Colonel Totten discussed the obstructions and means of removing them. On the Ohio a canal was direly needed around the falls at Louisville. As for other obstructions, rocks could be removed, and bars could probably be eliminated by the use of dikes. They advocated experiments to deepen the channel over these shoals by using dikes or wing-dams. Since this expedient was not certain to succeed, they recommended further study of the behavior of the river.

Obstructions of the Mississippi existed in the form of snags,

[7] Calhoun to Swift, Sept. 1, 1818, E.D., Doc. File B, Misc. Letters Received, 1813–18, No. 151; "Report of Col. Stephen H. Long's Western Expedition," Feb. 20, 1821, E.D., Bulky File, No. 107; Lippincott, "History," 634.

[8] A.R. of C/E for 1823, *ASP, MA*, II, 567–68; Calhoun to Secretary of State John Quincy Adams, April 28, 1823, E.D., Misc. Letters Sent, I, 391–92.

or trees caught in the bed of the river; rafts, or masses of matted trees; and shifts in the channel of the river. Machines could be designed to remove snags. Bernard and Totten strongly advocated snag removal, which would require continued effort to be successful. In the long run the danger of cross currents during floods might necessitate diking along the banks; but for the time being safety of navigation depended on snag removal, more skillful pilotage, and better boats. Since flatboats and keelboats were slow and difficult to steer, steamboats with their speed, precise steerage, and skilled pilots were the only boats well adapted for use on the Mississippi.[9]

As commerce and steamboating increased on the Great Lakes, Congress and the army engineers became interested in the condition of lake harbors. An act of March 3, 1823, appropriated funds for a survey of the harbor of Presque Isle on Lake Erie by a topographical engineer to prepare a plan and estimate for removing a bar obstructing its entrance. Calhoun considered this project of sufficient importance to justify the attention of the Board of Engineers for Fortifications. Chief Engineer Macomb informed Bernard and Totten that as a result of the great interest of Pennsylvania in its only harbor on Lake Erie, they were to study this harbor and means of improving it.[10]

The board examined the harbor of Erie and reported a plan and estimate for its improvement. Although a long sand bar obstructed the entrance of Presque Isle Bay, the basin was deep and well protected. The board proposed to use piers and piles to close most of the mouth of the bay so that the current would deepen its entrance. It emphasized the value of a good harbor on this part of Lake Erie. There was a rapid increase

---

[9] "Survey of the Ohio and Mississippi Rivers," Dec. 22, 1822, *ASP, Commerce and Navigation*, II, 740–46; Lippincott, "History," 634.

[10] May 7, 1823, E.D., Letters to Officers of Engineers, I, 419. Cf. Calhoun's letter of May 7, 1823, E.D., Misc. Letters Sent, I, 396.

in population and commerce throughout the region. Lake Erie was becoming a major channel of trade between the Atlantic and inland areas and needed unobstructed harbors to accommodate this growing navigation. This harbor should be accessible to boats of a deeper draft in order to benefit commerce and serve as a harbor of refuge during storms and a naval center to guarantee communication with the Erie Canal.[11]

By 1823 army engineers were thus investigating the navigability and planning the improvement of rivers and harbors in the interior as well as on the coast. With the growth of steamboating and the spirit of internal improvement, the army engineers were being called to aid navigation. Since the planning of such transportation improvements necessitated a great amount of technical skill, these engineers were assigned to plan canal, harbor, and river works. Although the Board of Engineers for Fortifications was created to prepare a system of coastal defenses, it was by 1823 extensively engaged in projecting waterway improvements. By that time it had examined several canal routes, surveyed the Ohio and Mississippi rivers, and prepared plans for harbor works on Lake Erie and the Atlantic Coast. This board and its engineers thus had charge of the first efforts of the federal government to improve harbors and rivers.

It had not been intended originally that the government and its army engineers enter this field. Until this time navigation improvements had been made by state and local agencies. Before steamboating became successful, these projects were not considered to be nationally important or to demand the technical skills of the army engineers. Roads and canals, however, were from an early date placed in a different category. Many national leaders believed that government aid,

---

[11] "Report of the Board of Engineers on the Harbour of Erie in Pennsylvania," Oct. 4, 1823, Corps of Engineers, Reports, 1812–23, 508–18.

both financial and engineering, was essential to the expeditious development of important roads and canals.

The term "internal improvements" was at first used more or less synonymously with roads and canals. These undertakings were technically more difficult, financially more costly, and nationally more beneficial than the earliest river and harbor works. In his report on internal improvements in 1808, for instance, Gallatin emphasized the necessity and utility of "artificial roads and canals." He proposed federal financing of a program of large canal and road projects which would not otherwise be built. He included only such river improvements as canals around waterfalls on large navigable streams. His plan, produced in answer to a Senate resolution directing his attention specifically to roads and canals, did not give a significant place to proposed river and harbor improvements. Before the War of 1812 there was apparently no general desire for the federal government to execute harbor or river improvements.[12]

There were many demands for an increase in the engineering branches of the army after 1815. Proponents of enlarging the strength and functions of the engineers advocated that they survey the country to learn more about its coasts, resources, transportation routes, and military features. They did not propose that these engineers participate in improvements of navigation, other than canals. Internal improvements still meant roads and canals.

Calhoun's "Report on Roads and Canals" in 1819 was essentially similar to Gallatin's earlier plan and to prevailing views about internal improvements. The House of Representatives had specifically directed him to submit a plan for applying federal means to construct roads and canals. He proposed that the government construct or help finance cer-

[12] Albert Gallatin, "Report on Roads and Canals" (April 4, 1808), *ASP, Miscellaneous*, I, 724–41.

tain road and canal projects which were clearly national in scope. He noted that navigable rivers connecting the Atlantic seaboard with the interior were of great military and commercial importance, particularly with the increasing use of steamboats. He felt, however, that the development of these east-west routes by means of canals or roads could be left primarily to the states and cities concerned.

Although the "spirit of rivalry between the great Atlantic cities" could be depended upon to complete the most important lines of communication with the West, the cities and states immediately interested should not bear the complete cost of these improvements. Since the federal government had a great interest in them, it ought to bear a proportional share of their cost.[13] To secure major river improvements Calhoun thus granted the desirability of federal financial aid. He also recommended that army engineers examine and survey proposed improvements considered eligible for federal aid. River improvements were thus not left completely outside Calhoun's plan. Congress authorized surveys of the Ohio and Mississippi by army engineers in the year of his report and again the following year to secure plans for improving the navigation of these rivers.

In his Annual Message of 1823, President Monroe spoke approvingly of the work of the army engineers and advocated a larger role for them in internal improvements. He noted their useful surveys for civil works. The Board of Engineers for Fortifications had prepared plans for a breakwater in Delaware Bay, for which Congress had appropriated $22,700 in 1822. Since this sum was inadequate for this important project, Monroe proposed that Congress consider making an adequate appropriation. He also noted the board's survey of the harbor of Erie in Pennsylvania and stated that a report containing a

[13] John C. Calhoun, "Report on Roads and Canals" (Jan. 14, 1819), *Works*, V, 43–48.

plan and estimate for its improvement was "submitted for the consideration of Congress."[14] He evidently approved of federal appropriations for harbor improvements and the use of army engineers in planning such projects.

Perhaps of even greater significance was Monroe's proposal that army engineers survey routes for the Chesapeake and Ohio and other canals. He stated that Congress had the right to appropriate money for national projects such as this, if jurisdiction remained with the states. His advocacy of federal financial and engineering assistance to this great project of civil engineering signified the temporary triumph of the movement for internal improvements. In 1824, the last year of Monroe's administration, Congress passed the General Survey Act and also made the first appropriations for river and harbor improvements. This marked the official beginning of government surveying of internal improvements and execution of river and harbor works by the army engineers.

The General Survey Act authorized the President to initiate the surveying and planning of road and canal projects he considered nationally important. River and harbor improvements were not specifically named in the act and, unlike railroads, were not later included by administrative decision. Even before 1824, Congress had adopted the practice of specifying the harbors and rivers to be surveyed. In acts passed during 1824 and in all later legislation, Congress designated the particular river and harbor projects to be surveyed and executed. Army engineers made the necessary surveys, plans, and estimates and reported the results to Congress, which then decided whether to make itemized appropriations for these projects on the basis of the plans submitted.

The river and harbor work of the army engineers was not completely separate, however, from their activities under the Survey Act. The Board of Engineers for Internal Improve-

14 Dec. 2, 1823, Monroe, *Writings*, VI, 338–39.

ments, organized by Monroe and Calhoun in 1824 to administer this act, was also in charge of many river and harbor surveys. It issued detailed instructions for these examinations, which its engineers then executed. The board systematized and accelerated all surveying, effected a better use of the limited number of engineers, and became a precedent for the later use of river and harbor boards. These benefits served to compensate for the losses and delays resulting from competing demands for the engineers' work on roads, canals, and railroads.

This "Board of Surveys" viewed the nation as a unit and considered its general transportation needs. It was able to weigh the national value as well as local advantage of each river or harbor project. It could also compare river navigation with roads, canals, and railroads and determine to what extent they were complementary. It could thus visualize river and harbor works as integral parts of a national scheme of internal improvements.

Congress made its first appropriation for river improvement on May 24, 1824, in "An Act to improve the navigation of the Ohio and Mississippi rivers." It was patterned after the proposals of General Bernard and Colonel Totten for improving these highways of commerce to accommodate the growing steamboat trade. It granted $75,000 for improving navigation over sand bars on the Ohio and removing fallen trees or "snags" from the Ohio below Pittsburgh and from the Mississippi below St. Louis. Six sand bars were named for improvement, but government engineers were to experiment with one or two before trying to deepen the channel over the others. The act committed river improvement to the federal government and indicated that army engineers were to take charge of this work.[15]

[15] *Laws of the United States relating to the Improvement of Rivers and Harbors from August 11, 1790, to March 4, 1907,* 58 Cong., 3 sess., H. Doc. 425, 27–28.

Two days later Congress made its first appropriation for harbor improvement. In "An Act making appropriations for deepening the channel leading into the harbour of Presque Isle, and for repairing Plymouth Beach" it set aside $20,000 for each of these projects, one on Lake Erie and the other on the New England coast.[16] The practice of combining river and harbor works in one appropriations bill originated two years later. These two acts, however, devoted $115,000 to the development of rivers and harbors and indicated that Congress was no less interested in these improvements, as shown by these grants, than in roads and canals, as shown by the General Survey Act.

Officers of the Corps of Engineers were placed in charge of the two harbor projects during 1824. Greatest attention was given to improving the Ohio River, the gateway to the West. Major Long of the topographical engineers started an experiment to deepen the channel over a bar on the Ohio. The Engineer Department advertised in several western newspapers for methods and machinery for removing snags and offered a premium of $1,000 for the best proposal. The Board of Internal Improvement was given the task of selecting the best method submitted. A contract was made for snag removal on the Ohio and Mississippi, with operations to be inspected by an engineer officer.[17]

The river and harbor work previously authorized by Congress was continued in 1825. Harbor projects were executed according to plans adopted by the Board of Internal Improvement. Major Long reported progress in his experiment to deepen the Ohio over a sand bar. The civilian under contract to remove snags from the Ohio and Mississippi was charged

[16] *Ibid.*, 28.

[17] Concerning river and harbor work by army engineers during 1824, see *Annual Reports* of the secretary of war and chief engineer, as well as correspondence of the Engineer Department. (These are the sources of much of the material of this chapter.)

*Wooden stringers, notched into crossties, with iron straps
laid on top; part of the original track of the
Baltimore and Ohio Railroad, 1830.*

Courtesy Baltimore and Ohio Railroad.


*The Carrollton Viaduct, begun in 1828, the oldest
railroad bridge in the United States.*

Courtesy Baltimore and Ohio Railroad.

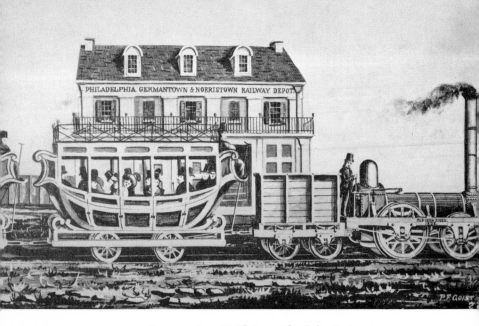

*Locomotive "Old Ironsides," built in 1832,
operated out of Philadelphia.*

Courtesy Reading Company.

*A track-laying gang in Missouri about 1854.*

Courtesy Association of American Railroads.

with defective works and failure to fulfill his contract, and the War Department started an investigation. The only new activity was the survey of three harbors in New England by two of the Board's topographical brigades. One party examined the island of Nantucket to plan an artificial harbor for the protection of shipping. Another party surveyed Marblehead and Holmes Hole to determine the practicability and value of improving their harbors.

The year 1826 witnessed a notable increase in river and harbor activities. Harbor works begun two years earlier were almost completed. A sand bar on the Ohio River had been removed by the use of wing-dams, although it was decided to await the permanent effects before attempting experiments on other bars. The civilian contractor and inspecting officer in charge of snag removal on the Ohio were withdrawn when it was shown that their work was deficient. The great increase followed passage on May 20, 1826, of the first pure "river and harbor bill." This act, containing more than twenty items, made appropriations for improving certain harbors and rivers and for surveying other bays and rivers.

These improvements and surveys were scattered along the Atlantic and Gulf coasts from Maine to Alabama and along the southern shores of Lakes Ontario and Erie. Many of them did not receive immediate attention because of the lack of engineers. Topographical engineers did most of the surveying, and officers of the Corps of Engineers took charge of improvements. Civil engineers or local superintendents were often employed to direct construction work, with supplies secured by contract. River and harbor improvements had suddenly become a major function of the army engineers, paralleling surveys for roads and canals.

The rapidly increasing use of steamboats made deeper harbors essential. Cities and regions jealously eager for more trade petitioned Congress for these improvements. There were proj-

ects to use piers to open channels into harbors, to create artificial harbors, to deepen harbors by dredging or removing
obstructions, and to make surveys and plans for creating or
improving still other harbors. Many of these works were on
Lakes Erie and Ontario, indicating the development of the
Great Lakes as a major commercial highway to the West,
thanks to the steamboat and the Erie Canal.

In 1827 army engineers were given additional projects for
improving rivers and particularly harbors. Works authorized
the previous year were started, and several new ones were
added. Topographical engineers made surveys for many river
and harbor works, and there was progress in removing snags
from the Ohio River and improving lake harbors. War Department officials complained that the number of engineers
was too small for their increasing duties and expressed strong
approval of leading river and harbor projects. Chief Engineer Macomb advocated removal of the "Great Raft" in the
Red River. He stated that to improve this river by removing
this mass of trees would have great military and economic
value. "When we consider the immense region which is wat-
ered by this river and its tributaries; the facility with which
the navigation of it may be improved, so as to open an easy
communication with its most distant settlements and *settle-
able* lands, passing also into the Indian Country, and into that
of our neighbours, the Mexicans; the sum proposed for improving the navigation, cannot but be regarded as very small,
compared with the advantages to be derived from its judicious
application."[18]

An officer examining the harbor of Stonington, Connecticut,
showed a comparable interest in the military and commercial
benefits of an improved coastal harbor. This harbor was in-
adequately protected from strong winds and heavy waves

[18] Macomb to S/W Barbour, Jan. 3, 1827, E.D., Misc. Letters Sent, IV,
9–10.

and was often unsafe for vessels anchored there. He proposed the erection of a pier to make the harbor secure for local ships, coastal trade, and naval vessels. Since a safe harbor at this location would benefit the coasting trade and would be advantageous in time of war, its improvement was highly advisable.[19]

Congress in 1828 made appropriations for many new river and harbor projects, thereby greatly increasing the work of the army engineers. Local agents were employed to supervise immediate operations on most projects, with engineer officers commonly exercising general inspection over several projects in a given area. Sometimes construction of projects was completed by contract. Several agents were appointed to construct works in New England and were paid an amount equal to 5 per cent of the funds disbursed on their projects.

At this time, Henry M. Shreve, a famous Mississippi steamboat captain, superintended improvement of the Ohio and Mississippi. He had built and sailed several early steamboats and had originated a plan for removing snags by a specially constructed snag-boat. A Jackson supporter politically, Shreve was not at first given much attention regarding plans for river improvements. After the initial failure of these plans, the Secretary of War, upon the recommendation of Vice President Calhoun, appointed Shreve in 1826 to superintend improvement of the Ohio and Mississippi. Shreve urged that the government build a special steam snag-boat, and in June, 1828, the Secretary of War finally gave his approval. Shreve supervised the construction of this twin-hulled boat, which was completed in 1829.[20]

---

[19] "A Report on a Survey of the Harbor of Stonington with a view to the erection of a Sea-wall for the protection of said Harbor," by Lieut. Jonathan Prescott, Dec. 1, 1827, T.B., Reports of the Board of Internal Improvements, I, 337–41.

[20] E.D. to S/W and Shreve, June 25 and 27, 1828, E.D., Misc. Letters Sent, V, 125, 128; Florence L. Dorsey, *Master of the Mississippi; Henry Shreve and*

Additional river and harbor works were assigned to army engineers in 1829. Most of the fifty-three civil constructions handled that year by the Engineer Department were of this type. Eighteen of the nineteen special surveys made on the call of Congress were for rivers or harbors. With his new snagboat Shreve had great success in removing snags from the Mississippi. He attacked the most dangerous places with the "United States Steam Boat *Heliopolis*" and succeeded in breaking off and removing trees lodged in the river bed. He stated that snags six feet in diameter were broken off below the surface of the sand and that he could remove every snag from the Mississippi.[21]

Colonel James Gadsden was given the choice between contract and government execution for improving a harbor in Florida. Since the work involved dredging, the contract method meant that the government would not have to furnish the equipment. If the officer himself directed the work, he could hire a local superintendent. Secretary of War Eaton proposed that an appropriation for improving Cape Fear River in North Carolina be placed in the hands of a state engineer to be spent according to a plan the latter had already adopted.[22]

River and harbor works continued to increase in 1830 and to attract greater attention. Most of the civil construction supervised by the Engineer Department was again of this type. Army engineers concluded several surveys ordered by Congress, including studies of the harbors of Baltimore and

the Conquest of the Mississippi, 140–50. After detailed study a recent investigator concludes that historians have commonly given Shreve too much credit for his part in improving the river steamboat and developing the steam snagboat. (Louis C. Hunter, *Steamboats on the Western Rivers*, 13–20, 75–76, 89–90, 133, 137–39, 150, 193–94.)

21 Dorsey, *Master of Mississippi*, 150–53; Shreve to C/E Gratiot, Aug. 25 and Sept. 24, 1829, E.D., Letters Received, II, Nos. S754 and S766. Shreve called his boat the "Helepolis."

22 Eaton to Gov. John Owen of North Carolina, April 1, 1829, E.D., Misc. Letters Sent, V, 494; E.D. to Gadsden, Aug. 21, 1829, *ibid.*, VI, 212–13.

Chicago. Baltimore had already spent large sums to deepen its harbor and desired federal funds for this work. The proposed Illinois and Michigan Canal had signified the need for a harbor at the mouth of the Chicago River. William Howard, U. S. civil engineer, reported that this river could easily accommodate steamboats except for a bar at its entrance. This bar could be removed by extending two parallel piers from the mouth of the river into the deeper water of the lake. On this principle the mouths of several rivers had been converted into harbors on Lake Erie. A harbor at Chicago formed by piers and dredging would raise the value of public lands, protect shipping, and increase commerce.

Greater efforts were made during 1830 to improve western rivers. The Board of Internal Improvement studied proposals to improve navigation on the Ohio and Tennessee rivers by means of canals. It planned projects for canals at the Louisville falls on the former and Muscle Shoals on the latter. Snags and other obstructions were removed from the Ohio and Mississippi, with heartening results for navigation and trade. The Chief Engineer praised Shreve's work with his snag-boat and informed Congress of the need for additional boats to clear the Mississippi and its tributaries. Since 1824, appropriations for improving the Ohio and Mississippi had amounted to $205,000, of which $53,000 had already been spent on the Ohio and $96,000 on the Mississippi.[23]

Secretary of War Eaton approved of the river improvements of the army engineers, saying that "The advantages to our commerce from the improvements which have been made in the navigation of the Mississippi and Ohio rivers have already been sensibly felt; and great good to the community at large is to be anticipated from further efforts to be made."[24] He

[23] Gratiot to Hon. C. A. Wickliffe, House of Representatives, April 14, 1830, E.D., Misc. Letters Sent, VII, 55–58.
[24] A.R. of S/W, Dec. 1, 1830, *ASP, MA*, IV, 586.

noted the low cost of these improvements relative to the great benefits of increased commerce, lower insurance rates on shipping, and more rapid and continuous navigation. Since these improvements were necessary and practicable, and since their value greatly outweighed their cost, he thought it surprising that they had been so long neglected.

Congress kept close check on river and harbor development. This work was not considered to be within the scope of the General Survey Act, and Congress alone could order surveys or provide funds for specific improvements. Although the Board of Internal Improvement merely administered these special surveys, it was disposed to consider the general importance of each project in a national scheme of transportation. Congress made the final decisions and was prompted by the spirit of public improvement, annual revenue surpluses, and pressure of city and regional rivalries to authorize numerous works in all parts of the country. The number of items in the annual river and harbor bills grew rapidly; and Congress was charged with logrolling, sectional favoritism, and inclusion of purely local works.

A comprehensive plan for river and harbor development was not evolved. Appropriations were of a piecemeal nature, with each congressman attempting to secure improvements in his area. The chief problem became that of distinguishing between works of national and local value. President Jackson and many others felt that Congress could appropriate for works of a general nature but not for local projects. He made a pocket veto in 1830 of "An act for making appropriation for building light-houses, light-boats, beacons, and monuments, placing buoys, and for improving harbors and directing surveys" on the ground that it authorized surveys of a local character. He intimated that previous grants had been extravagant and had invited projects so local in nature as to be neither necessary nor useful.[25]

Although the Board of Internal Improvement passed out of existence in 1831, the General Survey Act permitted extensive surveying for roads, canals, and railroads until 1838. The volume of river and harbor improvement also increased greatly in this period and demanded the services of a greater portion of the army engineers. River and harbor projects competed with and gradually exceeded government surveying for other internal improvements and thus contributed to the decline of the Survey Act.

During 1831 there was renewed interest in improving western rivers, especially the upper reaches of the Mississippi and Ohio. The Engineer Department wanted to build another steam snag-boat, improve navigation around rapids so as to give a thousand miles of navigation above St. Louis on the Mississippi, and use wing-dams to deepen the Ohio between Pittsburgh and Cincinnati. The Board of Internal Improvement, before its dissolution, revised plans for a canal around Muscle Shoals on the Tennessee River. The Topographical Bureau made surveys for river improvements and solicited greater functions of this kind. The head of this bureau and the Secretary of War recommended that topographical engineers make military, geographical, and scientific investigations of a general nature and examine minutely all coasts and rivers.

In 1832 there were further demands for general surveys of the coasts and navigable streams. A second snag-boat, the *Archimedes*, was constructed; and topographical engineers made several river surveys. Although the lateness of annual appropriations caused delay, there was extensive construction of river and harbor works by the Engineer Department. This agency also proposed improvement of the Red and Arkansas rivers. On Jackson's instructions, it classified projects contained in a river and harbor bill which he had failed to ap-

25 Annual Message, Dec. 7, 1830, 21 Cong., 2 sess., S. *Doc. 1*, 9–12.

prove. Twelve were for improving harbors on the seaboard, two for removing temporary obstructions on navigable rivers below ports of entry established by law, six for improving harbors on the rivers and Great Lakes used by vessels in foreign commerce, and twenty-one for "improvements which embrace water courses (or places thereon), that are not navigable, that are not in the direct line of communication between one port and another established by law, and which do not pertain to the established harbours, or ports of entry, and that are to be made in rivers on which no such harbours or ports of entry exist, or at points on the Lakes that are not situate at one, or between the different ports established by law to afford facilities to our Foreign Commerce."[26] Jackson was seeking, with some success, to substantiate his charge that many proposed works were purely local and thus, in his view, neither expedient nor constitutional.

The Engineer Department in 1833 wanted more engineers to execute river and harbor works in progress, and the Topographical Bureau wished to assign officers to survey the coast and lakes. Colonel Abert particularly noted the "increased necessity for an accurate survey of our extensive western lakes now so much frequented, and of which comparatively so little is known."[27] Further grants for river improvement enabled the Engineer Department to extend Shreve's snag removal operations to the Red and Arkansas rivers. Difficulties again resulted from late appropriations. In many cases either part of the working season was lost or operations were suspended.

In 1834 the Engineer Department commended Shreve on his progress in clearing the Arkansas and Red rivers. It was also interested in improving the upper reaches of the Mississippi and its main tributaries. It felt that the Illinois and

[26] Gratiot to the President, Oct. 27, 1832, E.D., Misc. Letters Sent, VIII, 494.
[27] A.R. of T.B., Oct. 19, 1833, *ASP, MA*, V, 218.

Michigan Canal should have the dimensions of a ship canal to facilitate continuous steamboat navigation from the St. Lawrence to the Gulf of Mexico. The Engineer Department and Topographical Bureau again demanded more engineers, the former for construction work and the latter for surveying. Many local agents had to be employed as construction engineers and disbursing agents. Since they were often inexperienced and unreliable, speed and efficiency were sacrificed by their employment. An inspection system had been devised, but each officer supervised more than six projects and could not secure careful, economical construction.

The Engineer Department pushed the improvement of lake harbors and western rivers during 1835 despite its lack of engineering personnel. Although it reported delays and losses in public construction, its officers supervised more than twenty river and harbor projects as well as the construction of lighthouses, beacon lights, and roads. The Topographical Bureau made several river and harbor surveys, some of which were for local groups and authorities. If surveys were desired which had not been ordered by Congress, this bureau provided engineers and instruments on condition that all other expenses be paid by local sponsors. This bureau asked to be enlarged in order to make surveys of the coast, lakes, rivers, roads, railroads, and canals and to take charge of civil works. In his request for construction duties, Colonel Abert stated that the corps making the survey, plan, and estimate for an improvement was best qualified to superintend its construction.

River and harbor improvement reached a high and critical point by 1836. There was a great increase in the number of works and volume of appropriations. All line officers serving with the Engineer Department and Topographical Bureau and most topographical engineers were withdrawn to serve with troops in the field. The result was a crisis in river and harbor development. The Engineer Department had charge of fifty-five works, as well as several lighthouse, beacon light, and road projects. Each officer was in charge of ten or twelve improvements, and local agents had to superintend most works. The Chief Engineer reported that adequate, economical construction was impossible and urged that his department's duties be reduced or its size doubled.

The Topographical Bureau was also much too small for its increased duties, particularly after the loss of personnel. Although it employed several civil engineers, surveying operations were reduced. It still made surveys of the coast and of rivers and harbors, including the mouth of the Mississippi. The most significant change in its duties was its execution of river and harbor works. It was assigned several projects for deepening channels, improving harbors, and building piers and breakwaters, primarily on the Great Lakes. It had to rely on civil agents for directing most of this work. Nevertheless, Colonel Abert's proposal that his bureau become a construction agency had been adopted, and he had a better basis for urging a larger topographical corps.

The task of securing competent agents for their many works faced both engineering corps. Superintending officers commonly selected local agents to direct operations. These officers were given some discretion as to the pay of agents, which often ranged from 2.5 to 5 per cent of disbursements on their projects. The Engineer Department suggested that where possible the officials of cities benefiting from improvements could superintend operations and disburse funds. It had been arranged for the port wardens of Baltimore to take charge of operations to improve their harbor, with one warden receiving 2.5 per cent of all disbursements for handling the funds and correspondence.

Many localities failing to receive their favorite projects requested surveys either to attract attention to their projects or to plan locally financed improvements. The Topographical

Bureau was willing but usually unable to supply engineers for such studies. Secretary of War Lewis Cass explained that Congress always took the first step in securing an appropriation for a new project. The established procedure was for Congress to authorize a survey, for the report on the survey to be submitted to Congress, and for Congress to decide whether to appropriate funds for the project. Once the original grant had been made, later appropriations were requested upon the estimates of engineer officers.[28] Congress was thus the strategic federal body to which cities and regions turned for surveys as well as appropriations.

River and harbor improvement experienced another critical year in 1837, for total appropriations and the number of projects again increased. The Engineer Department directed over fifty works, and it necessarily had to employ about fifty civil agents. The Chief Engineer again urged that his corps be doubled in size. The Topographical Bureau had charge of improving several rivers and harbors and surveying several others, mostly around the Great Lakes. It desired to facilitate the growing lake commerce, which acutely needed improved lake harbors. It employed about thirty civil engineers in addition to its own ten topographical engineers.

Secretary of War Poinsett and Colonel Abert recommended an immediate increase of the topographical corps and proposed that it survey and execute all river and harbor projects. Poinsett wanted all federal civil construction to be directed by an enlarged Corps of Topographical Engineers. Since their public duties were so important, topographical engineers should be withdrawn from aid to state and corporate enterprises and their number greatly increased. Until these changes were made, however, Poinsett feared that their public duties would be slowly and imperfectly done. Colonel Abert noted in addition that small, late appropriations were causing fur-

[28] Jan. 8, 1836, E.D., Misc. Letters Sent, XI, 451–52.

ther losses and delays. The final costs of this postponed, rushed, and inefficient construction inevitably exceeded original estimates.

In 1838 the river and harbor act was again so late that many projects were temporarily suspended before funds became available. Appropriations were greater than in any previous year, however, and were not to be as large again until 1852. There were other notable changes that year. The General Survey Act was repealed; the Corps of Engineers was enlarged; and the Corps of Topographical Engineers was reorganized, increased, and given greater civil functions. The principle was adopted of assigning civil works to the Corps of Topographical Engineers. All new civil works and several old ones were assigned to the Topographical Bureau.

The War Department also instituted a system for administering civil works. With more officers available for directing projects, districts were formed and experienced officers designated as permanent supervisors of improvements in their districts. They directed individual projects through local agents. Rules were formulated for disbursing funds, making periodic reports, and preventing supervising officers or agents from having any financial stake in works under their control. Great interest was shown in systematizing annual reports, collecting statistics on internal navigation, and making general surveys of lakes and large rivers to locate obstructions and prepare charts.

The volume of river and harbor work reached an impressive level between 1824 and 1838. By 1837 topographical engineers had made about 120 surveys for these projects, and the Engineer Department had executed about 90 of these.[29] Most works received rather small appropriations, but several improvements were quite large. Among the rivers receiving major expenditures were the Mississippi, Ohio, Red, Arkansas,

[29] Report of S/W, Jan. 23, 1837, 24 Cong., 2 sess., S. Doc. 115, 3-53.

Missouri, Cumberland, Hudson, Cape Fear, and Savannah. Large expenditures on harbors were made at Deer Island (Massachusetts), Delaware Bay, Ocracoke Inlet (North Carolina), Mobile, and on the Great Lakes at Oswego, Sodus, Rochester, Buffalo, Erie, Cleveland, and Chicago. The large western rivers and lake harbors thus received great attention in the first two decades of river and harbor work. In point of time these improvements followed the advance of the steamboat, occurring first along the Ohio, Mississippi, and eastern lakes and later along the western lakes and the other large tributaries of the Mississippi.

Since rivers and harbors were not specifically included in the General Survey Act, army engineers were not empowered to make general surveys of rivers and harbors. Congress designated every survey made by these engineers. During the 1830's several topographical engineers were engaged in the coast survey, which was directed by the Treasury Department without reference to river and harbor improvement. They also made surveys of the Great Lakes, but this work had not yet taken the form of systematic surveying. The only general surveying attempted by the army engineers was for roads and canals under the Survey Act.

By 1838 it had been decided that the Topographical Bureau should direct all river and harbor work. Consequently, all new works were assigned to it and also those works in progress which could be conveniently transferred. Since the number of engineers was inadequate, many local agents were employed to superintend individual projects under the general supervision of engineer officers. A more systematic plan of operations was finally evolved. Qualified inspecting officers were placed in permanent supervision of projects in districts of limited size. This system of inspection was further implemented by regulations concerning accountability for funds, reporting on operations, and gathering of data on commerce.

Although these practices and regulations evolved somewhat slowly, they constituted by 1838 a fairly systematic procedure for river and harbor improvement.

Congress played the initiating and guiding role in this system from the very beginning. Except for the popular desire to develop the principal rivers and most essential harbors needed for steamboat navigation, Congress had no general plan for their development. It adopted a piecemeal approach of making small appropriations for numerous projects. Local and sectional pressures tended to become the dominant force through logrolling to gain support for individual improvement projects.

Although the first appropriations for these works were made in 1824, the first itemized river and harbor bill was enacted in 1826. From then on, the number of works and total appropriations increased steadily. Despite the fact that army engineers showed greatest interest in projects of national importance, many secondary and local improvements were authorized. The engineers frequently complained about small, late appropriations. Since too many projects were executed at once, each had to be completed over a period of many years; and part of the working season was often lost in waiting for the annual grant of funds.

Among the typical criticisms of river and harbor bills were sectionalism, logrolling, and inclusion of useless and expensive local works. Sometimes the army engineers were criticized for failure to construct works at a cost within the original estimates; but they admitted that the very nature of the appropriations made delay, inefficiency, and loss inevitable. Most criticism was directed toward Congress rather than the engineers. Annual revenue surpluses during most of the period from 1824 to 1838 and rapid retirement of the public debt enabled Congress to make increasingly larger grants for improving navigation. Although the general policy of waterway improvement appeared to have been adopted, there were many complaints of logrolling and wastefulness.[30]

Although Jackson was a less ardent supporter of internal improvements than Adams, he was a less strict constructionist than Van Buren. He favored a policy of river and harbor development as long as it produced national and not local improvements. He supported the removal of obstructions from navigable rivers and the improvement of harbors which added to the ease and safety of foreign commerce. He argued that only those improvements at or below established ports of entry for foreign trade were constitutional. He favored such major works as improvement of the Ohio and Mississippi and the lake harbors as long as they aided foreign trade.[31]

River and harbor development made great strides after 1824, with some $9,000,000 appropriated before 1838. River and harbor work and government surveying for roads and canals under the General Survey Act commenced and developed together. Until its dissolution in 1831, the Board of Engineers for Internal Improvements co-ordinated government surveying and river and harbor activities; but after that date these two functions of the army engineers became less interrelated and more competitive.

It has been noted that opposition to government surveying for railroads was instrumental in undermining the Survey Act. The great increase in river and harbor activities had a similar effect, for both river navigation and railroads became

[30] Albert S. Bolles, *The Financial History of the United States, from 1789 to 1860,* 556–57, 563–64; Davis R. Dewey, *Financial History of the United States,* 170, 216, 219; Johnson, "River and Harbor Bills," 788–90; Schermerhorn, "Rise and Progress," 259.

[31] Dewey, *Financial Hist. of U. S.,* 216; Johnson, "River and Harbor Bills," 788–90; Harold Kelso, "Inland Waterways Policy in the United States" (Ph.D. dissertation; University of Wisconsin, 1942), 121–22; Lippincott, "History," 647; Edward C. Mason, *The Veto Power,* 98; E. C. Nelson, "Presidential Influence on the Policy of Internal Improvements," *Iowa Journal of History and Politics,* Vol. IV (1906), 41, 67; Ralph G. Plumb, *History of Navigation on the Great Lakes,* 36–37.

more practicable and popular than roads or canals. The success of steamboats and steam locomotives ended public enthusiasm for other internal improvements. Progress of steamboat navigation required so much engineering activity that army engineers could hardly be made available for the objects of the Survey Act. The success of steamboating and involvement of the army engineers in improving navigation thus weakened this act and contributed to its repeal in 1838. River and harbor improvement itself diminished after 1838, no doubt for reasons similar to those leading to repeal of the General Survey Act.

# VII: Later River and Harbor Work

RIVER AND HARBOR improvement encountered increasing political and constitutional criticism after 1838 and was greatly reduced in volume. Appropriations became intermittent and reached extensive proportions only for two brief intervals before the Civil War.

Acting on the principle that the Topographical Bureau should supervise all civil works and the Engineer Department all defense works, the Secretary of War during 1839 transferred some fifty-six river and harbor projects to the former. The War Department ordered rigid economy in executing improvements. Engineers were told to restrict or, if possible, suspend operations. Lack of funds and probable reduction or failure of appropriations were given as reasons for reducing operations.

Secretary of War Poinsett advocated revision of the system of river and harbor improvement, both in principle and in procedure. Too many works had been authorized without a careful determination of their commercial usefulness and a comparison of their cost and value. Congress had often restricted the army engineers by requiring that funds be used according to some inflexible plan. He described the system the government should adopt:

The already important and daily increasing trade of the great lakes and estuaries which encompass and indent the United States, demands the fostering care of the Government; but, in order that its interference may be effectually and constitutionally exerted, it ought to be confined to such works as are of general utility, and not extended into every creek or inlet where a favored village may require easier access for a market boat. This abuse, which is cal-

181

culated to bring the whole system into deserved disrepute, can only be remedied by directing a previous examination to be made by this department into the nature of the proposed work, and a full report on the proper method of obtaining the object contemplated, setting forth the public, not partial, advantages likely to result from it, as well as the probable cost of its completion.[1]

Like President Van Buren, Poinsett wanted river and harbor improvements based on a strict construction of the Constitution; but he saw their great value and wanted them continued on a systematic basis.

Since there were no appropriations in 1840 and none in prospect, all operations were halted. Unfinished works and durable equipment were preserved; civil agents were discharged; and perishable property was sold. The two engineering agencies were willing to lend idle snag-boats and dredging machines to local authorities if this involved no expense to the government. Poinsett again insisted that "the system requires to be revised, both with regard to the principle upon which such improvements ought to be authorized, and the manner in which they ought to be conducted."[2]

River and harbor operations remained suspended in 1841. Improvements and equipment were preserved, although in several cases additional funds were needed for this purpose. The secretary of war and engineer officials noted the injuries and losses to unfinished projects and recommended that those of general usefulness be completed as soon as possible. Only a limited number of important works should be executed, and none should be started before full examinations had been made by competent engineers. Particular notice was given to the growth of trade on the Great Lakes and the need of lake surveys and harbor improvements.

Additional civil works were transferred to the Topograph-

[1] A.R. of S/W, Nov. 30, 1839, 26 Cong., 1 sess., S. *Doc. 1*, 48.
[2] A.R. of S/W, Dec. 5, 1840, 26 Cong., 2 sess., S. *Doc. 1*, 24.

ical Bureau in 1842. It divided river and harbor improvements into two classes according to their importance and urgency. It was in charge of the systematic survey of the Great Lakes, which had been started the year before. It secured improvement of the Red River by contract. Congress appropriated $100,000 for improving the Ohio, Mississippi, Missouri, and Arkansas rivers; and this bureau prepared boats and equipment for the work. These operations were superintended by Colonel Long and consisted of removing snags, rocks, and wrecks and examining bars to be improved later by wing-dams or sluice structures. Great interest was shown in plans for resuming river improvement, and President Tyler and his secretary of war recommended that Congress adopt vigorous measures for improving major western rivers and lake harbors.

The Topographical Bureau in 1843 directed work on the western rivers and the lake survey. This bureau emphasized the growth of population and trade along the Great Lakes, the need of more data on this commerce, and the benefits to be derived from improved lake harbors.

In 1844 work was resumed in constructing and deepening major lake harbors. The last appropriation prior to this resumption had been in 1838. Army engineers became concerned with means of improving navigation between Lakes Erie, Huron, and Superior as commerce flowed westward. Colonel Abert favored constructing a large canal at Sault Ste Marie, in order to avoid the mistake made at Louisville of building a canal with dimensions too small for large vessels and expanding commerce. To remove all doubt as to its national character, it should accommodate naval vessels and steamers of the first class. A deeper channel was also needed at the Straits of Detroit and the St. Clair Flats to facilitate trade between Lakes Erie and Huron.

Secretary of War William Wilkins favored vigorous improvement of western rivers and lake harbors. Suspension of unfinished projects caused great sacrifice of boats and machinery, interruption of navigation, and unprofitable use of previously appropriated funds. Only a small number of important works should be begun, and these should never be abandoned until completed.

President Tyler granted that funds for rivers and harbors were being judiciously spent but cautioned that Congress must appropriate only for improvements of a demonstrably national character.[3] To receive his approval, river and harbor projects had to pass a strict constitutional test: necessity for the safety of interstate or foreign commerce. Since the Topographical Bureau presented only estimates approved by the President, Congress was called upon to consider only projects passing this test. Colonel Abert refused to present to the House Committee on Commerce a list it requested of estimates for seaboard rivers and western harbors adding up to about $1,000,000. Official estimates had already been prepared under instructions of the War Department and submitted to Congress. Abert strongly opposed numerous small estimates which would not permit efficient, economical improvement. The final cost of small works invariably exceeded original estimates.

Failure of Congress to pass a river and harbor bill in 1845 caused reduction or partial suspension of these improvements. The secretary of war and Colonel Abert insisted on the military and commercial importance of lake harbors. These harbors on the "inland seas" were described as essential ports of refuge for naval and commercial vessels. The growth of lake commerce was emphasized, and efforts were made to determine annual imports and exports of each harbor. The large rivers were said to be national highways and arms of the sea

[3] Annual Message, Dec. 3, 1844, 28 Cong., 2 sess., S. *Doc. 1*, 17. Tyler warned Congress not to appropriate funds for "improvements which are not ascertained, by previous examination and survey, to be necessary for the shelter and protection of trade from the danger of storms and tempests."

possessing military and commercial value. The Ohio, Mississippi, Hudson, Missouri, Arkansas, and Red rivers unquestionably merited improvement by the federal government.

In 1846, during the war with Mexico, many engineers served with armies in the field. No river and harbor bill was passed by Congress, and the administration presented no estimates for works in progress. All improvements were once again suspended as in 1840. All equipment was sold or preserved, and local agents were discharged. This situation continued in 1847 and 1848.

The Topographical Bureau attempted to collect data on the commerce of the lakes and western rivers but complained that the government lacked an adequate system for gathering such information. It was willing to make dredge boats and other equipment available for local execution of suspended river or harbor works. War Department regulations prevented the outright loan of equipment, but it could be operated at local expense under a United States officer or agent. President Polk believed that the river and harbor category should remain narrow and that a general system of internal improvements was unconstitutional. He would permit improvements of a national character but wanted other works financed locally.

In 1849 the Topographical Bureau submitted estimates to continue certain river and harbor works. New projects were not included, for Congress alone could initiate them. Secretary of War George W. Crawford stated that estimates for old works were as large as could be judiciously applied without increasing the Corps of Topographical Engineers. He warned that Congress should not appropriate for new works before surveys and estimates had been made by competent engineers. President Taylor, whose friendly attitude toward river and harbor improvements caused estimates to be presented, recommended without success that Congress consider new as well as old projects.

The story was much the same in 1850 and 1851. Practically the same estimates were again presented, but no appropriations were made. President Fillmore approved of plans for resuming these improvements, particularly of the Mississippi, its tributaries, and major lake harbors. He stated that improvements which were local in position, as the proposed ship canal at Sault Ste Marie, were nevertheless general in their benefits. He proposed to complete projects already begun and to commence such new ones "as may seem to the wisdom of Congress to be of public and general importance."[4]

River and harbor improvement was finally resumed in 1852. Congress appropriated over $2,000,000 for more than one hundred projects. Individual grants were typically small, and many were for surveys to prepare plans and estimates for future works. Since the act was passed rather late, little was done that year beyond preparing plans and equipment. Although funds were commonly inadequate to complete individual projects, the administration assumed that further grants would be made for their eventual completion.

The War Department attempted to institute a systematic procedure for their execution. Since the topographical engineers were also engaged in surveys, explorations, and other duties, and since defense works of the Corps of Engineers were suspended for lack of funds, the War Department divided the many river and harbor works between the two corps. It assigned improvements on the western rivers and Great Lakes to the Topographical Bureau, whose officers were familiar with the West and had other duties there, and works on the Atlantic and Gulf Coasts to the Engineer Department, whose officers were in charge of defense projects along these coasts. Each corps created a "board of engineers for river and harbor improvements" to supervise preparation of all plans and estimates and inspect the progress of work.

[4] Annual Message, Dec. 2, 1850, 31 Cong., 2 sess., *S. Ex. Doc. 1*, 15.

Officers were assigned to supervise projects in specified districts, and local agents were employed. The two boards approved project plans on the premise that later appropriations would be made for their ultimate completion. Necessary surveys were made; and measures were taken to secure snagboats, dredges, and other equipment. Officers making surveys were often instructed to consult local supporters or interested congressmen concerning proposed improvements. All project plans and estimates, whether for old or new works, had to be approved by the appropriate board and bureau head and by the secretary of war. These boards classified each suggested project as national or local in character, and Chief Engineer Totten informed his board members that "their conclusions, founded on a full and deliberate consideration of each proposition, in connection with the general or national benefits to be derived from it, will be entitled to much weight before Congress. In every instance, therefore, it is desirable that the Board should state distinctly, their opinion whether the project is, or is not, of such general interest and importance—considering moreover the expenditure likely to be involved—as to deserve the support of the nation."[5]

Totten also told this board that it had power to originate estimates for new projects which had never received congressional attention. The board in its studies might discover "instances in which works not before proposed, are nevertheless desirable and necessary to the well-being of the Country." Furthermore, "to bring any such to the notice of the Government, with suitable plans, descriptions and estimates, will be among the most valuable and important labors of the Board."[6] Until this time the government had never granted

[5] Totten to Lt. Col. R. E. DeRussy, Dec. 1, 1852, E.D., Letters to Officers of Engineers, XIX, 499–500.

[6] *Ibid.*, XIX, 500. When Totten instructed the board to prepare estimates for Congress, he stated that "Any case that the Board may deem of great national importance, and requiring immediate attention, may be included in

army engineers the authority to initiate river and harbor projects. Congress still had the ultimate power of appropriation, but the engineers were given an opportunity to select projects according to their own criteria and knowledge.

President Fillmore assured Congress that economical and efficient arrangements had been made for executing river and harbor work on what he hoped would be a continuing basis. He explained that further appropriations were needed for their completion and that projects once begun should never be discontinued. He cautioned against commencing any work "which is not of sufficient importance to the commerce of the country to be viewed as national in its character."[7]

Although the Pacific railroad surveys made heavy demands on the army engineers in 1853, river and harbor projects were executed on a large scale. The two boards of engineers for river and harbor improvements inspected these works and reviewed plans and estimates for new projects. A major change took place, however, in the manner in which improvements were planned and executed. Jefferson Davis, President Pierce's secretary of war, ruled that individual projects must be planned so as to be completed with existing appropriations. He noted that most plans approved previously had been based on a different principle—the assumption that further grants would be made. Plans had sometimes been adopted which necessitated funds ten times as large as the original appropriations to complete them. He stated his new policy as follows:

The general provision in regard to these works is a simple direction to apply a certain sum to a specified object, without any intimation of an intention on the part of Congress to make further appropriations, and I deemed it to be improper to expend those appropriations in commencing works on a scale which the depart-

those estimates altho not provided for in the late River and Harbor law." (Dec. 6, 1852, *ibid.*, XIX, 506.)

[7] Annual Message, Dec. 6, 1852, 32 Cong., 2 sess., S. *Ex. Doc. 1*, 14-15.

ment has not means to complete, and which must in a great measure be lost, unless Congress make further appropriations for them.[8]

Davis believed that the government should not construct or improve commercial harbors. If it acquired ownership and jurisdiction of the sites, it might construct harbors of refuge to protect naval and commercial vessels from storms and enemy attacks. Navigable rivers "washing several states" were of national concern and were under federal jurisdiction. Such rivers were actually national highways essential to the functions of the federal government, even though the Constitution had not explicitly provided for their maintenance. Congress must decide whether their importance justified "further operations for the removal of temporary and accidental obstructions in their natural channels." All local improvements, such as small rivers and commercial harbors, should be financed locally, perhaps through the collection of tonnage duties.

Since many works had been started with inadequate funds, the problem had arisen of deciding on what conditions to accept voluntary contributions from local sources. This problem arose when localities attempted to borrow public equipment to continue operations and when they offered local funds with the hope of eventual refunds from federal appropriations. The War Department refused to accept gifts or loans of local funds. It was willing to continue work on federal projects if local parties paid all expenses except compensation of the supervising United States officer or agent.

On June 4, 1853, Davis issued a War Department regulation stating that local funds could be used to continue unfinished river or harbor works for which Congress had previously made appropriations if certain conditions were met. These were that such projects must be continued according to original War Department plans, that an army engineer must

[8] A.R. of S/W, Dec. 1, 1853, 33 Cong., 1 sess., S. *Ex. Doc. 1*, 26.

supervise operations, that this officer must not handle or be responsible for the disbursing of funds, and that his supervisory work must not be construed to imply any claim for reimbursement or any expectation of further appropriations by Congress.[9] Engineer officials explained that this rule was not intended to withhold the professional services of army engineers from unfinished improvements but rather to prevent claims for reimbursement of funds spent on works directed by these engineers.

The year 1853 was a great engineering year. In addition to military, geographical, and lake surveys, the Pacific railroad explorations were in progress. More river and harbor surveys and improvements took place than in any other year prior to the Civil War. Army engineers were also constructing other civil works such as roads and lighthouses. Both corps needed additional officers for their greatly increased duties. The two boards of engineers for river and harbor improvements were busily engaged in checking project plans and inspecting construction activities. Their planning of new works gave way to inspection of going operations, however; and they became inactive by the end of the year. They were not kept alive to exercise the authority given them by the previous administration to originate plans for new projects. This was a short-lived effort to have army engineers share more fully in planning and programming waterway improvements.

President Franklin Pierce disagreed with Fillmore concerning the policy of river and harbor improvement. Pierce informed Congress that on the basis of his strict interpretation of the Constitution he had refused to present estimates for local works. He opposed all local improvements for the benefit of either inland or coastal trade. If his view should become settled policy, localities would make such improvements.

River and harbor works remained unfinished in 1854, with

[9] *Ibid.*, 53–54.

most of the appropriations spent. Many works were closed down, but there was nevertheless a good deal of surveying and construction. Supervising officers were called upon to present more detailed data on the estimated cost and benefit of each improvement. The War Department instituted a rule that officers having served at one station longer than four years must be rotated elsewhere, but the two engineering corps were displeased to see experienced officers transferred from projects with which they were familiar. A few officers supervised projects whose continuation was financed locally.

Secretary of War Davis still demanded that army engineers plan river and harbor works so as not to depend on later appropriations for completion. He stated that their final cost often exceeded their limited benefits and refused to submit estimates for works which would not produce commensurate benefit. Failure of Congress to make grants for the repair and preservation of completed works allowed their destruction and decay. The removal of snags and rocks from navigable channels had permanent benefit, whereas the value gained by artificial structures to improve harbors was temporary and demanded continuing maintenance. He felt that the government must have exclusive jurisdiction over the sites of all artificial improvements it constructed.

President Pierce insisted on strict interpretation of the power to improve harbors and rivers. He vetoed a river and harbor bill on the grounds that it contained purely local items and constituted a general system of improvements which the government lacked power to execute. He proposed that each appropriation be in a separate bill to aid determination of its national or local character and its relation to the exercise of delegated powers. He approved of harbor improvement by individual states and noted that the Constitution permitted states to levy tonnage duties for this purpose with the consent of Congress. Such Democratic leaders as Stephen A. Douglas also favored this method of local improvement. Critics of the scheme wondered how western states with little or no commerce could finance their improvements through levies on commerce.

River and harbor appropriations were exhausted by 1855, and these improvements were again suspended. The administration presented no estimates for their resumption, sold the snag-boats on the western rivers, and recommended sale of dredge boats on the Great Lakes. In a few cases dredging operations were continued locally with expenses paid by those benefiting. This general situation prevailed until the Civil War. The President did not present estimates, and Congress passed no regular river and harbor bills. Army engineers had few duties in this field except the lake survey and repair of government equipment and unfinished projects. They made frequent demands for funds to preserve existing improvements, and a few of them directed locally financed work on unfinished projects.

Waterway improvements were obviously made in an intermittent manner after the repeal of the General Survey Act in 1838. Regular river and harbor bills were passed very infrequently from that date to the Civil War, and funds for many individual projects were secured by special acts or riders attached to other bills. Although this work was a major duty of the army engineers, it was never put on a systematic, stable basis. After 1838 all river and harbor works were transferred to the Topographical Bureau. Its other duties increased rapidly during the following decade, while these improvements were in great part suspended. The large-scale resumption of these improvements in 1852 necessitated a sharing of river and harbor works between the Topographical Bureau and Engineer Department.

The basic procedure of river and harbor development gave Congress the major role and left the army engineers subservient to the demands of Congress and wishes of the Executive. Congress alone could initiate proposals for new projects. The only exception to this was a brief attempt in 1852 under President Fillmore to allow army engineers through special boards to originate projects for the consideration of Congress.

Having been ordered by Congress to do so, army engineers made plans and estimates for a new work. If Congress then authorized this project, they executed it according to approved plans. They could later submit estimates for its continuation. At this point, however, the President and secretary of war could indicate the old works for which estimates would be made and the size of estimates. Most administrations allowed estimates to be submitted only for old works which they considered by rather strict standards to be of national value.

The administration controlled the army engineers in their use of funds on individual improvements. Since individual grants were usually small, completion of the original project plans necessitated piecemeal appropriations over a period of years. Funds were applied on the premise that further grants would be made by Congress. The army engineers executed individual projects according to such long-range plans until 1853, when Secretary of War Davis decreed that funds be applied according to plans which did not require future appropriations for completion. They were obliged thereafter to plan and execute projects of limited size so as to complete them with funds already authorized.

A system of supervision was formulated for executing river and harbor improvements. Experienced officers were made general superintendents of a small number of works in districts of limited size. They directed civil agents and junior officers in charge of individual works. Rules for accounting for funds and making periodic reports were evolved, and officers and agents collected data on the volume of navigation in their vicinity. This system of inspection was complemented in 1852 by the use of two boards of engineers which examined and approved all project plans and inspected their execution. These boards served a useful purpose for two years but became inactive with the decline of river and harbor work prior to the Civil War. This system of supervision was also weakened in the 1850's by the regulation requiring frequent rotation in the station of officers.

The philosophy of the army engineers regarding river and harbor development was fully as important as their procedures. Their attitudes may be compared with those of Congress and the Presidents. These engineers visualized the development of rivers and harbors as a major area in which they could apply their professional skills to promote rapid national growth. They felt it to be their professional duty to participate in this work, and they never raised constitutional questions as to the power of the government to engage in such activities.

Recognizing the stimulus of steam navigation to national expansion, they desired to improve the major inland rivers and lake harbors. They conceived the Mississippi River, its chief tributaries, and the Great Lakes as national highways, "arms of the sea," and inland seas. They desired fundamentally to secure rapid completion of a limited number of large improvements. They insisted on careful surveys before appropriations were made and tried to distinguish between national and local works. They opposed small grants for numerous works, which spread operations over several years, caused inefficient and wasteful piecemeal construction, and even risked suspension and loss of money and effort expended.

The army engineers attempted to collect information on the growth of commerce so as to estimate the potential value of individual improvements and determine the general transportation needs of the nation. They admitted their inability to gather adequate statistics on trade and requested funds for the systematic collection of such data. They desired to examine all lakes, rivers, and harbors to determine their navigability and prepare charts. They secured funds for a systematic survey of the lakes and provided engineers for the coast survey.

Congress, however, reserved the privilege of designating surveys to plan particular improvements. Congress often made appropriations for improvements which had not been studied by army engineers, and it passed river and harbor bills with numerous items. Cities and regions urged their congressmen to secure projects of local and regional benefit. The epithet of logrolling aptly described the process by which inclusion of additional improvements in an appropriation bill secured additional votes for the bill. The inevitable tendency was to grant funds for many small, local projects.

Among the results of this congressional system were overloading of army engineers with small works requiring years for completion, growing unpopularity of river and harbor improvements, and likelihood of failure or veto of river and harbor bills and suspension of work. Since there was never a consensus in Congress after 1838 regarding the constitutionality or expediency of these improvements, such unsatisfactory results were inevitable. Despite widespread agreement that the government should make improvements of a clearly national character, Congress could never agree on the scope of the river and harbor category, the distinction between national and local works, and the exact constitutional basis of its power to appropriate for these improvements.

Questions of the expediency and legality of river and harbor improvements became involved in such issues as the protective tariff and disposal of the revenue surplus, which increasingly assumed a sectional character. The Whigs commonly supported and the Democrats opposed large river and harbor bills. Many Democrats, particularly from western states, favored federal development of major harbors and rivers. As a result of deadlocks over the wisdom and legality of less important works, no appropriations were made during many sessions of Congress. River and harbor bills were either defeated or vetoed, and the only appropriations secured were those in special acts or riders attached to other legislation.

Attitudes of the Executives were also of strategic importance in the river and harbor activities of the army engineers. After 1838 there was a major change in national policy toward river and harbor improvements. All Presidents after Jackson except Taylor and Fillmore, who were Whigs, followed such a strict interpretation of the Constitution that Jacksonian policies were later regarded as liberal by comparison. There was increased hostility toward these policies from term to term with Van Buren, Tyler, Polk, Pierce, and Buchanan. These five Presidents either submitted estimates for only a few strictly national improvements or presented none at all. They urged execution of minor works by state or local government and vetoed several river and harbor bills on the premise that they authorized local works which were unrelated to delegated federal powers and thus unconstitutional.[10]

River and harbor improvements were brought to a standstill on three occasions under Van Buren, Polk, and Pierce. Failure to agree on the question of constitutionality in a period of increasing sectional antagonism prevented continuous execution even of major improvements admitted by all parties to be of a national character and within the government's power. Under these conditions the government was unable to formulate an effective system for administering these improvements, and the army engineers failed to achieve extensive or lasting benefits. Despite the unavoidable inadequacy of their river and harbor development, the engineers were

10 For views of these presidents on river and harbor improvements, see Johnson, "River and Harbor Bills," 788–90; Kelso, "Inland Waterways," 122–23; Mason, *Veto Power*, 106; Nelson, "Presidential Influence," 52–53, 67–68; Plumb, *Navigation*, 36–37; and Schermerhorn, "Rise and Progress," 259–60.

greatly interested in this task and established precedents for their later exercise of this function.

In their river and harbor activities the army engineers were buffeted about by both Congress and the President. They could make only the improvements authorized by Congress and could execute these only to the liking of the President. In this situation they were not able to make improvements in an economical way or to develop systematic procedures. Appropriations were infrequent, projects too many in number, other duties increasingly large, and the number of engineers too small. Their procedures also had to conform to War Department regulations, such as the rule that officers change stations every four years.

The army engineers were probably more independent and influential in this period than a civilian agency could have been, and they had the technical skill to promote the material development of the nation, skill which no other agency possessed. They have always been solely responsible for executing federal improvements of rivers and harbors. They saw that defense and commerce were dependent upon each other and necessitated development of river navigation and safe harbors. Since this development has been their primary civil function, they attempted to formulate systematic procedures for effecting these river and harbor improvements. They matured a scheme of military defense which included development of interior communications. Congress, however, had no general plan for these improvements. Instead, it made appropriations in a piecemeal fashion for a large number of works.

Limited by Congress, the President, and their own conception of their duties, the army engineers were never permitted to engage in comprehensive planning of river and harbor development. They took a broader view of their work during the time of the General Survey Act than afterwards. The army engineers remained aware of their professional ability to improve waterways and the stimulus this gave to national advancement. This workmanlike use of their engineering skill to improve navigation indicated an attitude of selective encouragement which was quite significant, even in the absence of generalized planning.

# VIII: Beyond the Call of Duty

THE ARMY ENGINEERS engaged in several civil functions in which they made important contributions to the internal improvements movement. Attention has already been given to certain major areas in which they encouraged public improvement, including surveying for roads, canals, and railroads and the execution of river and harbor works. In these as well as in other fields, the army engineers applied their engineering skills in a purposeful manner highly stimulative to the geographical and economic expansion of the nation. These additional civil functions and areas of encouragement may be classified as technical education, surveying and exploration, and civil works.

The early development of the United States Military Academy as a national school of engineering was reviewed in Chapter I, and its contribution to the early progress of railroads was discussed in Chapter V. A part of the Engineer Department until the Civil War, West Point was developed as the first and most prominent school of technology and engineering in the nation. For several decades it produced most of the academically trained engineers to be found in the United States. At a time when trained civil engineers were quite scarce, the fact that the army engineers had both theoretical and practical training made it almost inevitable that they would be drawn into activities of public improvement.

Presidents Jefferson, Madison, and Monroe linked education with internal improvements in advocating national programs for their advancement; and they actively supported the building of West Point into a technical school. Calhoun proposed an additional military academy and a school of application as well as a national plan for constructing roads and canals. President John Quincy Adams even more strongly advocated national promotion of technology and internal improvements. With the encouragement of such national leaders as these, West Point, in a sense the only "national seminary of learning" to be established, became an early fountainhead of technology in this country.

The Military Academy had developed quite rapidly between 1817 and 1824, while the movement for internal improvements gained momentum. Adams proposed greater national support of its growth and explained that its graduates provided "the means of multiplying the undertakings of public improvements, to which their acquirements at that institution are peculiarly adapted."[1] In urging greater federal aid to internal improvements, Adams declared that the most essential instrument was knowledge, the acquisition of which necessitated public seminaries of learning. He noted that for this purpose the Military Academy had been developed but that a national university had not been created.

West Point was made to serve a double purpose, to be both a military school and a national university. It was operated to fulfill both military and civilian needs, particularly the promotion of internal improvements. Secretary of War James Barbour in 1825 called the Military Academy the "nursery of military science." Several branches of this "science" were well adapted to the peacetime needs of the nation. The most important among these was civil engineering, which "promises to be among the most beneficial acquisitions in the whole range of science."[2] In 1828, Secretary of War Peter B. Porter stated that West Point was effectively "scattering the fruits of its science" and concluded that "the interchange of the theoretic science of this national school with the practical skill

[1] Annual Message, Dec. 6, 1825, 19 Cong., 1 sess., S. Doc. 2, 9.
[2] A.R. of S/W, Dec. 1, 1825, ASP, MA, III, 109.

and judgment of our citizen engineers, which is now going on throughout the United States, will soon furnish every part of the country with the most accomplished professors in every branch of civil engineering."[3]

There is no indication that Jackson attempted to change the function of the Military Academy, and it continued to develop and to stimulate internal improvements during his administration. In 1829, he recommended its support as "one of our safest means of national defence." It produced graduates who were extremely useful in the army and militia and in private life.[4]

Secretary of War John H. Eaton also emphasized the military value of West Point and stated that its benefits greatly exceeded its costs. He strongly opposed any reduction in its size and urged that graduates not needed in the army be allowed to enter civilian pursuits of their own choice. It would be far better, he thought, to enlarge the school and create another than to reduce it.[5]

West Point was sometimes criticized for having gone beyond and perverted its original purpose. The House Committee on Military Affairs answered such criticism in 1834 by asserting that this school had benefited the nation in many essential ways. It had improved the performance and reputation of the War Department, provided skilled engineers for constructing internal improvements, and produced teachers for other educational institutions.[6] Jackson later felt that the Military Academy had some imperfections needing correction

[3] A.R. of S/W, Nov. 24, 1828, *ibid.*, IV, 2.
[4] Annual Message, Dec. 8, 1829, 21 Cong., 1 sess., S. *Doc. 1,* 14.
[5] A.R. of S/W, Dec. 1, 1830, *ASP, MA,* IV, 585; Report "On the Subject of a Change in the Organization of the Military Academy at West Point," Jan. 28, 1831, *ibid.,* IV, 676–77.
[6] "Statement of the History and Importance of the Military Academy . . . and Reasons Why it Should Not Be Abolished," May 17, 1834, *ibid.,* V, 355. The committee remarked that West Point "has sent forth principles and professors to ornament and sustain colleges and literary seminaries."

but that it should not be abolished. Its system of military education had proved its usefulness by producing a valuable group of officers possessing the requisite "fidelity, science, and business habits" to execute the diverse functions of the War Department.[7]

A House select committee in 1837 was much more critical of the Military Academy than Jackson, who justified it on the basis of its necessity to qualify officers for public service. This committee argued that many more cadets were being educated at West Point than the needs of the public service demanded. It objected to the training at public expense of persons not needed by the War Department and wished to convert West Point into an advanced school of application for army officers only. It preferred to "abolish entirely the system of educating cadets in the elementary and theoretic sciences," since colleges and seminaries then being established could teach such sciences. These changes would encourage the teaching of science in colleges and the study of science by individuals desiring to become army officers and gain access to the widespread engineering activities of the army. Collegiate education and scientific study would then receive a great stimulus throughout the country.[8]

Soon afterwards President Van Buren took an approving view of the Military Academy quite unlike that of the select committee and easily as favorable as that of Jackson. Van Buren declared that West Point was providing the country with officers and civilians possessing military knowledge and "the scientific attainments of civil and military engineering."[9] His only criticism was that the minimum term cadets were expected to serve was too short. At that time this period was five years, extending only one year beyond graduation. He

[7] Annual Message, Dec. 7, 1835, 24 Cong., 1 sess., S. *Doc. 1*, 22.

[8] Report of Select Committee on the Military Academy, March 1, 1837, *ASP, MA,* VII, 1–18.

[9] Annual Message, Dec. 5, 1837, 25 Cong., 2 sess., S. *Doc. 1*, 18.

went no further, however, than to recommend a strictly enforced enlistment of seven years.

Reports of the annual Boards of Visitors on the progress of the Military Academy clearly illustrated its development of technical education and its role as a school of technology and engineering. These boards annually proclaimed the success of West Point in teaching civil and military engineering and emphasized the value of its curriculum and graduates to the army, internal improvements, and technology and education in general. In 1830 the board stated that West Point was expected to provide technical training not only for the army, militia, and internal improvements but also for "exploring the hidden treasures of our mountains, and ameliorating the agriculture of our valleys" and for securing a sound national educational system. The board declared in 1831 that civil engineering had become a fundamentally important branch of education. Other schools had failed to cultivate this field which was so essential to developing the transportation and resources of the country. Consequently, promoters of useful improvements were compelled to demand of the War Department the services of its skilled engineers.

The Board of Visitors stated in 1837, as in other years, that West Point graduates were ably fitted for positions in the public service and in civil life. Their education was of general benefit to the nation, and they could not be more usefully employed than in "imparting to others" the knowledge acquired at West Point. In 1840 a minority of the board was alarmed by the "tendency to resignation" and felt that too many cadets were being educated for private careers. It insisted that West Point had become a school for civil engineers instead of a school of military science.[10]

[10] "It has been urged by many of the advocates of the present plan of instruction at West Point, that though it may fail to furnish the country with a competent and accomplished military man in every graduate, still the public

In 1842 the board again described the unique contribution of the Military Academy to technology and education. It lucidly explained how West Point was stimulating national advancement of science by "devoting a large portion of its course to mathematical and physical science, and being supplied by the munificence of Congress with ample means to procure able instructors and all necessary apparatus, it is enabled by these means to exhibit to other seminaries the model of a high and rigorous course of scientific instruction, and thus to incite those seminaries to a generous emulation. It also trains up young men, who are eminently qualified to fill professorships in colleges and other institutions of learning, and others, again, who are employed with distinguished advantage to the public in civil engineering, both in the service of the States and in that of private corporations. This country has not yet been able to contribute greatly to the extension of the empire of science; but for a service so calculated to benefit mankind and to illustrate our national character, the board would look more confidently to no class than to those who, through the severe and thorough elementary training given in this academy, have become accomplished in the use and application of the most powerful instruments of modern discovery."[11]

The board unanimously felt in 1848 that the Military Academy had been of incalculable value to the country. Referring to the many activities of its graduates as skillful engineers,

---

is amply compensated by the number of skilful engineers which it supplies for other useful purposes.

"We will not hesitate to say that the course of instruction is probably well calculated to impart a knowledge of civil engineering, but we repudiate the idea that this institution was created for such purposes. . . ." (Minority Report of Board of Visitors, June 25, 1840, 26 Cong., 2 sess., S. *Doc. 1*, 152. For reports of these boards for 1830, 1831, and 1837 referred to above, see *ASP, MA*, IV, 603–609, 736–39, and VII, 709–12.)

[11] Report of Board of Visitors, June 20, 1842, 27 Cong., 3 sess., S. *Doc. 1*, 272–73.

topographers, and explorers, the board described it as "the cheap school of science of this nation."[12]

This strategic role of West Point in the early development of engineering in this country has been substantiated by later historical analysis. It pioneered in teaching such subjects as civil and military engineering, architecture, geology, and mineralogy. It was until 1824 the only school of engineering in the nation and remained the leading technical school until the Civil War. Literary colleges traditionally remained aloof from technical disciplines, and engineering schools were not common until after the Civil War. As other schools started teaching engineering in later decades, the Military Academy served as model, stimulus, and source of well trained professors.[13]

Before the Civil War, manufacturing had not developed to the point where the industrial community could support schools of technology. If technical education was to be developed, it had to be done largely by the government. The greatest early needs for technical training were for military defense and internal improvements, both of which were thought to fall within the responsibility of the federal government. The army engineers thus inherited the function of advancing the engineering potential of the nation, first in the form of military science and later in the form of civil as well as military engineering.

At first the army utilized several foreign military engineers, particularly as fortification engineers and West Point professors. American engineers were trained through an enlarged and improved curriculum at West Point and through practical duties which increased rapidly in variety and volume. The best West Point graduates were utilized as professors at their

[12] Report of Board of Visitors, June, 1848, 30 Cong., 2 sess., *H. Ex. Doc.* 1, 282–83.

[13] Alstaetter, "Ohio River," 35; *Centennial*, I, 289, 835, 875–78; Dickinson, "River Improvement," 77–78; Dupuy, *Where They Have Trod*, xiii, 182, 368; Youngberg, "Civil Activities," 73–74.

alma mater and as field engineers. The most technical branches of the Army received the most able graduates: the Corps of Engineers took the best cadets; the Corps of Topographical Engineers, artillery, and ordnance received the next best; and cavalry and infantry took the remainder. Cadets competed scholastically to earn commissions in the two engineering corps, which were the most technical and most generally preferred services.

The army engineers imported technical knowledge not only by securing foreign military engineers as teachers and field engineers, but also by purchasing technical books from Europe and sending American engineers there to study. It is recalled that after the War of 1812 the government sent two famous engineer officers, Colonel McRee and Major Thayer, to France for military and technical research and publications. Soon after their return, the former became a member of the Board of Engineers for Fortifications and the latter superintendent of the Military Academy.

The importation of French military science was particularly great. West Point continued to secure books from France and to send officers there for further study. A notable instance of this was the research of Dennis Hart Mahan in Europe from 1826 to 1830. Mahan graduated at the head of his cadet class in 1824 and immediately became an assistant professor of mathematics and engineering at West Point. He was granted a furlough in 1826 to study military education and public works in Europe. He was particularly urged to secure knowledge of engineering science, and he was instructed by the Secretary of War to obtain "any information concerning roads, canals, bridges, the improvement of rivers and harbors, construction, labor-saving machinery, etc., which will be new to this country and of sufficient importance to render its acquisition desirable. To fulfil the end in view in seeking such information, viz., its successful application to useful purposes in this country, it should be distinct and accurate as well as minute."[14]

In Europe, Mahan examined foundries, bridges, naval bases, harbors, and railroads, the construction of which he carefully described in written reports. For more than a year he studied at the French School of Application for Artillery and Engineering at Metz, then considered the finest military school in Europe. He so greatly admired French advances in military engineering that he asked for extensions of his leave and recommended that other officers be sent to study in French military schools.[15]

Mahan spent most of his time in France studying civil and military engineering and returned in 1830 to be professor of engineering at West Point. He prepared textbooks on military and civil engineering during his long teaching career. In summers he inspected new constructions in civil engineering, and his treatise on this subject became a standard textbook in the United States. Other American officers followed Mahan to France to study military science, but he was perhaps the most famous and did much to make West Point a "national academy of science."[16]

Only slowly did other institutions arise to share with the Military Academy the task of teaching and expanding engi-

[14] Dupuy, *Where They Have Trod*, 192.

[15] Mahan informed the Engineer Department that "our own service and that of England are the only two who are not at this time reaping the advantages of the labors of the most scientific and intelligent corps in the world, the French Corps of Engineering and Artillery." (*Ibid.*, 199.)

[16] *Ibid.*, 191–201; W. D. Puleston, *Mahan. The Life and Work of Captain Alfred Thayer Mahan, U.S.N.*, 1–10. For an analysis of the process by which professional competence was transferred from Europe to America, see Fox, "Civilization," 753–68. According to Fox, the four general stages of this process were the use of foreign specialists in America, the study of Americans abroad, the starting of American professional schools initially dependent upon teachers trained abroad, and the final development of these schools as independent, self-sufficient institutions. It would seem that by the 1830's West Point had about reached the final stage and that for another four decades or so it helped other American scientific schools through the first three stages.

neering. West Point had definite advantages in the form of access to foreign knowledge, reputation of and demand for its graduates, and federal appropriations and encouragement. Total funds granted for the development of West Point had reached four million dollars by 1843 and seven million by 1863.[17] It was able to obtain as professors experienced officers who were familiar with domestic and foreign accomplishments in all fields of engineering. Besides their own wealth of experience, they possessed good models and textual material to use in their instruction. They gave an intensive four-year course and graduated about forty cadets annually. Between 1802 and the Civil War they trained two thousand graduates. Four thousand other cadets attended West Point but withdrew before graduating.

Although West Point had no close rivals before the Civil War, other engineering schools were coming into existence by that time. Rensselaer Polytechnic Institute at Troy, New York, was created as early as 1824. Initially, however, it did not emphasize engineering. It did not give a degree in civil engineering until 1835 and did not give instruction exceeding one year in length until 1850. After that date it was primarily a school of engineering on a level more comparable to West Point. They were the only engineering schools in the country until the 1840's when several others were established.[18]

In 1845 the Naval Academy at Annapolis, Maryland, and a school of engineering at Union College in Schenectady, New York, were founded. The Lawrence Scientific School was begun at Harvard University in 1846 or 1847, as was the Sheffield

17 Boynton, *West Point*, 311–12.

18 Ray Palmer Baker, *A Chapter in American Education: Rensselaer Polytechnic Institute, 1824–1924*, 30–31, 153; *Centennial*, I, 875–76; Russell H. Chittenden, *History of the Sheffield Scientific School of Yale University, 1846–1922*, I, 33–34; Charles R. Mann, *A Study of Engineering Education*, 4–6, 11–12, 16–18; Palmer C. Ricketts, *History of Rensselaer Polytechnic Institute, 1824–1914*, 7–8, 71–74, 82–87, 93–97; A. Riedler, "American Technological Schools," *Report of the Bureau of Education*, 658–61.

Scientific School at Yale. The University of Michigan decided to offer an engineering course in 1847 and organized an engineering department in 1852. The Chandler School of Science at Dartmouth College was founded in 1851, and Brooklyn Polytechnic Institute started teaching engineering in 1854. These new technical schools grew slowly and did not gain importance until after the Civil War. In their early years they had the Military Academy as an example and source of textbooks and teachers. Courses in engineering and related technical subjects at Harvard, Yale, Michigan, and Brooklyn Polytechnic, for instance, were offered by West Pointers.[19]

By this time West Point was furnishing many of the country's professors and practitioners of engineering science. The report of the Board of Visitors in 1848 indicated that this institution had produced many educators, civil engineers, and manufacturers among its 1,365 graduates. There were 72 graduates in the educational field, including 5 presidents and 42 professors of colleges, 20 principals of academies, and 5 other teachers. In the field of application were some 173 graduates, including 103 civil engineers, 3 presidents and 29 chief engineers of railroads or canals, 11 manufacturers, and 27 United States civil agents.[20]

An analysis in 1868 showed that of the 2,218 graduates between 1802 and 1867, some 139 had entered the field of education and 334 had taken up pursuits of a technical nature. Those in education included 26 presidents of universities and colleges, 23 principals of academies and schools, 5 regents and chancellors of educational institutions, and 85 professors and teachers. In specialized callings were 1 superintendent of the Coast Survey, 6 surveyors-general of states and terri-

[19] Chittenden, *Sheffield*, 34, 61; Dupuy, *Where They Have Trod*, 368–69; Mann, *Engineering Education*, 4–6, 11–12, 16–18; Samuel E. Morison, *Three Centuries of Harvard, 1636–1936*, 279–80; Riedler, "Amer. Tech. Schools," 660–63; Struik, *Yankee Science*, 347–48.
[20] Report of Board of Visitors for 1848, 30 Cong., 2 sess., *H. Ex. Doc. 1*, 295.

tories, 14 chief engineers of states, 35 presidents of railroads and other corporations, 48 chief engineers and 41 superintendents of railroads and other public works, 155 civil engineers, 30 manufacturers, and 4 architects.[21]

It is quite significant that West Point made this great contribution to the advancement of technical education before schools of engineering started developing in this country and that it facilitated their later growth.[22] Older educational institutions opposed introduction of technical subjects and engineering schools as dangerous to academic traditions. As a result, engineering came to be taught mainly by the newer polytechnical schools. In the meantime, the government and army engineers, with their need of military and civil engineering, helped cultivate this field until modern industrialism was able to sustain its rapid growth after the Civil War. They greatly facilitated the transition from self-taught to college-trained engineers and from practical to systematic engineering training.

The government may be said to have fostered the development of the technology of the nation. Only by assuming much of the social cost of improving technical education was it able

[21] Cullum, *Biographical Register,* I, 7. Sidney Forman states that 393 of the 1,787 West Point graduates of the period 1802–60 went into some kind of civil engineering. ("First School," 112.)

[22] One military historian states that among West Point's main influences on American life, "The first, and perhaps the most important, is the field of education, in which as Henry Adams says, the American Government projected, through West Point, 'the first systematic study of science in the United States.'" He adds: "To put it conservatively, the influence of the Military Academy was predominant in scientific educational activities during the most sensitive period of national growth—from 1820 to 1870. This was due first to the direct affiliation of its graduates actively teaching in other institutions, second to the scientific texts compiled by graduates and used not only at West Point but in other schools." (Dupuy, *Where They Have Trod,* 368, 369. Cf. Puleston, *Mahan,* 2.) Two recent historical studies which deal with the contribution of West Point to engineering science are R. Ernest Dupuy, *Men of West Point: The First 150 Years of the United States Military Academy,* and Sidney Forman, *West Point: A History of the United States Military Academy.*

to train engineers for their task of building the military defenses and major internal improvements of the country. The army engineers were acutely conscious of the national need for engineering assistance and were eager to utilize their engineering skills to encourage economic development. They visualized these skills as the scarcest resource of the nation and the greatest requisite for material progress. Their determined efforts to advance and diffuse technical training were of vital importance in the development of transportation, particularly during the early internal improvements movement.

One of the notable ways in which army engineers diffused the benefits of technical training was by surveying and exploration. These engineering activities implemented the work of the War Department and other federal agencies and aided the progress of state and private enterprises. Surveys were made for roads, canals, railroads, lighthouses, river and harbor projects, government buildings, and other civil works. They were also made to prepare maps, locate natural resources, guide the flow of westward migration, and determine state and Indian boundaries. These explorations and surveys were essential for planning federal improvements, assisting important nonfederal projects, and determining the main lines along which national development could occur.

Army engineers had already started exploring the country before passage of the General Survey Act in 1824. They surveyed coastal inlets and harbors to plan defense works and explored frontier areas to locate forts and map the terrain. The War of 1812 caused a great increase in these activities and the creation of a body of topographical engineers who became famous as the explorers and surveyors of the nation. While examining the coast they made surveys after 1816 for local navigation improvements, and by 1823 they made several canal surveys for state and private enterprises. They made several explorations of western rivers starting in 1817, and they also made surveys of lead mines and turnpikes in that area. Their topographical activities grew so rapidly that in 1823 alone they made surveys of roads, canals, lead mines, rivers, and harbors.

Even more important was the attitude of government officials and army engineers toward these new engineering duties. They were strongly committed to increasing topographical knowledge and mapping the country. In 1816, Chief Engineer Swift recommended a large increase in engineer officers for inspecting the frontiers, staffing the Military Academy, surveying the coast, and working on canals and bridges to gain a practical knowledge of engineering. John Anderson and Isaac Roberdeau, two topographical engineers who had just explored around the Great Lakes, favored increasing the topographical functions of the government, a "branch of public economy" which had not received adequate support. They pointed out the military and civil need for surveys of the natural resources, seacoasts, transportation routes, national frontiers, and general economic conditions of the country.[23]

In his "Report on Roads and Canals" in 1819, Secretary of War Calhoun advocated extensive use of army engineers for surveys of these undertakings. In 1822 a survey bill was proposed in Congress which would have required these engineers to prepare surveys, plans, and estimates for road and canal projects considered eligible for federal aid. Roberdeau again urged that army engineers be given civil engineering functions. This course was essential because of lack of civil engineers, demand for internal improvements, military and civil value of these surveys, and necessity that the government foster civil engineering. He proposed a large corps of topographical engineers to develop engineering science for the benefit of public improvement and military defense.[24]

[23] Swift to S/W, Jan. 8, 1816, E.D., Misc. Letters Sent, I, 9–10; Memoir of Anderson and Roberdeau, Jan. 15, 1816, E.D., Bulky File, No. 207.

General Bernard also advocated a large topographical corps with broad civil functions. He predicted that if army engineers were allowed to develop the fields of "geography, topography, hydrography, critical and military history . . . a rich harvest of scientific glory will become the share of the American topographical engineers."[25] President Monroe recognized the part army engineers could play in internal improvements when he recommended in 1823 that they make surveys and plans for canals between Chesapeake Bay, the Ohio River, and Lake Erie.

The General Survey Act of 1824 formalized the introduction of army engineers into civil engineering and instituted a pattern for using their scientific skills in making surveys, plans, and estimates for roads and canals worthy of national support. Their extensive surveying for roads, canals, and railroads has been analyzed in Chapters II–IV. Investigations for canals were initially dominant; but engineering aid to railroads, which began in 1827 with government surveys for the Baltimore and Ohio Railroad, was most important after 1831. Surveying for river and harbor improvements also increased steadily between 1824 and 1838, as shown in Chapter VI.

Despite the volume of these engineering activities, army engineers carried on other exploring and surveying activities during the life of the Survey Act. They made several surveys on the Great Lakes during the 1830's; and when the coast survey was re-established in 1836, they assisted with this work. They made numerous military reconnaissances and surveys for defense works and about ten exploring expeditions west of the hundredth meridian. Military field work increased rapidly after 1836; and in 1837, army engineers examined the national frontiers in Maine, Florida, and the Southwest. They also

[24] Roberdeau's report of Dec. 25, 1822, E.D., Bulky File, No. 114, pp. 10–15.

[25] Bernard to Roberdeau, Dec. 11, 1823, E.D., Letters Received, I, No. E1501.

made surveys to determine political boundaries, and starting in 1834 they made geological and mineralogical investigations and maps. These activities must obviously be added to surveys of roads, canals, railroads, rivers, and harbors to indicate the amount of surveying done by army engineers in this period.

Engineer officers and government officials had a great interest in this surveying activity and understood its value in national expansion. President Monroe and Secretary of War Calhoun created the Board of Engineers for Internal Improvements to apply the Survey Act. President Adams and Secretary of War Barbour actively supported this work and were deeply interested in promoting canals and railroads through surveying aid. These four men and Engineer Department officials repeatedly advocated an increase in the number of army engineers so as to make their technical skills more widely available.

Although President Jackson opposed financial aid to canal, road, and railroad enterprises, he allowed engineering assistance to these enterprises to increase. Government surveying for railroads reached its highest level during his second term. He and his secretaries of war actively urged an increase in the engineering agencies. In 1831, Secretary of War Eaton explained that surveys for internal improvements had military as well as civil value and recommended complete surveys of the inland and coastal frontiers of the nation. Eaton's successor, Cass, repeated demands for surveys of the coast and lakes and topographical examinations of the interior—"dissecting the country in all directions, and particularly along its streams or routes where roads already are or probably will be established." These tasks "require an intimate knowledge of the most abstruse investigations of the present day in mathematics and physical science" and could only be done by the government.[26]

[26] A.R. of S/W, Nov. 21, 1831, *ASP, MA,* IV, 710–11.

The Topographical Bureau was always eager to increase its surveying personnel and to extend its work into new fields. In 1833, Colonel Abert requested an appropriation for geological investigations. He felt that "national encouragement of a regular system of scientific investigation" would stimulate commerce, science, and national prosperity. His proposal was adopted in 1834, and at the end of the year he referred proudly to "geological and mineralogical surveys and researches" in Arkansas Territory which would promote science, industry, and the profitable employment of capital. In 1835, he stated that his bureau had the duty of surveying for coastal defenses, roads, railroads, and canals, as well as surveying harbors, rivers, lakes, inland frontiers, and the coast.[27] At this time President Jackson recommended increase of both engineering corps and stated that the work of the topographical engineers "is at all times interesting to the community, and the information furnished by them is useful in peace and war."[28]

During the 1830's great objection arose in Congress and elsewhere to government surveys for railroads. In 1836 and 1837 the secretaries of war opposed the loan of engineers to state and private enterprises, although the Topographical Bureau did not share their view. At this time surveying for internal improvements diminished while that for military purposes increased. With the repeal of the General Survey Act in 1838, military surveying received greatly increased emphasis. That these so-called military surveys were of a broad and essential character was indicated by Secretary of War Poinsett in 1838: "It is deemed very important that the annual appropriation for military surveys should be made. We are still lamentably ignorant of the geography and resources of our country; and it is essential to its defence, as well as to its

[27] A.R.s of T.B., Oct. 19, 1833, *ASP, MA,* V, 219; Oct. 30, 1834, *ibid.,* V, 425; and Nov. 2, 1835, *ibid.,* V, 715–16.
[28] Annual Message, Dec. 7, 1835, 24 Cong., 1 sess., S. *Doc. 1,* 22.

improvement, that the boundaries, the course of the rivers, the size and form and obstacles to navigation of the lakes, and the direction and height of the mountains should be accurately determined and delineated."[29] With the Survey Act repealed, the War Department and army engineers had no intention of curtailing their surveying. They were ready to make broader investigations of the physical character and natural resources of the country to promote national defense and development.

After 1838 there was a great increase in western explorations and military surveys. Expeditions west of the hundredth meridian increased during the 1840's and became very numerous in the 1850's. Besides the regular military and geographical explorations, there were surveys to locate military roads in the territories, wagon routes to the Pacific, and political boundaries. Surveys for river and harbor improvements were not numerous, but systematic surveying of the Great Lakes was energetically pushed after 1841. Army engineers also aided the coast survey. The war with Mexico greatly increased engineering activities in the Southwest and Far West, and after 1846 there was much exploring between Texas and the Pacific.

Topographical engineers started serving with the different military commands; and in this service they made surveys in such areas as Oregon, California, New Mexico, Texas, and Florida. These field engineers located military posts, wagon roads, Indian boundaries, and state and national borders. Appropriations were made in 1849 for examining routes from the Mississippi to the Pacific, and army engineers began to think in terms of planning a transcontinental railroad route. Many topographical expeditions crossed all parts of the West, with from five to fifteen exploring parties in the field each year in the decade prior to the Civil War.

The greatest increase in western exploration came in 1853

[29] A.R. of S/W, Nov. 28, 1838, 25 Cong., 3 sess., S. *Doc. 1,* 197–98.

with the start of the Pacific railroad surveys. Congress granted $150,000 for surveys to find the most practicable route for a railroad from the Mississippi to the Pacific. Having urged the desirability of such a railroad for several years, army engineers examined four different routes and collected information relevant to constructing a railroad and settling the country along its route. They were engaged in these and supplementary railroad surveys almost to the Civil War.

The attitude of the army engineers was always that of a marked desire to facilitate national expansion and the westward movement. They surveyed the Great Lakes, charted their waters, and marked reefs and shoals with buoys to stimulate commerce and settlement in the region. They surveyed and improved western rivers, located wagon routes, surveyed and built military roads, and made extensive examinations for a Pacific railroad route to speed development of the West. They explored and mapped its terrain and resources to facilitate settlement and growth. They continually asked for more army engineers to speed the exploring of unsettled territory. Their reputation as western explorers and Pacific railroad explorers reflects both their purposes and accomplishments.

Their insatiable desire for knowledge of the West was revealed in the Pacific railroad surveys. They collected meteorological data on the rainfall, snowfall, temperature, and humidity of the country through which railroads might pass. They made geological researches on the nature of the soil, barriers to railroad construction, existence of coal, and possibility of securing water by artesian wells. Material was amassed on questions of zoology and botany affecting possibilities of settlement and choice of a railroad route. In submitting reports on these surveys in 1855, Davis declared that they had involved investigation into many branches of science. Explorations on this large scale greatly contributed to knowledge of the interior, could be made only by the government, and should be continued.[30]

John B. Floyd as succeeding secretary of war strongly supported military explorations and surveys in the West. Noting the substantial benefit of the previous work, he concluded that much remained to be done to overcome the national ignorance of the region between the Mississippi and the Pacific.[31] In 1858 he again urged western exploration and stated that "Important additions to our geographical knowledge have been made by these surveys, and extensive information upon many scientific subjects has been procured at the same time." He proposed to issue a geological map to present the valuable scientific data collected by army engineers.[32] In 1860, on the eve of the Civil War, Floyd once more praised the work of exploring the West to find new routes to the Pacific and gain knowledge of topography, hydrography, climate, and geology. He emphasized that this work had great military value, aided settlement and resource development, and produced valuable contributions in several fields of science. Colonel Abert recommended an increase of the topographical corps and creation of a "company of pioneers" to aid in military and geological explorations.[33]

In summary, the army engineers, particularly the topographical engineers, were explorers and surveyors from the very beginning. They were for several decades practically the

[30] A.R. of S/W, Dec. 3, 1855, 34 Cong., 1 sess., S. *Ex. Doc. 1*, 13–15.

[31] A.R. of S/W, Dec. 5, 1857, 35 Cong., 1 sess., S. *Ex. Doc. 11*, 13.

[32] "The extensive deposits of precious metals throughout our vast dominion, in search for which such immense sums are annually expended, would be accurately marked; whilst the great articles of national wealth and prosperity, iron, coal, and salt, would be so clearly defined that no money need ever be thrown away in fruitless search for them in localities where they do not exist. Such a map would direct wisely the expenditure of money and labor, and would restrain losses likely to arise from ignorance or willful misrepresentation." (A.R. of S/W, Dec. 6, 1858, 35 Cong., 2 sess., S. *Doc. 1*, 12–13;)

[33] A.R. of S/W, Dec. 3, 1860, 36 Cong., 2 sess., S. *Ex. Doc. 1*, 10; A.R. of T.B., Nov. 14, 1860, *ibid.*, 301.

only academically trained engineers. Since civil engineers were at first relatively scarce, these military engineers were soon drawn into civil engineering. Their chief desire, and presumably the wish of national leaders, was to make engineering science available throughout the country. They started making surveys for civil purposes prior to the General Survey Act; and before its repeal in 1838 they had made many surveys for canals, roads, and railroads. Their surveying for river and harbor improvements was also extensive in this period. Most of this engineering activity before 1838 was to encourage internal improvements. Surveys, plans, and estimates were made for individual projects, including federal, state, private, and "mixed" undertakings. The objective was to stimulate all major transportation improvements through engineering aid. Better transportation was the basic need in securing national development, and engineering skill was a primary need of transportation undertakings.[34]

With the repeal of the General Survey Act, government surveying for internal improvements diminished. Engineering aid to state and private undertakings ceased, and the army engineers made surveys only for federal projects. Instead of decreasing, however, surveying by these engineers increased after 1838. Surveys and explorations became more general in character and less directly concerned with internal improvements. They were intended to encourage national development and westward expansion in an indirect but essential

[34] Andrew A. Humphreys, chief engineer soon after the Civil War, explained that the army engineers "were to a great degree the repositors, in this country, of that knowledge which was requisite for the purpose of making accurate surveys. The location and construction of the roads, canals, and bridges built for the development of the resources of the country, and the accurate methods of surveying, geodetic, topographic, and hydrographic, now in use, are in a great measure due to the talents and labors of its officers." He asserted that "Almost all the great routes of internal communication . . . were first explored, located, and projected by the officers of this corps." ("Historical Sketch of the Corps of Engineers," 45 Cong., 3 sess., *S. Rept.* 555, 348.)

fashion. The plan was to explore the West and make known its geographical features and natural wealth. After the war with Mexico and the California gold rush, military and geographical surveys of the West became quite numerous.

The role of the army engineers changed from that of directly aiding improvement enterprises to that of spearheading the winning of the West. As explorers and mappers they located wagon routes, military roads, army posts, and boundaries. To aid the westward movement they surveyed and charted the Great Lakes and made geological and mineralogical investigations. In 1853 they started the great Pacific railroad surveys. Even prior to this they had become interested in a Pacific railroad and had made military surveys with this goal in mind.

These railroad surveys and geographical explorations in the West were tremendous engineering undertakings which amassed great knowledge of topography and resources and materially aided national expansion. They represented effective application of engineering to promote economic development. This engineering activity was undoubtedly as important to westward expansion as earlier surveying aid had been to the growth of internal improvements. With both types of encouragement, the army engineers were the instrumentality by which the government developed and disseminated engineering science to foster the growth of the country.

The army engineers were engaged in constructing extensive public works of many kinds for four decades before the Civil War. Although they had built military defenses from 1794 onward, they did not execute civil works until 1824. They then started making river and harbor improvements, and a year later they began to extend the Cumberland Road. Their road work, practically all of which was in the West, increased steadily during the late 1820's and the 1830's, although it was shared with the Army Quartermaster Department. Military engineers surveyed, located, and inspected the construction of these roads, which were commonly built by civilian contractors. Although the eastern part of the Cumberland Road was returned to individual states in 1835 and work on its western part ceased by 1840, construction of territorial roads increased rapidly.

Despite the great increase in river, harbor, and road projects by 1838, army engineers were given other construction activities during the 1830's. They were assigned such civil works as lighthouses, beacon lights, monuments, and even bridges and aqueducts. These works were clearly secondary to river and harbor improvements and roads, but the building of lighthouses assumed increasing importance. During this decade several army engineers were also loaned to railroads to superintend construction of their lines. These construction activities were sufficiently widespread and important to compare favorably with the surveying for internal improvements which took place before the Survey Act was repealed in 1838.

For several years all civil works were directed by officers of the Corps of Engineers. The Topographical Bureau desired to become the national civil works agency, and by 1831, Jackson's secretaries of war, Eaton and Cass, shared this view. Topographical engineers were gradually assigned to construct lighthouses and river and harbor works. Colonel Abert insisted that the Topographical Bureau should construct all civil works; since it already surveyed, planned, and prepared estimates for them, it was best qualified to superintend their construction.[35] Secretary of War Poinsett agreed that all civil works connected with the commerce of the country should be handled by this bureau; and its duties in this area mushroomed almost immediately.

After 1838 the civil constructions of the Topographical Bureau were augmented by the transfer of all works previously directed by the Corps of Engineers and by increased building

[35] A.R. of T.B., Nov. 2, 1835, *ASP, MA*, V, 716.

of lighthouses and western roads. It monopolized all federal civil works until 1852, when large river and harbor appropriations caused the return of many revived works to the Corps of Engineers. Between 1840 and 1852, topographical engineers were also in charge of such varied construction projects as bridges across the Potomac, Washington Aqueduct, New Orleans customhouse, marine hospitals, and repair of Pennsylvania Avenue and other streets in Washington.

After 1852 the two engineer corps shared this work and also repaired the White House and constructed other government buildings. For a few years river and harbor improvements were again important, but the most notable increase was road building in the West. From 1849 onward the number of military and territorial road projects grew rapidly, so that by 1859 the Topographical Bureau directed road construction in Minnesota, California, and the territories of Nebraska, Kansas, New Mexico, Utah, Oregon, and Washington. The work of topographical engineers as western road-builders grew with surprising speed until the Civil War intervened.[36]

Although the army engineers had been brought into existence to build coastal defenses, their later construction activity lay primarily in the field of civil works. Their civil construction was extensive during the time of the General Survey Act but was greatest just before the Civil War.

The significant role which the army engineers achieved in the movement for internal improvements before the Civil War was indicative of the responsibility which the federal government took in this field. By the time of the War of 1812, it was

[36] Cf. A.R.s of E.D. and T.B.; and W. Turrentine Jackson, "The Army Engineers as Road Builders in Territorial Iowa," *Iowa Journal of History*, Vol. XLVII (1949), 15–33; "The Army Engineers as Road Surveyors and Builders in Kansas and Nebraska, 1854–1858," *Kansas Historical Quarterly*, Vol. XVII (1949), 37–39; "Federal Road Building Grants for Early Oregon," *Oregon Historical Quarterly*, Vol. L (1949), 3–29; *Wagon Roads West; A Study of Federal Road Surveys and Construction in the Trans-Mississippi West, 1846–1869.*

widely agreed that the government would have to guide and assist public improvement, and the most effective instrumentality at its command was its skilled army engineers. A comprehensive system of planning and encouragement was thought to be necessary, and each President asked for a federal system of roads and canals and for increased support of the engineering branches of the War Department.

This assumption of governmental responsibility for the progress of transportation eventuated in passage of the General Survey Act of 1824. The Board of Engineers for Internal Improvements was instituted as the technical planning agency to execute this act. The board completed surveys and plans for many important projects, studying the military, commercial, and political benefits of each proposed improvement, but no federal program was adopted for securing their systematic completion. As it became evident that plans would not be fulfilled, generalized planning became pointless. After a few years, therefore, the planning function of the army engineers declined and atrophied. There was a slow change in emphasis from surveying for internal improvements to exploring the West and executing public works necessary for national expansion.

This instance of abortive planning is noteworthy. For two or three decades the planning of internal improvements was extensively advocated and debated. It is significant that this attempted planning was often felt to be essential, that it took place primarily on the engineering level, that it was designed to promote private enterprise and economic development, and that its abandonment was due more to political factors than to the opposition of private business.

The task of planning a national system of transportation projects was committed to the army engineers in recognition of the basic role of engineering science in public improvement. The early scarcity of trained civil engineers and the technical character of planning and executing transportation projects made the employment of army engineers advisable, for they made up the most concentrated group of school-trained engineers, as contrasted with the self-trained engineers developed on some of the earlier works of internal improvement. Because of the systematic body of knowledge at their command, the army engineers were considered capable of undertaking the comprehensive planning of internal improvements.

The planning which the government attempted through its army engineers was intended to aid national defense and stimulate economic expansion through positive measures to improve transportation. The plan was to encourage private as well as public undertakings in the field of internal improvements and thus to provide conditions facilitating general economic growth. The government was to furnish engineering aid to important transportation projects, to encourage eligible projects of state, private, and "mixed" enterprises through loans and investments, and to execute other essential improvements not attempted by these enterprises. The objective was clearly that of guiding economic development through fostering conditions beneficial to business enterprise.

This attempted planning did not fail because its engineering base was inadequate or because the defenders of private enterprise objected to it. Instead, much of its strength and appeal lay in its effective engineering basis and its great stimulus to transportation and commercial expansion. Opposition to this planning occurred mainly in the area of political, including constitutional and sectional, issues. Its chief critics were the proponents of a doctrine of limited powers. In the attempted selection of national projects the "logrolling" problem became insurmountable, and rival cities and regions found it impossible to agree on a scheme of improvements. The failure to institute a national system of internal improvements was thus due more to unresolved constitutional and sectional issues than to any lack of technical ability of the army engineers to plan internal improvements and assist enterprises in this field. This planning also lost much of its military justification in the long period of peace after 1815.

Like the attempted planning of internal improvements, their encouragement by the army engineers took place on the engineering level. Unlike planning, however, this encouragement continued to flourish and to stimulate transportation and economic activity. During the life of the General Survey Act there was a rapid increase in surveys for roads, canals, and railroads as cities and sections jealously fought for the trade of the interior. This act served, until its repeal in 1838, as a vehicle for providing engineering aid to many promising transportation projects.

In the fields of exploration, surveying, and civil construction, the army engineers also stimulated westward expansion and economic growth. Such leaders as Gallatin felt that private enterprise, if unaided, would never complete the most essential connections and that the government must take the initiative and bear the major burden in their development. They believed that scarcity of capital and sparsity of population were almost insuperable barriers to private enterprise, and that the government must take the lead in overcoming them and thus guide the progress of transportation in the interest of military and political security and commercial growth.

It is significant that, despite the failure of the government to give large financial aid to internal improvements, its engineering assistance was so stimulating. Labor and land were available for these undertakings; every city had its promoters of transportation ventures; and capital funds alone were relatively scarce, in the sense of being drawn into other, more profitable channels. The scarcest factor was civil engineering. School-trained engineers could not easily be secured except from the government. Government engineering was for a time popular as well as effective. It was quite useful in determining whether undertakings would be profitable, and with this aid improvement companies were better able to overcome technical difficulties and secure capital funds.

It is not surprising that government encouragement through engineering aid and promotion of technical training was popular, that it was thought essential, and that it continued throughout the period under discussion. This activity was beneficial to private business rather than restrictive or competitive. Government surveying was not so vulnerable to constitutional issues as federal execution of improvements. The training and civil functions of the army engineers could be justified on military grounds; and there was no problem of federal jurisdiction when they aided state or incorporated enterprises or resigned to become civil engineers. Government participation in economic activity was widely demanded and was fairly consistent with prevailing economic attitudes during the internal improvements movement prior to the Civil War.

The internal improvements movement had lagged alarmingly before government engineering became available. The accelerated improvement of transportation speeded the growth of markets, specialization, and industrial output—thus increasing the rate of economic development. This purposeful promotion of technology by the federal government undoubtedly played a strategic part in early national expansion and was the key to the final triumphant conquest of the Great American West.

# Bibliography

## 1. MANUSCRIPT MATERIAL

THE CENTRAL MATERIAL of this study consists of the manuscript records of the Engineer Department, located in the War Records Division of the National Archives in Washington, D. C. These manuscripts are primarily letters issued, letters received, and reports. Letters issued are contained in large letter books and are indexed only by the name of the receiver. Letters received are indexed in register books by the name of the sender, but many of these letters are missing. Reports issued and received by the Engineer Department are found in large report books. Many of these reports were never published.

The following manuscript records were used in this study:

Corps of Engineers. Reports, 1812–23. 1 vol.
Engineer Department. Bulky File. This file consists mainly of large reports, many of which were never published. There is an index of these documents giving their author, title, and date.
———. Communications to Secretary of War. I–IV, VII–X. These volumes cover the periods 1836–44 and 1850–63.
———. Document File B, Miscellaneous Letters, 1813–18. One box of letters received. Registered in Engineer Department, Miscellaneous Papers, 1789–1831, File B.
———. Letter and Report Book of the Board of River and Harbor Improvements, 1852–53. 1 vol.
———. Letters Received. I–II, V. These volumes contain indexes of letters received for 1819–30 and 1838–40.
———. Letters to Officers of Engineers. I–IV, VI–VIII, XIX–XX. These volumes cover the periods 1812–34, 1836–41, and 1851–53.
———. Miscellaneous Letters Sent. I–XVI, XIX–XX. This correspondence is for the periods 1812–48 and 1855–61.

———. Miscellaneous Papers, 1789–1831. File G. Some of the documents indexed and abstracted in this volume are missing.

———. Outgoing Correspondence of the Board of Internal Improvement, May 16, 1826 to Feb. 16, 1828. III. Other volumes are missing.

Office of the Chief of Engineers. Document File, 1894–1923. Box 1209, File 50734–72. This file contains information on the history of the Corps of Engineers.

Topographical Bureau. Internal Improvement Letters Issued. A. This volume covers the period May 3, 1824 to May 1, 1827.

———. Letters Issued. I–XXII. This correspondence is for the period 1829–61.

———. Letters Issued to Secretary of War. I–IX. These volumes cover the period 1843–62.

———. Record of Proceedings, Board of Engineers, Lake Harbors and Western Rivers. This volume contains the board's proceedings, letters, and reports for the period Dec., 1852 to Aug., 1853.

———. Reports of the Board of Internal Improvements. I–III. These three volumes contain reports from Nov. 5, 1823 to June 9, 1831. Some of these reports were never published.

———. Reports Received, Reports on Internal Improvements, Feb. 1, 1828 to Jan. 30, 1839. 1 vol.

Totten, Colonel Joseph G. Official Letters and Papers. I, VII–VIII. These letters cover the periods 1803–25 and 1848–61. Totten kept separate letter books for all his official correspondence.

## Unpublished Theses

Cranmer, H. Jerome. "Internal Improvement in New Jersey: Planning the Morris Canal." M.A. thesis, Columbia University, 1949.

Kelso, Harold. "Inland Waterways Policy in the United States." Ph.D. dissertation, University of Wisconsin, 1942.

### 2. GOVERNMENT PUBLICATIONS

Frequent use has been made in this study of government documents, particularly Congressional Documents containing Annual Messages of the President and Annual Reports of the Secretary of War, Engineer Department, Topographical Bureau, and Board of

Visitors of the U. S. Military Academy. In addition, many special reports by these officials and by army engineers relating to internal improvements which were printed by order of Congress were found useful. The Congressional Documents which have been used are footnoted at appropriate places in the text.

Other United States government sources cited in the text include the following:

*Abridgement of the Debates of Congress, from 1789 to 1865.* Edited by Thomas Hart Benton. 16 vols. New York, D. Appleton, 1857–61.

*Acts of the Twenty-fifth Congress,* in Vol. V of *Public Statutes at Large of the United States of America.* Edited by Richard Peters. Boston, Little and Brown, 1846.

*American State Papers.* Edited by Walter Lowrie *et al.* 38 vols. (*Commerce and Navigation, Military Affairs, Miscellaneous.*) Washington, Gales and Seaton, 1833–61.

*Annals of the Congress of the United States, 1789–1825.* Washington, Gales and Seaton, 1834–56.

*Congressional Globe, 1834–1873.* Edited by Blair & Rives *et al.* Washington, Blair & Rives, 1834–73.

Humphreys, A. A. "Historical Sketch of the Corps of Engineers," 45 Cong., 3 sess., S. Rept. 555, 327–53.

Riedler, A. "American Technological Schools," *Report of the Bureau of Education,* 53 Cong., 2 sess., H. Ex. Doc. 1, 657–86.

Upton, Emory. *The Military Policy of the United States.* 62 Cong., 2 sess., S. Doc. 494. Washington, G.P.O., 1912.

U. S. Department of the Interior, Census Office. "Statistical Report of the Railroads of the United States," by Armin E. Shuman. Pages 5–639 in *Report of the Agencies of Transportation of the United States.* Washington, G.P.O., 1883.

U. S. Office of Federal Coordinator of Transportation. *Public Aids to Transportation. II. Aids to Railroads and Related Subjects.* Washington, G.P.O., 1938.

### 3. BOOKS

Albion, Robert Greenhalgh. *The Rise of New York Port.* New York, Charles Scribner's Sons, 1939.

Albright, George Leslie. *Official Explorations for Pacific Railroads.* University of California Publications in History, Vol. XI. Berkeley, University of California Press, 1921.

Armroyd, George. *A Connected View of the Whole Internal Navigation of the United States.* Philadelphia, H. C. Carey and I. Lea, 1826.

Baker, Ray Palmer. *A Chapter in American Education. Rensselaer Polytechnic Institute, 1824-1924.* New York, Charles Scribner's Sons, 1924.

Bolles, Albert S. *The Financial History of the United States, from 1789 to 1860.* New York, D. Appleton, 1883.

Boynton, Edward C. *History of West Point, and Its Military Importance During the American Revolution: and the Origin and Progress of the United States Military Academy.* 2d ed. New York, D. Van Nostrand, 1871.

Burgess, John W. *The Middle Period.* New York, Charles Scribner's Sons, 1897.

Calhoun, John C. *The Works of John C. Calhoun.* Edited by Richard K. Cralle. 6 vols. New York, D. Appleton, 1854-57.

*The Centennial of the United States Military Academy at West Point, New York, 1802-1902.* 2 vols. Washington, G.P.O., 1904.

Chevalier, Michel. *Society, Manners and Politics in the United States.* Trans. from the 3rd Paris ed. by T. G. Bradford. Boston, Weeks, Jordan, 1839.

Chittenden, Russell H. *History of the Sheffield Scientific School of Yale University, 1846-1922.* 2 vols. New Haven, Yale University Press, 1928.

Clark, William H. *Railroads and Rivers; The Story of Inland Transportation.* Boston, L. C. Page, 1939.

Cullum, George W. *Biographical Register of the Officers and Graduates of the U. S. Military Academy at West Point, N. Y., from Its Establishment, in 1802, to 1890, with the Early History of the United States Military Academy.* 3d ed. 3 vols. Boston, Houghton Mifflin, 1891. (1st ed. New York, D. Van Nostrand, 1868.)

———. *Biographical Sketch of Brigadier-General Joseph G. Swift, Chief Engineer of the United States Army, July 31, 1812, to Nov. 12, 1818.* New York, Charles A. Coffin, 1877.

Dewey, Davis Rich. *Financial History of the United States.* Twelfth edition. New York, Longmans, Green, 1934.

Dorsey, Florence L. *Master of the Mississippi; Henry Shreve and the Conquest of the Mississippi.* Boston, Houghton Mifflin, 1941.

Dunbar, Seymour. *A History of Travel in America.* . . . 4 vols. Indianapolis, Bobbs-Merrill, 1915.

Dupuy, R. Ernest. *Men of West Point: The First 150 Years of the United States Military Academy.* New York, William Sloane Associates, 1951.

———. *Where They Have Trod: The West Point Tradition in American Life.* New York, Frederick A. Stokes, 1940.

Folmsbee, Stanley John. *Sectionalism and Internal Improvements in Tennessee, 1796–1845.* Philadelphia, 1939.

Forman, Sidney. *West Point: A History of the United States Military Academy.* New York, Columbia University Press, 1950.

Ganoe, William Addleman. *The History of the United States Army.* Rev. ed. New York, D. Appleton-Century, 1942.

Godson, William F. H., Jr. *The History of West Point, 1852–1902.* Philadelphia, 1934.

Haney, Lewis Henry. *A Congressional History of Railways in the United States.* 2 vols. Madison, Wisconsin, Democrat Printing, 1908–10.

Hart, Albert Bushnell. *National Ideals Historically Traced, 1607–1907.* New York, Harper & Brothers, 1907.

Heitman, Francis B. *Historical Register and Dictionary of the United States Army, from Its Organization, September 29, 1789, to March 2, 1903.* 2 vols. Washington, G.P.O., 1903.

Holt, W. Stull. *The Office of the Chief of Engineers of the Army.* Baltimore, Johns Hopkins Press, 1923.

Hungerford, Edward. *The Story of the Baltimore and Ohio Railroad, 1827–1927.* New York, G. P. Putnam's Sons, 1928.

Hunter, Louis C. *Steamboats on the Western Rivers.* Cambridge, Harvard University Press, 1949.

Ingersoll, L. D. *A History of the War Department of the United States.* Washington, Francis B. Mohun, 1880.

Jackson, W. Turrentine. *Wagon Roads West; A Study of Federal Road Surveys and Construction in the Trans-Mississippi West,*

*1846–1869.* Berkeley and Los Angeles, University of California Press, 1952.

Jefferson, Thomas. *The Writings of Thomas Jefferson.* Edited by Paul Leicester Ford. 10 vols. New York, G. P. Putnam's Sons, 1892–99.

Johnson, Emory R. *Inland Waterways, Their Relation to Transportation.* Supplement to *The Annals of the American Academy of Political and Social Science.* September, 1893.

Johnston, James Houstoun. *Western and Atlantic Railroad of the State of Georgia.* Atlanta, Stein Printing Co., 1931.

Kirkland, Edward Chase. *Men, Cities, and Transportation: A Study in New England History, 1820–1900.* 2 vols. Cambridge, Harvard University Press, 1948.

Lane, Wheaton J. *From Indian Trail to Iron Horse; Travel and Transportation in New Jersey, 1620–1860.* Princeton, Princeton University Press, 1939.

Long, Stephen H. *Rail Road Manual, or a Brief Exposition of Principles and Deductions in Tracing the Route of a Rail Road.* Baltimore, William Woody, 1829.

——— and McNeill, William Gibbs. *Narrative of the Proceedings of the Board of Engineers of the Baltimore and Ohio Rail Road Company.* Baltimore, Bailey and Francis, 1830.

MacGill, Caroline E., and Meyer, Balthasar. *History of Transportation in the United States before 1860.* Washington, Carnegie Institution of Washington, 1917.

Madison, James. *The Writings of James Madison.* Edited by Gaillard Hunt. 9 vols. New York, G. P. Putnam's Sons, 1900–10.

Mann, Charles Riborg. *A Study of Engineering Education.* Bulletin No. 11 of the Carnegie Foundation for the Advancement of Teaching. New York, 1918.

Mason, Edward Campbell. *The Veto Power; Its Origin, Development and Function in the Government of the United States.* Boston, Ginn, 1891.

Monroe, James. *The Writings of James Monroe. . . .* Edited by Stanislaus Murray Hamilton. 7 vols. New York, G. P. Putnam's Sons, 1898–1903.

# Bibliography

Morison, Samuel Eliot. *Three Centuries of Harvard, 1636–1936.* Cambridge, Harvard University Press, 1936.

Park, Roswell. *A Sketch of the History and Topography of West Point and the U. S. Military Academy.* Philadelphia, Henry Perkins, 1840.

Phillips, Ulrich Bonnell. *A History of Transportation in the Eastern Cotton Belt to 1860.* New York, Columbia University Press, 1908.

Plumb, Ralph G. *History of the Navigation of the Great Lakes.* Washington, G.P.O., 1911.

Puleston, W. D. *Mahan. The Life and Work of Captain Alfred Thayer Mahan, U.S.N.* New Haven, Yale University Press, 1939.

Reizenstein, Milton. *The Economic History of the Baltimore and Ohio Railroad, 1827–1853.* Johns Hopkins University Studies in Historical and Political Science, Series XV, Nos. 7–8 (July–Aug., 1897).

Ricketts, Palmer C. *History of Rensselaer Polytechnic Institute, 1824–1914.* 2d ed. New York, John Wiley and Sons, 1914.

Ringwalt, J. L. *Development of Transportation Systems in the United States.* Philadelphia, Railway World Office, 1888.

Russel, Robert R. *Improvement of Communication with the Pacific as an Issue in American Politics, 1783–1864.* Cedar Rapids, Iowa, The Torch Press, 1948.

Sanderlin, Walter S. *The Great National Project; A History of the Chesapeake and Ohio Canal.* Baltimore, Johns Hopkins Press, 1946.

Semmes, John E. *John H. B. Latrobe and His Times, 1803–1891.* Baltimore, Norman, Remington, 1917.

Spaulding, Oliver Lyman. *The United States Army in War and Peace.* New York, G. P. Putnam's Sons, 1937.

Struik, Dirk J. *Yankee Science in the Making.* Boston, Little, Brown, 1948.

Stuart, Charles B. *Lives and Works of Civil and Military Engineers of America.* New York, D. Van Nostrand, 1871.

Swift, Joseph Gardner. *Memoirs.* Worcester, Mass., F. S. Blanchard, 1890.

Taylor, George Rogers. *The Transportation Revolution, 1815–1860.* New York, Rinehart and Company, 1951.

Thian, Raphael P. *Legislative History of the General Staff of the Army of the United States from 1775 to 1901.* Washington, G.P.O., 1901.

Thurston, Robert H. *A History of the Growth of the Steam-Engine.* Ithaca, Cornell University Press, 1939.

Turner, Frederick Jackson. *Rise of the New West, 1819–1829.* New York, Harper and Brothers, 1906.

Vose, George L. *A Sketch of the Life and Works of George W. Whistler, Civil Engineer.* Boston, Lee and Shepard, 1887.

Ward, George Washington. *The Early Development of the Chesapeake and Ohio Canal Project.* Johns Hopkins University Studies in Historical and Political Science, Series XVII, Nos. 9–11 (Sept.–Nov., 1899).

Waugh, E. D. J. *West Point.* New York, Macmillan Co., 1944.

#### 4. ARTICLES

Abbot, Henry L. "The Corps of Engineers," *Journal of the Military Service Institution,* Vol. XV (1894), 413–27.

Allan, Carlisle. "George W. Whistler, Military Engineer," *The Military Engineer,* Vol. XXIX (1937), 177–80.

Alstaetter, F. W. "The Ohio River," United States Army, Corps of Engineers, *Professional Memoirs,* Vol. II (1910), 35–41.

Beers, Henry P. "A History of the U. S. Topographical Engineers, 1813–1863," *The Military Engineer,* Vol. XXXIV (1942), 287–91, 348–52.

Callender, G. S. "The Early Transportation and Banking Enterprises of the States in Relation to the Growth of Corporations," *Quarterly Journal of Economics,* Vol. XVII (1902), 111–62.

"Corps of Engineers," *Niles' Weekly Register,* Vol. XXIX (October 22, 1825), 121–22.

Dickinson, J. M. "The Army Engineer and River Improvement," United States Army, Corps of Engineers, *Professional Memoirs,* Vol. II (1910), 73–81.

Forman, Sidney. "The First School of Engineering," *The Military Engineer,* Vol. XLIV (1952), 109–12.

Fox, Dixon Ryan. "Civilization in Transit," *The American Historical Review,* Vol. XXXII (1927), 753–68.

# Bibliography

Goodrich, Carter. "National Planning of Internal Improvements," *Political Science Quarterly*, Vol. LXIII (1948), 16–44.

———. "Public Spirit and American Improvements," American Philosophical Society, *Proceedings*, Vol. XCII (1948), 305–309.

———. "The Revulsion Against Internal Improvements," *The Journal of Economic History*, Vol. X (1950), 145–69.

———. "The Virginia System of Mixed Enterprise: A Study of State Planning of Internal Improvements," *Political Science Quarterly*, Vol. LXIV (1949), 355–87.

Hill, Forest G. "Government Engineering Aid to Railroads Before the Civil War," *The Journal of Economic History*, Vol. XI (1951), 235–46.

Jackson, W. Turrentine. "The Army Engineers as Road Builders in Territorial Iowa," *Iowa Journal of History*, Vol. XLVII (1949), 15–33.

———. "The Army Engineers as Road Surveyors and Builders in Kansas and Nebraska, 1854–1858," *Kansas Historical Quarterly*, Vol. XVII (1949), 37–59.

———. "Federal Road Building Grants for Early Oregon," *Oregon Historical Quarterly*, Vol. L (1949), 3–29.

Jewett, Henry C. "History of the Corps of Engineers to 1915," *The Military Engineer*, Vol. XXXVIII (1946), 340–46.

Johnson, Emory R. "River and Harbor Bills," *The Annals of American Academy of Political and Social Science*, Vol. II (1892), 782–812.

Kirby, Richard Shelton. "Some Early American Civil Engineers and Surveyors," Connecticut Society of Civil Engineers, *Papers and Transactions*, Vol. XLVI (1930), 26–47.

Lippincott, Isaac. "A History of River Improvement," *Journal of Political Economy*, Vol. XXII (1914), 630–60.

Nelson, E. C. "Presidential Influence on the Policy of Internal Improvements," *Iowa Journal of History and Politics*, Vol. IV (1906), 3–69.

Schermerhorn, I. Y. "The Rise and Progress of River and Harbor Improvement in the United States," *Journal of the Franklin Institute*, Vol. CXXXIX (1895), 252–71.

Sidell, W. H. "Red and Mississippi Rivers Rail-Road," *DeBow's Review*, Vol. XII (1852), 409–20.

Symons, Thomas W. "The Army and the Exploration of the West," *Journal of the Military Service Institution*, Vol. IV (1883), 205–49.

Way, R. B. "The Mississippi Valley and Internal Improvements, 1825–1840," Mississippi Valley Historical Association, *Proceedings*, Vol. IV (1910–11), 153–80.

Youngberg, Gilbert A. "The Civil Activities of the Corps of Engineers," *The Military Engineer*, Vol. XIII (1921), 73–77.

# Index

Abbot, Gen. Henry L.: 141
Abert, Col. John J.: 13n., 49, 64–65, 73ff., 82–90, 114f., 119–31, 133–38, 140, 146f., 150, 173–75, 183f., 215, 218, 221; *see also* Topographical Bureau
Adams, Henry: 210n.
Adams, Pres. John: 12
Adams, Pres. John Quincy: 44, 61–62, 68, 71, 112, 179, 200, 214
Akron (Ohio): 113
Alabama: 54, 151, 165
Alabama River: 53
Albemarle Sound, project to improve navigation: 24f., 154–55
Alexandria (Va.): 100
Allegheny River: 52, 53n., 54
Altamaha River (Ga.): 59, 108
Alton (Ill.): 131
Alum: 26
American Revolution: 3, 5, 10f.
"American system": 44
Anderson, Maj. John: 10, 22, 28, 212
Apalachee Bay (Fla.): 52n.
Aqueducts: 79, 221
*Archimedes* (snag-boat): 171
Arkansas River: 171f., 176, 183, 185
Arkansas Territory, geological surveys in: 84, 215
Armroyd, George: 97
Army, U.S.: 9, 14, 19, 35, 41, 83, 85, 114f., 201; topographical engineers with general staff, 10; officers employed on useful undertakings, 13n., 41; line officers assigned to topographical duty, 26, 36, 49, 51, 60, 62f., 78f., 83ff., 91, 105n., 110, 147, 173; used to improve transportation, 41; Quartermaster Department, 220; *see also* army

engineers, Engineer Department, *and* Topographical Bureau
Army engineers: *vii*, 4ff., 19ff.; lent or furloughed to railroad companies, 4, 68, 87–89, 111–17, 120–30, 137, 144–51, 221; sent to Europe for study, 14–15, 103–104, 110, 206–207; early civil activities, 21–36; role in internal improvements, 21, 34, 42–43, 51, 90–91, 199; demands for additional, 22, 27, 33, 51, 61–65, 68f., 71, 81–86, 89, 120, 160, 166, 172–75, 190, 212–15, 217f.; qualifications for civil functions, 35–36; felt duty to aid transportation enterprises, 68, 75, 88–90, 123–27, 137, 150; attitude toward alternative means of transportation, 71–72, 109; policy criteria under General Survey Act, 8off., 90–91; service with transportation companies restricted and opposed, 81f., 86–94, 103, 112, 114–15, 118, 121–23, 128–32, 137, 147, 151, 173, 215; compensation while with transportation companies, 87–88, 92–93, 103, 107, 112, 124–25, 128, 129n.; planning function declines, 91–95; resign (usually to enter railroading), 93, 114–15, 117, 122–24, 127, 142–49, 203; rotation in station, 191, 197; qualifications for river and harbor improvement, 194–98; as western explorers, 212, 217–20; role in public works construction, 220–22
Artillery: 12, 14, 19, 206
Astronomy: 81n., 83
Athens (Ga.): 119
Atlantic Coast: 8, 29, 41, 53, 120, 125, 131, 159, 186
Augusta (Ga.): 119

237

# Index

Carroll, Charles, of Carrollton: 103
Cass, Secretary of War Lewis: 8of., 84, 123, 175, 214, 221
Catskill (N.Y.): 107f., 110, 113
Catskill and Canajoharie Railroad: 108, 110, 113
Cavalry: 14, 206
Cedar Key (Fla.): 131
Central America, plans for canals or railroads across: 133, 137
Chandler School of Science, Dartmouth College: 209
Charleston (S.C.): 28, 53n., 103, 109, 119, 122, 126
Charleston and Hamburg Railroad: 103, 108, 117, 119, 143
Chemung Canal (N.Y.): 117
Chesapeake and Delaware Canal: 30, 58, 155
Chesapeake and Ohio Canal: 43–45, 49, 52–54, 57, 100, 116, 162; survey proposed by Pres. Monroe, 33–34, 44–45
Chesapeake Bay: 24, 44, 52n., 57, 213
Chevalier, Michel: 4
Chicago (Ill): 169, 177
Chicago River: 23, 156, 169
Cincinnati (Ohio): 122, 126, 171
Cincinnati and Charleston Railroad: 128f.
Civil engineering: see engineering
Civil engineers: 49f., 148f.; early scarcity of, 5, 12, 26–27, 68, 70, 88–89, 92–94, 124, 127, 152, 146, 149, 199, 212, 219, 223–26; War Department opposition to employment of, 62–63, 83–87, 89, 91; corps of, opposed by Barbour, 62–63; corps of, favored by Mercer, 63–64; army engineers compete with, 137, 141–42; U.S. civil engineers, 144
Civil War: vii, 141, 192, 205, 210, 216, 218, 220, 222, 226
Civil works, construction by army engineers: 59, 79–80, 9of., 94, 220–22; see also lighthouses, river

and harbor improvements, roads, and Topographical Bureau
Clay, Henry: 44, 46
Cleveland (Ohio): 177
Clinton, C. A.: 113n.
Clinton, Jr., De Witt (U. S. civil engineer): 113, 116f.
Coal: 26, 31f., 84, 218n.
Coast survey: 10, 21f., 33, 79ff., 122, 128, 171f., 177, 195, 212, 214f.; "school of practice" for engineers, 81, 83
Coastal defenses: 5f., 11, 13, 22, 34f., 38, 153–54, 157, 159, 211, 215, 220, 222; planning of, 8–9; see also Board of Engineers for Fortifications and military defense
Coastal trade: 29, 41, 156, 167, 190
Colleges and universities: early opposition to technical education, 202f., 205, 207–10; see also U. S. Military Academy
Columbus (Ga.): 120, 122, 126
"Company of pioneers," proposed: 218
Connecticut: 114, 122f., 166
Connecticut River: 52n., 57
Conrad, Secretary of War Charles M.: 135
Construction: see civil works
Continental Army (U.S.): 5, 10
Continental Congress (U.S.): 5, 11
Cook, Lieut. William: 105n., 111, 113–14, 146n.
Copper ore: 26, 28
Corps of Artillerists and Engineers: 5, 12
Corps of Engineers: vii, 11n., 19, 21, 206, 221–22; origin, 4–5, 12; early activities, 5–10; division of labor with Corps of Topographical Engineers, 91, 181, 186; see also army engineers and Engineer Department
Corps of Invalids: 11
Corps of Topographical Engineers: 11n., 22–23, 33, 81–85, 91, 128, 206; see also Topographical Bureau

239

# Index

# Index

Proprietors of Locks and Canals on the Merrimack River: 118, 145
Providence (R. I.): 114, 117, 126
Providence and Stonington Railroad: 114, 117, 120
Public debt, retirement of: 18n., 178; *see also* revenue surpluses
Public lands: 26, 169
Public works, constructed by army engineers: 220–22; *see also* coastal defenses, lighthouses, river and harbor improvements, *and* roads
Puget Sound: 138

Quartermaster Department: *see* army
Quebec (Canada): 120, 122

"Rafts": 26, 158, 166
Railed highway: 98
Railroad routes surveyed by army engineers: Boston (Mass.) to Hudson River, 106–107; Ithaca to Catskill (N. Y.): 107–108; Ithaca to Owego (N. Y.), 107; Catskill to Canajoharie (N. Y.), 108, 110, 113; Akron (Ohio) to Jersey City (N. J.), 113, 116–18; Winchester to Harpers Ferry (Va.), 113, 116, 126; New London (Conn.) to Providence (R. I.), 114; New London (Conn.) to Worcester (Mass.), 114, 117, 126; Providence (R. I.), to Stonington (Conn.), 114, 117, 126; Potomac Creek to Fredericksburg (Va.), 116; Mad River (Ohio) to Lake Erie, 117f.; St. Francisville (La.) to Woodville (Miss.), 117; Williamsport (Pa.) to Elmira (N. Y.), 117f., 126; across southern Vermont, 118; Detroit to St. Joseph (Mich. Terr.), 119–21, 126; Memphis (Tenn.) to the Atlantic, 119–20; Boston (Mass.) to Whitehall (N. Y.), 120; Detroit to Pontiac (Mich. Terr.), 120, 126; in Indiana, 120; proposed New Orleans (La.) to Nashville (Tenn.), 120; Pensacola (Fla.) to Columbus

(Ga.), 120, 122, 126; Portland (Me.) to Quebec, 120; Belfast (Me.) to Quebec, 122; Charleston (S. C.) to Cincinnati (O.), 122, 126, 128f.; Alton to Springfield (Ill.), 131–32; across Florida from Cedar Key to Jacksonville and the St. Johns River, 131; across Panama, 137; *see also* Pacific railroad surveys
Railroads: surveys by army engineers, 58–60, 69–70, 72, 74, 79, 88, 96ff.; government engineering aid opposed, 86, 90, 92, 123, 128–29, 151, 215; growth, 93, 111, 150–52; early federal interest, 97ff.; turnpike principle applied in early charters, 98f.; craze, 99; military value, 102, 109, 130–31, 140; bridges, 104, 138, 145n.; land grants, 149; milage, 150–51; *see also* railroad routes surveyed
Raritan River (N. J.): 52
Red River: 135–36, 166, 171f., 176, 183, 185
Rensselaer Polytechnic Institute: 208
Revenue surplus, use of annual: 18n., 170, 178, 195
Rhode Island: 114, 122f.
Río Grande: 135
Rivalry for internal improvements and trade: 39, 41, 55, 69, 76f., 92–94, 100, 109, 111, 151, 161, 165, 170, 178–79, 195, 224–25
River and harbor bills: first, 163–64; logrolling, 170, 178–79, 195, 224; vetoed, 170, 191, 195–96
River and harbor boards: 163, 186–88, 190, 194
River and harbor improvements: 153–80, 181–98, 221–22; early local execution, 21, 154, 159; government engineering aid to local projects, 34, 154–55, 173–75, 211; value to military defense, 29, 34–35, 40, 72–73, 140, 166–67, 197; role of Congress, 58, 72, 162, 170, 173, 175, 178, 184f., 187–88, 192–93, 195, 197; relation to General

245

209–10; Frenchmen as professors, 15–16; Thayer's improvements, 15–17; Board of Visitors, 16, 142–43, 148, 203f.; relation to internal improvements, 17–21, 141–49, 199ff.; criticisms, 20–21, 143, 201–202; resignation of officers trained at, 93, 127, 142ff., 203; contribution to progress of railroads, 96, 141–49, 151; civil careers of graduates, 141–42, 146–49, 201, 203, 209–210; sciences taught, 142, 200, 203–205, 210n.; source of professors for educational institutions, 142, 201, 203–205, 209, 210n.; term of enlistment of cadets, 147, 202–203; advancement of technical education, 203–205, 207n., 209–210; best graduates commissioned into the army's most technical branches, 206; textbooks secured from Europe, 206; source of textbooks in engineering, 207–209, 210n.

U. S. Naval Academy (Annapolis, Md.): 208
Universities: see colleges
University of Michigan: 209
Utah Territory: 222

Van Buren, Pres. Martin: 147, 179, 182, 196, 202
Vermont: 118
Vicksburg (Miss.): 134
Virginia: 63n., 113, 119n., 125, 151, 154

Wabash River (Ohio, Ind.): 23
Wagon roads: see roads
War of 1812: vii, 3, 5f., 10, 14, 18, 21f., 38, 154, 156, 160, 206, 211, 222
War with Mexico: 185, 216, 220
Warren, Gen. G. K.: 141
Washington, Gen. George: 5, 11
Washington, D. C.: 53ff., 67, 100, 116, 134; street repair by army engineers, 222

Washington Aqueduct: 222
Washington Territory: 222
Western and Atlantic Railroad, state of Georgia: 127–30, 145n.
"Western Engineer, United States Steam Boat": 24n., 157; see also Long
Western Railroad (Mass.): 128, 130, 145
West Point (Ga.): 119
West Point (N. Y.): early engineering schools at, 11, 13; see also U. S. Military Academy
Westward expansion: vii, 133, 211, 217, 219–20, 225
Wever, Casper W.: 106n.
Whigs, attitude toward river and harbor improvements: 195–96
Whistler, Lieut. George W.: 103–105, 110f., 113, 116–18, 144–45, 146n.
Whistler (locomotive): 113n.
White, Canvass: 30
White House, repaired by army engineers: 222
Whitehall (N. Y.): 120
Wilkins, Secretary of War William: 148, 183
Williams, Capt. W. G.: 122, 126–28
Williamsport (Pa.): 117f., 126
Williamsport (Pa.) and Elmira (N. Y.) Railroad: 117n.
Wilson, Maj. John: 111n.
Winchester, George: 110
Winchester (Va.): 113, 116, 126
Winchester and Harpers Ferry Railroad (Va.): 113n., 116, 118f.
Wing-dams: 157, 165, 171, 183
Woodville (Miss.): 117
Worcester (Mass.): 114, 117, 126
Wright, Benjamin: 30

Yale University: 209
Yazoo River (Miss.): 118

Zoology: 139, 217

UNIVERSITY OF OKLAHOMA PRESS

NORMAN

...panese automakers own on average over 60 per-
...r sales companies. The only other automaker
...ership level is anywhere near as low as Toyota's is
...y small-scaled competitor, Honda.

...emphasis on having local business interests capi-
...gional sales companies was part of the sales expan-
...developed early on by Kamiya. This policy reaped
...ng advantages.

...l managers running these regional sales compa-
...ore serious about succeeding when they know that
...ness interests have their money invested in these
...panies.

...wnership also makes it easier for profits to be re-
...in the sales companies that earn them. After all,
...nagers at sales companies that are fully owned by
...t automaker are employees on loan from the parent
...y. They tend to think profits should be channeled
...the parent company. Also, they tend to be less con-
...with the regional sales company's long-term interests.
...les power of locally owned regional sales companies
...ed by double support — support from the parent com-
...d support from local investors and the local people
...ake up almost all of the sales company management.
...ddition, the fact that these regional sales companies
...ned and operated almost entirely by local people
...it easier to increase sales through social and family
...the community.

## ...VANTAGES OF WHOLLY OWNED DEALERSHIPS

...mentioned earlier, Toyota has thirteen wholly owned
...rships. Most of these are in the two largest metropolitan
...ctures of Tokyo and Osaka, where competition among
...rships is the greatest.

Table rows (under side label "Trucks" for the lower group); right-hand column heading: "Handles all Toyota models":

- Toyota MR2
- Sprinter Carib
- Dyna
- Toyoace
- Hiace
- Master Ace
- Town Ace
- Liteace
- Hilux
- Publica Pick-up
- Land Cruiser
- Blizzard
- Coaster
- Industrial vehicles

1. Solid squares indicate dealers that handle only passenger cars and solid triangles dealers that handle only vans.
2. Toyota industrial vehicle dealers include 32 Toyota Forklift dealers. The Toyota dealer handles districts that do not have their own Toyota Forklift dealer (except for the Tokushima District, which is handled by a Toyopet dealer).

[Translator's Note: The above car model names are those used in Japan. Some of these models may use different names in overseas markets.]

models just prior to the introduction of the new model. They would feel pressured to resort to absorption sales and their business results would have bigger fluctuations. By contrast, the mutual-aid system enables the impact of model changes to be spread out. That, plus the fact that each dealership group handles several models, helps spread the sales risks associated with specific models.

2. The mutual-aid system also makes for a more extensive network for parts supply and after-sales service. Again using the previous example of mutual aid in Crown and Corona sales, both dealerships are required to maintain parts supply and after-sales service for both car models. This results in a broader-ranging and stronger after-sales service organization.

Table 5-2 shows the specific relationships between dealership groups and car models handled.

### COMPETITION AMONG DEALERSHIP GROUPS

Formally, there is no competition between Toyota dealerships in the same territory, since each belongs to a different group and sells different models aimed at different consumer strata. However, the fact is that the expansion of Toyota's selection of models has caused overlapping among targeted consumer strata. This in turn has led to increasingly severe competition among Toyota dealerships belonging to different groups in the same territory. In other words, the dealership groups are not as distinctive from each other as they used to be.

Let us take as an example the Kanagawa Toyota dealership, which was established in October 1946. This was Toyota's first dealership in Kanagawa Prefecture following the war. Noting the principle that one cup can only hold one cup's worth of

water, Toyota's Kamiy
nel for Toyota cars i
Toyopet dealership in
January 1956. Later, tl
Toyopet dealerships joir
lish a Corolla dealership
dealership in 1968, and fi
the years, the competitio
the same territory has stea

Obviously, competition
tories is a positive factor fo
factor behind the strength o

### ADVANTAGES OF

Of the 314 sales compani
Toyota group, Toyota directl
ment) only thirteen companie
(about 96 percent of the tota
capital. The thirteen wholly ov
six Tokyo-based companies (i
Toyopet, and Tokyo Corolla),
(Osaka Toyopet), five in Sappor

By contrast, nationally, Japan
ership of 20 percent of their si
majority ownership (ranging fr
company equity) in another 11 p
ship (less than 50 percent of sales
19 percent. The industry average t
local capitalization is the case at
companies. By and large, these loc
panies are invested in by prominent

When we subtract Toyota, who o
sales companies, from the industry

remaining J
cent of the
whose own
the relativel
Toyota's
talize its re
sion policy
the followi

The loc
nies are m
local busi
sales com

Local
invested
most ma
the paren
compan
back to
cerned

The s
is boost
pany a
who m

In a
are ov
makes
ties in

A
As
deale
prefe
deale

All of these wholly owned dealerships were established by the Toyota Motor Sales Company, the formerly separate sales company that has since merged with Toyota Motor. These dealerships were established to secure a solid position in Japan's major urban markets. This strategy stood in stark contrast to the common strategy among rival automakers in the early postwar period of linking up with a foreign-owned company to facilitate the importation of technology for improving production and sales. As such, Toyota's plan posed a direct challenge to dealerships allied with its chief rival , Nissan.

On the other hand, the presence of the Toyota-owned dealerships provided a healthy stimulus to locally owned dealerships. For example, one might think that the goal at the Yokohama Toyopet dealership is to replace the rival Nissan dealership as Number 1 in Kanagawa Prefecture. But they have already achieved that goal. Now, their goal is to become number one in sales results among all Toyopet dealerships, and to do that they must outsell the Toyota-owned Tokyo Toyopet dealership.

Thus, by being the first to carry out strategic investment in certain sales channels, Toyota has achieved the highest level of sales competitiveness among Japan's automakers.

Toyota began taking the lead in this respect in the late 1940s, when it established its strategy of rapidly building up sales strength via the efforts of locally owned dealer/distributors, sales channels, and sales outlets. It goes without saying that the sales network is the nucleus of any company's sales strength. We should also affirm, however, that a good sales network is essential for obtaining good information and communication and for providing extensive after-sales service. Toyota did just these things and thereby reached a prominent position during its formative years.

## CHAPTER 6

# New Product Development System

FOR ANY automobile manufacturer, car production and sales involves a large and lengthy process. At Toyota, this process can be broken down into three stages: (1) new product research and development (R&D), (2) manufacturing, and (3) sales. Specifically, this first stage of new product R&D consists of conceptual research and development and concrete new product development, the latter of which usually is done in-house. In contrast, the manufacture of parts, an activity within the manufacturing stage, is done usually by outside suppliers. Primarily, Toyota's in-house manufacturing work consists of pressing out car bodies and assembling finished products. The work at the sales stage is handled by Toyota's affiliated sales companies. Any automaker's overall management system must cover the entire group of companies involved in this long process.

Chapter 6 describes Toyota's new product development system, which is part of the first stage, new product R&D. This description is based on three new model development case studies for the car models known in Japan as the Toyota Celica, the Carina ED, and the Corona EXIV. The material used in this chapter comes primarily from two sources: first, an article by Takehiko Morozumi entitled "The Development Story of the New Line of Toyota Celica Cars" *(Nyu Moderu ga Dekiru made: Serika Keiretsu no Baai)* that appeared in the January 1990 issue of *Motor Fan (Motoru Fuan)*; and second, interviews with members of Toyota's product planning division.

## OVERVIEW OF TOYOTA'S NEW PRODUCT · DEVELOPMENT SYSTEM

At Toyota, new product development falls into three categories: new car models, full model changes, and minor model changes. Rarely does the company come out with a brand new car model, so the great majority of new product development work falls in the two model-change categories. In principle, full model changes follow a four-year cycle and minor model changes a two-year cycle. Each new model is estimated to have a market life of four years. Consequently, once a new model reaches full production and sales, developers begin the conceptual planning work for its successor. The process that begins at this stage and ends with full-scale production takes four years, the same length as the product's estimated market life.

If we include the time required for the basic research that goes into the new car model, product development and initial production stages end up going way beyond the model's market life. Toyota carries out a wide range of basic research at its main R&D center in Toyoda City. More specialized and concrete new-model research is done at other R&D centers, such as the Higashi-Fuji Center and the Parts Center.

The following lists the organizational structure and main activities of the Higashi- Fuji R&D Center.

• *Development Section #11:* Initial development of body, chassis, and drive system.

For example, people in this section perform early design and development of new body structures and steering systems.

• *Development Section #12:* Initial engine development for Engine Sections #1 and #2 of the Design Division.

For example, this section works on reducing exhaust emissions and developing super chargers and engines for motor shows.

• *Research Section #11:* Research on fuel control technologies, alternative fuels, and engine development (prior to the engine development work done by Development Section #12).

For example, this section works on gas turbine engines, methanol engines, fuel analysis, and so on.

• *Research Section #12:* Research on materials (both structural and functional). Also, R&D in electric automobiles and automotive communications technologies.

For example, this section studies ceramic materials, PZT, new types of batteries, and the like.

In addition, the R&D division at Toyota's head office includes the following sections:

• *Material Technology Section:* Development of automotive materials.

For example, they develop new varieties of chrome, resins, rubber, urethane, leather, plastics, superconductors, and composite materials.

• *Microelectronics Development Section:* Development of automotive electronic components (semiconductors, etc.).

For example, they develop ICs and other electronic components.

There is a chief engineer for each car model. This person is the core member of the new product planning team within the Product Planning Division and receives initial technological developments made by the various R&D centers and the head-office R&D division as well as market information gathered by the Merchandise Planning and Sales Divisions.

This transfer of technology and information occurs about three years before the new model reaches its final form.

While the more specific product development work after this point is handled primarily by the head office's Engineering Division, the outside suppliers participate in their respective areas (such as car body suppliers taking part in the model's body development and parts suppliers in the development of various parts).

Figures 6-1A and 6-1B outline Toyota's new product development organization and shows how the new product development process is divided up among the organization's various divisions and sections. The encircled numbers 1 to 10 in Figure 6-1A approximate the temporal sequence of development steps within this organization.

As already mentioned, Japanese automakers generally produce new models on a four-year cycle. However, most European automakers work on a much longer cycle. Mercedes-Benz, for example, has a new model cycle of seven to nine years. According to automotive journalist Takehiko Morozumi, the Japanese build cars from a commercial total quality control (TQC) perspective while Europeans build them from a philosophical perspective. In other words, before getting into the nitty-gritty of technology, the Europeans undertake extensive research on factors such as humankind's relationship with cars, present and future road systems, and the outlook for distribution.

The purpose of undertaking basic scientific research and extensive research into the philosophical question of how cars fit into society is to study how well automobiles serve as a vehicle toward human happiness. This is the focal point from which all new car development should begin.

Figure 6-2 provides a flowchart that counts backward from full-scale production to show approximately how many months before that point each stage of the product develop-

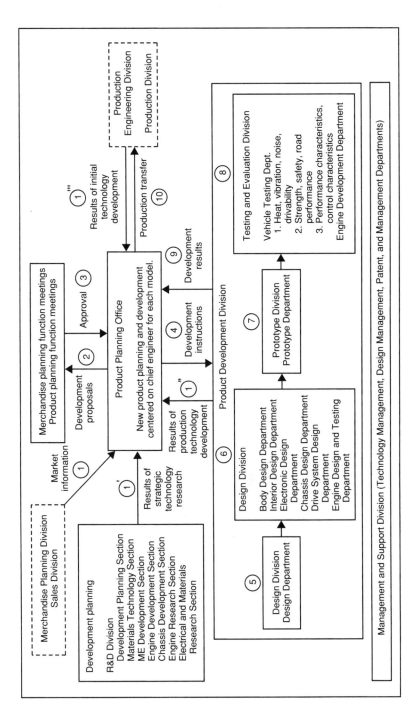

**Figure 6-1A. New Product Development Organization**

| Division/Department/Section | | Main tasks | Themes and products |
|---|---|---|---|
| Head office | Development Planning Section | ▲ R&D planning and promotion | R&D themes: materials, electronics, engines, chassis, drive systems, resin body parts, air conditioning, vehicle characteristics, communications, safety, welded body parts, electric cars, batteries, etc. Products: full or minor model changes for Crowns, Corollas, and development of completely new models such as the MR2. |
| | Product Planning Center | ▲ New product planning<br>▲ Liaison and coordination with other departments as needed for new product development | |
| | Technology Management Division | ▲ Management of Engineering Division's organization, equipment, costs, and technical data (reports, etc.)<br>▲ Cost planning and estimation | Computer processing, CAD, LA, etc. |
| | Region-specific testing grounds | ▲ Evaluation of characteristics in cars for cold-weather regions<br>▲ Evaluation of high-speed road performance conditions | Starting performance, drivability |
| | Design Management Division | ▲ Management and design support for technical data (diagrams, CAD data, standards, etc.)<br>▲ Certification processing | Legal processing required for certification and sales |
| | Patent Department | ▲ Acquisition and management of industrial property rights (patent claims, utility model rights, design rights, trademark rights) | |
| | Design Department | ▲ New product style design development | Style design: exterior and interior design, color design, clay model design, style CAD |
| | Body Design Department | ▲ Body design | Body design includes the main body, exterior parts, lamps, mirrors, exhaust pipes, wipers, etc. |
| | Interior Design Department | ▲ Design of interior parts | Interior design includes the instrument panel, interior door handles, seats, seat belts, air conditioning, etc. |
| | No. 1 Engine Section | ▲ Design and testing of commercial-model engines | Development of engines for next production cycle |
| | No. 2 Engine Section | ▲ Design and testing of passenger-model engines | Development of EFI system, carburetors, turbo chargers, etc. |

| | Department | Activity | Details |
|---|---|---|---|
| Head office | Electronic Engineering Department | ▲ Design and testing of various electronic control systems | EFI systems, cruise control, battery, TEMS, pneumatic suspension, ABS, navigation, displays, audio, wire harness, etc. |
| | Chassis Design Department | ▲ Chassis parts design | Suspension, steering, brakes, exhaust pipes, fuel system, etc. |
| | Drive Train Department | ▲ Design and testing of drive train systems and parts | Transmissions, differential gears, 4WD, etc. |
| | Product Testing Department | ▲ Comprehensive testing and evaluation of vehicle characteristics | |
| | No. 1 Vehicle Testing Section | ▲ Vehicle testing (heat, vibration, noise, drivability) | Evaluation of cooling and air conditioning, vibration and noise, drivability, field of vision, and visual indicators |
| | No. 2 Vehicle Testing Section | ▲ Vehicle testing (strength, safety, road performance) | Evaluation of body, chassis, drive strength, seats, wipers, rubber parts, exhaust pipes, collision testing, and durability testing |
| | No. 3 Vehicle Testing Section | ▲ Vehicle testing (performance characteristics, control characteristics) | Evaluation of operational safety, drivability, etc. |
| | Prototype Department | ▲ Manufacture of prototypes (preparation and management of prototype parts and manufacturing processes such as presses, sheet metal processing, and assembly) | |
| | Material Technology Department | ▲ Development of automotive materials | Development of paints, chroming, resins, rubber, urethane, leather, plastics, superconductor, composites, etc. |
| | Microelectronics Development Department | ▲ Development of electronic components (semiconductors, etc.) | Development of ICs and other electronic components |
| | Motor Sports Department | ▲ Planning, development, and support for motor sports activities | |

**Figure 6-1B. Engineering Division Organization**

ment process takes place. Now we will have a closer look at the product development stages shown in Figure 6-2.

## NEW PRODUCT PLANNING PROCESS

Almost all Japanese automobile manufacturers have a section that exercises comprehensive control over the entire new product development process. The people in this section assume overall responsibility for the new product and help coordinate the development process, such as by issuing instructions to the various relevant departments.

At Toyota, this section is called the Product Planning Center. It is here that we find the new model's chief engineer, the person with ultimate responsibility for the new model. The chief engineer establishes the direction of the new model's development and oversees the development process. Consequently, each new model clearly reflects the thinking and approach of its chief engineer. Figure 6-3 shows a matrix chart that plots the relationship between the chief engineer and the people in the various departments related to the new product's development.

While the product managers usually are graduates of the engineering departments, occasionally they rise up the management ranks instead. The product manager who handled the Nissan Cima's development was a nonengineer manager. It is thought that product managers from the management ranks generally are better able to develop new car models that anticipate market trends than are the more technical-minded engineers. The marketability factor is, of course, very important. However, engineers generally show themselves to be better at supervising the design stages while manager-types are usually better at supervising the product promotion stages.

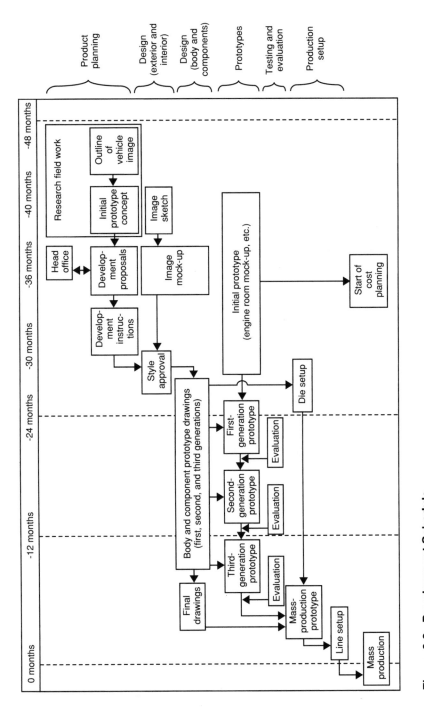

**Figure 6-2. Development Schedule**

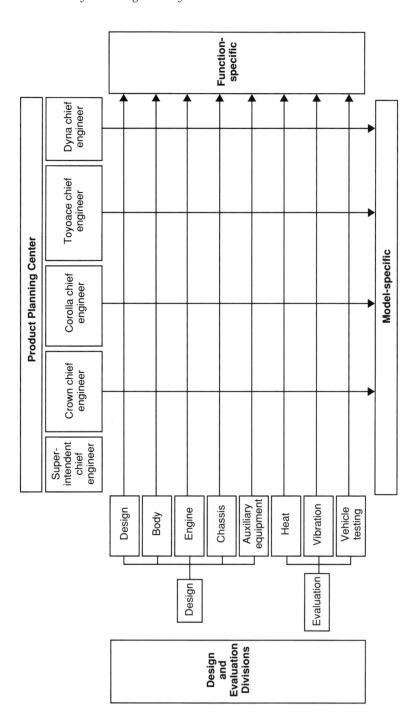

**Figure 6-3. The Chief Engineer System Behind New Car Development at Toyota**

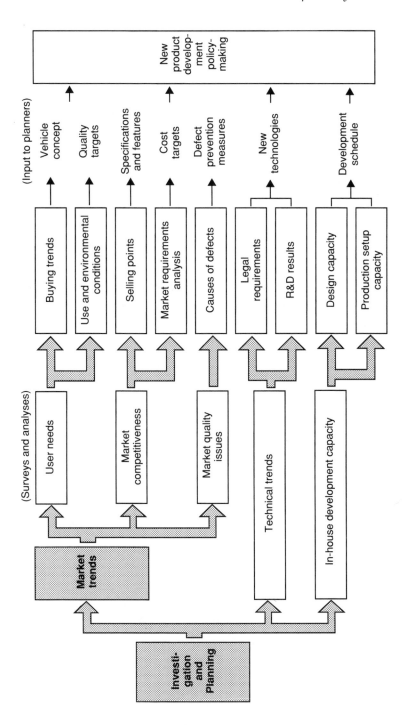

**Figure 6-4. New Model Planning Process**

Basically, chief engineers take one of the following two approaches to new model development:

1.  A *decentralized approach* in which the product planning center plays a pivotal role but the various related departments operate with a relatively large degree of autonomy.
2.  A *centralized approach* in which the entire new product development organization is centered on and represented by the project team that is headed by the chief engineer.

The first approach generally works better for the routine work in new product development. The second approach enhances the chief engineers' ability to put their personal stamps on the new product. We will look more closely at the chief engineer's job in a forthcoming section.

As we see in Figure 6-4, the planning process for a new car model is based on a new model image that combines market trends with technical trends. The basic planning process in this figure shows considerations such as user needs, product positioning in the market, and ways to address quality problems in current models form the backbone of the market research. This strict approach is part of the strength of Japanese cars and is undoubtedly one reason for their high quality.

Market research begins with surveys to understand the public's reaction to recently introduced current models. This involves more than simply collecting data. Often, the chief engineer personally interviews domestic dealers or overseas importers to find out firsthand what salespeople and users are saying in various sales regions. In addition, members of the Merchandise Planning Office, who look at the merchandise value of automobiles, interview domestic and overseas dealers and sales managers to get input they can use when planning the next model.

However, considering that all of this market research data concerns only reactions to previous or current products, the new product planners must also try to look four years ahead and anticipate the social environment and trends that could affect product marketability. Product planners know that they can never rely completely on data based solely on current opinions and perceptions. They should place a high value on input from younger people in the company. By introducing its new flat organization, Toyota is doing just that.

## NEW CAR STYLING PROCESS

The exterior design process at Toyota uses an initial development team in addition to the line team in the Design Division, which enables the design planning process to get started earlier. Usually, this process begins about forty months before the new car's market debut.

Once the line team has finished preparing minor changes for the most recent new model on the market, it switches over to design work for the next-generation new model. This means that they cannot begin work on the next-generation model until about ten months after the new model has been brought to market.

Design work begins with idea sketches as a method of image development to create a new concept. After that, they begin to make three-dimensional models, such as ceramic models, to study and evaluate the aesthetic features of the car's form.

Next, they draw more sketches to render a more detailed picture of the car design. Often, this step is followed immediately by the creation of a five-to-one scale model. Since there is only so much time available for this design work, designers tend to prefer three-dimensional models over two-dimensional drawings because the 3-D renderings give a better idea of the image. These models are called "mock-ups." It takes from twenty to thirty days to complete each mock-up.

The following step is to make a full-size clay model. This model is submitted for approval as part of the new car's planning proposal. This approval should come within a year after the start of the design work, which leaves about thirty months before the new car hits the market.

The interior design is started later than the exterior design, but it is submitted for approval at about the same time.

Because the design team is given only one year to come up with its new car planning proposal, the question of how much time to allot for initial concept development is critical.

## NEW CAR DESIGN PROCESS

The timetable for each model change design is built around the body design work.

Once the new car design proposal ("style") is approved, the designers draw up a line chart for the car body. They use this line chart as a basis for the body sheet metal design. When completed, the body sheet metal design drawings — which are the original drawings for the body structure — are given to the die-cast and press engineers who begin preparing dies for manufacturing the car body.

Toyota and other automakers that manufacture many types of cars and trucks treat component/part design and development as a separate process from new model design. They usually select basic component designs from among the wide variety of designs available and then make detailed design changes to suit the new model design. Nowadays, many design departments use Computer-aided Design/Computer-aided Manufacturing (CAD/CAM) systems. Among other tasks, these systems simplify and accelerate the process of determining the three-dimensional data for basic body designs. Some CAD systems are equipped with style programs that program numerically controlled (NC) machines to make first-draft "clean models." Others can automatically make line drawings based on the dimensional measurements of the final mock-up. There are also some systems that can make design drawings for the detailed body design.

The CAM technology of the CAD/CAM system has been used to design press dies and to make them using CAM-programmed NC machining centers. Almost every Japanese automaker now uses a CAM system for die design and fabrication.

Another popular computer application in car design work is the computer-based simulation system, which is often used in structural analysis. In this instance, the computer simulates the vibration stroke against the suspension to check the suspension's vibration characteristics. These kinds of computer applications fall under the category of Computer-aided Engineering (CAE).

### NEW CAR PROTOTYPE PROCESS

The design process runs concurrently with the prototype fabrication and test/evaluation process. This prototype process is needed early on so that the designers can see as soon as possible how their designs actually work and can make corrective changes. The prototype process is a cycle with several steps.

As illustrated in Figure 6-5, the three main steps in the prototype process are the (1) initial prototype, (2) official prototype, and (3) production prototype. The development of each prototype takes place via the following process.

*Make and/or buy prototype dies and jigs → Make and/or buy prototype parts → Conduct acceptance inspection of*

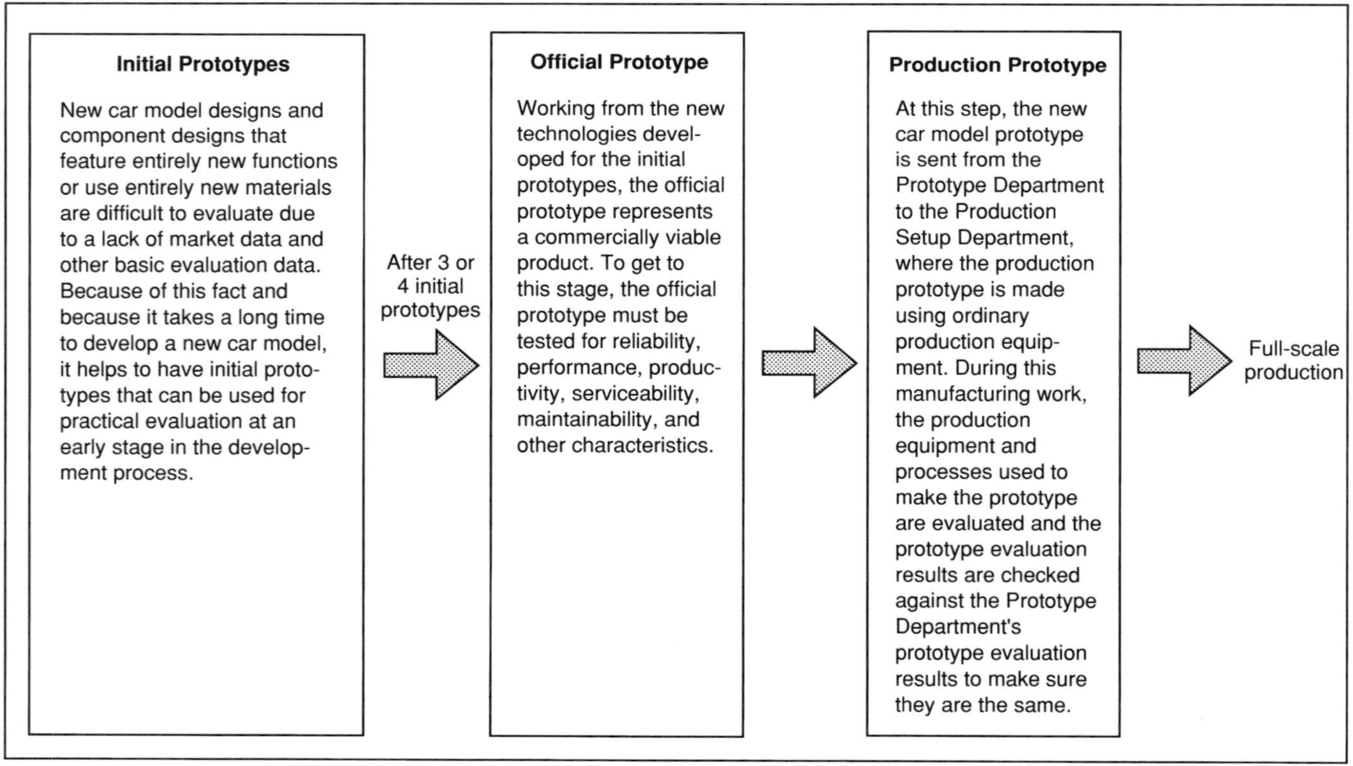

## Initial Prototypes

New car model designs and component designs that feature entirely new functions or use entirely new materials are difficult to evaluate due to a lack of market data and other basic evaluation data. Because of this fact and because it takes a long time to develop a new car model, it helps to have initial prototypes that can be used for practical evaluation at an early stage in the development process.

After 3 or 4 initial prototypes

## Official Prototype

Working from the new technologies developed for the initial prototypes, the official prototype represents a commercially viable product. To get to this stage, the official prototype must be tested for reliability, performance, productivity, serviceability, maintainability, and other characteristics.

## Production Prototype

At this step, the new car model prototype is sent from the Prototype Department to the Production Setup Department, where the production prototype is made using ordinary production equipment. During this manufacturing work, the production equipment and processes used to make the prototype are evaluated and the prototype evaluation results are checked against the Prototype Department's prototype evaluation results to make sure they are the same.

Full-scale production

**Figure 6-5. Prototype Process Flow**

*prototype parts → Send parts to presses → Press parts →*
*Weld on sheet metal parts → Assemble body shell → Paint*
*body shell → Assemble prototype vehicle → Inspect finished*
*prototype vehicle*

Naturally, a schedule must be made for all of the production processes required for this sequence of steps.

Almost all of the body welding work is done manually. After the body panels have been pressed, veteran welders perform the finish welding ("brazing") along with some spot welding. Recently, CAD/CAM systems and sophisticated industrial robots have taken over some of this work.

At the initial prototype step, the new car model's unit components are manufactured and tested even before the car's style has been finalized. In many cases, the people who make initial prototypes simply remodel unit components from current car models to make them resemble the new-model design.

Also at this step, the engine room produces a full-size engine mock-up as realistically as possible and studies the layout and assembly logistics of the various unit components in the engine. Sometimes, the new car model is scheduled to offer a wide selection of engines and transmission types, and in such cases several mock-ups must be made at the initial prototype step.

The official prototype step includes three generations of prototypes. The prototype testing process at this step involves checking characteristics ranging from reliability and performance to productivity, serviceability, and maintainability. Reports on problems identified during this testing are fed back to the designers who must then come up with corrective improvements.

The processing of manufacturing and testing three generations of official prototypes easily can involve the manufacture of more than 300 prototype cars. The production cost for each prototype, exclusive of labor costs, comes to several hundred thousand dollars, and even more for luxury models. Consequently, Toyota and other car makers must budget nearly $8 million for the prototype process for each new car model.

Toyota carries out four or five model changes per year, which means its prototype factories turn out more than 1,000 prototypes in a year. When the final, third-generation official prototype has been produced, the prototype work shifts to the production prototype step. Here, too, there are at least two generations of prototypes, and various detailed checks are made on each prototype.

## NEW CAR TESTING AND EVALUATION PROCESS

This is the most time- and labor-consuming part of the new car development process. The people involved in new car development estimate that about half of all the energy they spend to develop a new car is spent in the new car testing and evaluation process.

The multitude of test categories include dynamic characteristics, ride comfort, drivability, and safety. All together, there are some 200 kinds of tests and 3,200 specific test items. Because each new car model has thousands of possible component combinations, the evaluation standards must differ from one combination to the next to account for each combination's different characteristics that require evaluation.

To help rationalize the complex testing schedule, most automakers have established a Computer-aided Testing (CAT) system. The tests are broadly divided into two groups:

1. *Tests to confirm basic functions and reliability.*

    The contents and evaluation criteria for these tests have been standardized to a large degree, so that much of these tests have become routine work. Usually, the results are fed back to the designers. Some of these tests have been moved back to earlier development stages, such as the initial prototype step or steps where CAE systems are used.

As mentioned earlier, there are thousands of test items, and these are carried out thoroughly to check the quality of each part. Typical of the best Japanese manufacturing, these tests are based on the user's perspective and are designed to take into account every imaginable user need.

2. *Running tests to check for road performance characteristics.*

These tests, which include indoor tests, test-course performance tests, and road tests on actual public roads, are designed to evaluate the car's overall performance characteristics and its "feel" for the driver and passengers.

## TOYOTA'S CHIEF ENGINEER SYSTEM

As mentioned earlier, a chief engineer is assigned to each new Toyota car under development as the person most responsible for that development project. In other words, the chief engineer is the chief developer. Let us now take a closer look at Toyota's chief engineer system. (Much of the material in this section is borrowed from Shigeru Shiozawa's book *Toyota Motor's Development Chief System* [Toyota Jidosha Kaihatsu Shusa Seido], published by Kodansha in 1987.)

It has long been thought that sales is Toyota's greatest strength. Just after World War II, Toyota's Shōtarō Kamiya successfully led an ambitious campaign to build a comprehensive nationwide sales network. Without a doubt, a company's sales strength is derived largely from the numbers of its sales outlets and sales staff. This was definitely the case at Toyota.

However, no matter what the product is, it takes more than a sales organization to make it sell — the product must also have sales appeal. In Japan, Nissan's Cima model of luxury cars and Asahi's "super-dry" beer are two recent examples of hot-selling products whose success has been based primarily upon product sales strength. In other words, if a company can develop a product that responds to user needs with perfect accuracy, it will be a big seller. Product strength, or marketability, therefore remains a key factor in product development.

How, then, does the chief engineer system operate at Toyota for the development of new car models?

Toyota's Product Planning Office occupies the fifth and sixth floors (about 300 square meters) of Engineering Building No. 6 at the company's head office in Toyoda City.

On the fifth floor, there are eleven chief engineer teams for passenger cars (private vehicles); on the sixth floor, there are almost twenty chief engineer teams for commercial vehicles (including wagons, vans, trucks, and buses). Each team has its own group of desks.

The members on each chief engineer team for passenger cars number between ten and fifteen. Most of them are of middle-management rank such as section chief or chief clerk, who do not work directly on the line but have specialist management duties.

The Product Planning Center is a relatively small division staffed by about 500 people, including managers. However, four of these people are of executive-director rank. This attests to the decidedly strong emphasis Toyota places upon new car development. It can even be said that the Production Planning Office is the nucleus of the entire company.

What is the role of the chief engineer team members? Let us suppose that, for example, a member of a particular chief engineer's team is someone on loan from one of the design offices in the Design Division. His or her responsibilities naturally would include communicating the chief engineer's intentions to the design offices, listening to their reactions, and reporting back to the chief engineer. Thus, based on background, this individual becomes the chief engineer's design liaison agent.

Likewise, team members that come from other divisions function as liaison agents with their "home" divisions, facilitating two-way communication regarding new designs for engines, car bodies, interior components, and so on.

How does someone rise up through the ranks at Toyota to become a chief engineer? Let us consider a few typical examples. After graduating from a technical university (in the machinery department), Employee A joins Toyota and spends his first eight years there working in the Design Division. While in the Design Department, he participated in the design of Corolla and Corolla II models. Next, he was assigned to the Product Planning Office to be a member of the chief engineer teams for new models in the Celica and Carina lines. Finally, he was promoted to chief engineer for the next new Celica model.

Here is another example: Employee B graduated from the industrial design department at an industrial arts university and joined Toyota to put his specialty (design of mass-produced industrial products) to work. Naturally, he was also assigned to Toyota's Design Division. Later, he was promoted to the Product Planning Office, where he was a member of the chief engineer teams (an assistant chief engineer, in fact) for new models of the Corona and the Mark II. Finally, he was promoted to chief engineer for new models in the Soarer line and other lines.

A third and final example: This person graduated from the machinery department at a technical university, then joined Toyota, where he first worked in the Vibration Testing Department. After a stint there, as well as in the departments that test and evaluate chassis and handling characteristics, he was assigned to an R&D team and later to the Chassis Design Section to help design the chassis for a new Crown model. Next, he was promoted to the Product Planning Office, where he was a member of the chief engineer teams for new models of the Celica and Carina. After a time in the Product Technology Development Section, he was returned to the Product Planning Office and was made chief engineer for the fifth-generation Corolla, and later for the sixth-generation Corolla.

All three of these examples are typical of the process by which Toyota employees become chief engineers. Generally, they begin either as line-based designers or employees in the Design Division. In either instance they acquire experience by helping to develop new car models. Next, they join the Product Planning Office and serve as chief engineer team members for certain models. Finally, they are promoted to the position of chief engineer.

Incidentally, we might note that Toyota currently has twenty passenger car lines, each of which includes thousands of variations. The Corolla, for example, includes the following eight body types:

1. sedan four-door 1,500-cc GL Saloon
2. sedan five-door 1,660-cc ZX
3. three-door 1,600-cc FX-GT
4. five-door 1,500-cc FX-G
5. levin three-door GTV
6. levin two-door GT
7. wagon 1,800-cc diesel GL
8. four-door van 1,800-cc diesel GL

As a result, each car line competes for the same users, establishing a strong rivalry among the chief engineers of each car line.

There are other matters of interpersonal relations that come into play in the Design Planning Office. For example, if a chief engineer selects a certain newly designed part to use in his or her car but another chief engineer has already ordered the same part design, the latecomer must get permission from the earlier chief engineer before using the part.

Although all eleven passenger-car chief engineers have their desks on the same floor, there is still a keen sense of rivalry among them. Each works with a strong sense of independence. By contrast, there is little discord between chief engineers and their team members, who work very closely for the duration of the development project.

Since there are only eleven passenger-car chief engineers for twenty passenger car models, all but one of the chief engineers is responsible for at least two passenger car models. For example, the chief engineer for the Corolla, which alone accounts for about a quarter of Toyota's total sales, is also the chief engineer for the Sprinter and for the Nova cars produced in America by NUMMI, a Toyota-GM joint venture company.

Toyota adopted this chief engineer system back in 1953, when the growing variety of Toyota models made it no longer feasible for Toyota's president to assume direct responsibility for each new model's development.

### THE CHIEF ENGINEER'S ROLE IN THE MATRIX ORGANIZATION

In the previous section, we examined the chief engineer system at Toyota, in which a matrix organization mixes model-specific chief engineers with representatives from various company divisions such as design and testing and evaluation. In this matrix, the division representatives are the horizontal threads in the matrix and stand for line-based work; the chief engineers make up the vertical threads as independent product developers.

The chief engineer for each new car model is just one person and must be able to direct the thorough implementation of the development plan and assume the ultimate authority and responsibility for the overall product development process and its results.

As was shown in the matrix diagram, chief engineers are not line-based workers but management staff workers. Therefore, their authority is not limited to a particular part of the company. Their daily work mainly involves going from department to department to instruct and persuade people. Chief engineers have the authority to issue "development manuals" for their new car models to all relevant company divisions. However, there is no guarantee that the staff in those divisions will carry out the chief engineers' instructions to the letter.

For example, let us suppose a chief engineer issues instructions for a certain type of body design. If he or she gets firm opposition from the team member who represents the body design department (and is consequently ranked at about section-chief level), the idea must be dropped. Even though the chief engineer clearly outranks the opposing team member, the latter has the right to oppose the chief engineer's proposals. Therefore, it is very important that the chief engineer be able to persuade the team members of the value of his or her proposals. The team members are like the arms and legs of chief engineers — they must coordinate them and work closely with them to get anything done. This can be a difficult job, indeed.

Fortunately, chief engineers work directly with their team members, which facilitates this kind of persuasion. However, it is not always easy for the team members to get the instructions carried out by the divisions they represent, whether it be the design division, engine division, or whatever. In each division, corresponding team members have a series of managers

— supervisors, section chiefs, chief clerks, and so on down the management line — that they must persuade, and everyone's cooperation is needed to make the details of the development project happen.

Over the many years of the chief engineer system, Toyota has developed a smoothly functioning system in which the chief engineers enjoy very strong authority and influence in accordance with the "ten-point code of ethics for chief engineers" that will be described next. As a result, it rarely happens that instructions passed down from the chief engineer's team are not carried out as intended.

In a sense, chief engineers are like orchestra conductors. They alone have the baton and alone are ultimately responsible for the harmony of the music. They help to create the music by communicating their intentions to the orchestra members. Therefore, they must be more than managers — they also must inspire those whom they direct with their ideas and strong convictions. This type of inspiration runs throughout the orchestra or, in Toyota's case, throughout the company. Chief engineers must not only be conductors but also philosophers.

Recognizing that it takes a person of exceptional qualities to successfully fill the important post of chief engineer, Toyota promotes a code of ethics for chief engineers. It was written and handed down by Tatsuo Hasegawa, chief engineer of both the first and second generations of Toyota's biggest seller, the Corolla. Toyota's "Ten-point Code of Ethics for Engineers" states the following:

1. Chief engineers must cultivate wide knowledge and keen insight.
2. Chief engineers must possess a personal strategy and plan.
3. Chief engineers must spread a wide and beneficial web of influence.

4. Chief engineers must apply their knowledge and abilities to attain good results.
5. Chief engineers must not begrudge repetitive work.
6. Chief engineers must possess self-confidence.
7. Chief engineers must never pass the buck.
8. Chief engineers and their team members must all be of good character. Any criticism within the team should be made as self-criticism.
9. Chief engineers must make themselves well understood.
10. Chief engineers must possess the following qualities:
    * knowledge and skill
    * perceptiveness, keen judgment, and decisiveness
    * ability to see the large-scale picture
    * lack of emotionalism and a quiet, calm attitude
    * energy and persistence
    * concentration
    * leadership ability
    * expressiveness and persuasiveness
    * flexibility
    * selflessness (unselfishness).

Let us examine some of the more important of the ten points in the code of ethics.

Point 5, not begrudging repetitive work, has to do with the injunction that chief engineers should reflect each day on their day's thoughts and actions. They should not hesitate to emphasize repeatedly important matters when working with higher-ups or co-workers.

This relates to Point 6, which is to have self-confidence. While this does not mean self-confidence to the point of obstinacy, it does mean overcoming any sense of ambivalence about one's abilities. People who are self-confident can calmly devise good plans even under stressful circumstances. (This self-confidence should be tempered with the flexibility mentioned in Point 10.) The combination of self-confidence and flexibility is what we sometimes call "tact" — chief engineers should sense when it is necessary to make compromises and propose face-saving alternatives.

In sum, the purpose of the code of ethics is to help cultivate people who have both a broad perspective and a discerning, decisive sense of authority and leadership.

It might pay to ask why the post of chief engineer is a general management post (staff position) not directly attached to a line of authority in any particular division. The reason is that if chief engineers were at the direct top of a division, their instructions would have to be followed as direct orders. The managers and workers in the division would not work with as much energy or enthusiasm if they were simply following orders. No one at Toyota is too highly ranked to ignore the importance of major model changes when each model change incurs total development costs of more than $230 million. Model changes, although devised by chief engineers, do not get off to a real start until the chief engineers have convinced top management of their worth. If an initial presentation to top managers meets with objections, the chief engineer must come up with materials to persuade the objectors to change their minds.

### THE CHIEF ENGINEER'S PHILOSOPHY

What kind of concepts and philosophy do chief engineers embrace as a basis for gaining support from others?

This relates to the question of what kind of car will be in demand by society over the next few years. It takes four years to develop a new car model, and the market life of each new model is also four years. Therefore, from the initial planning stage, designers must look eight years forward in considering such marketing factors as social environment, economic conditions, industrial structure, consumer groups, life-styles, trends among competitors, and technological trends. In short, planners must attempt to predict what the market mainstream will appear like several years in the future.

Already, consumers in Japan have everything that would be considered a necessity. This has created a new era of greater discretion among consumers, who can choose from among various luxury products as well as necessities. Young people no longer simply try to accumulate fancy products. Instead, they are aiming toward a new kind of affluence in which the products they buy are expressions of their life-style. When they shop for a car, they evaluate the models they see not only in terms of price and functions but also in terms of their image as "urban" or "high-tech" and so on. In other words, they want to buy a car that fits in with what they perceive as their life-style and personal values. This point was emphasized by Mr. Fumio Agetsuma, who was the chief engineer of the fourth-generation Corolla. When designing this Corolla, he came up with five key points for ensuring a successful model change:

1. Attractive design.
2. Economy, not just in terms of low fuel consumption but also in terms of high durability and reliability, and superb serviceability. (The latter factors add up to lower maintenance costs.)
3. Riding comfort for driver and passengers.
4. The introduction of new technologies and mechanisms. Model changes have no impact if they use the same engine as the previous model.
5. Competitive pricing.

More recently, of the three key elements in any passenger-car "hit" product, namely style, engine, and suspension, style has come to the forefront as the most important element. Whether it be in a catalog or on a television commercial, the consumer's first impression of the car is always its style. A car whose style turns off buyers will not sell, no matter how excellent the engine and suspension might be. Conversely, if the car's style is attractive, that alone will bring prospective buyers into the dealerships, where they can begin looking at other features, such as the engine and suspension.

Does the chief engineer's philosophy become incorporated directly and wholly into the new model he or she is in charge of developing? In determining the most important element — the car's styling — and especially the car exterior design as described earlier, the chief engineer must work with other managers in the relevant departments in the manner to be described.

First, the chief engineer presents his or her ideas. Explaining the car exterior design ideas to the design managers may involve several rounds of discussions, during which everyone arrives at an understanding concerning not only the design dimensions but also the mood of the design. They draw image sketches to illustrate these ideas. Next, a 5-to-1 scale model is built and shown to sales managers. After that, a full-scale model is built. This model is then presented at a new car development meeting, where designers and sales managers can offer their opinions. These meetings are attended by top managers, such as the chairman or president, and usually produce some improvements to determine the final style.

While the chief engineer's ideas are the foundation, the final style also incorporates input, or suggested improvements, of other people from various departments. Therefore, the decision-making process that produces the final car design is a consensus-building process. This process of decision-making by consensus has been pointed out as a disadvantage by some critics who argue that it tends to produce cars that lack flair and distinctiveness due to the lack of individuality in the design process.

## CHAPTER 7

# Production Management System: Integration of SIS, CIM, and JIT

ADVANCES IN computer-based data communications technologies have enabled manufacturing companies to build in-house information networks and to set up data communications linkages with sales companies, parts contractors, and material suppliers.

## SIS, CIM, AND JIT

Strategic Information System (SIS) utilizes the word "strategic" because the very existence of such an information system has strategic significance. It is *not* an information system that serves the company by distributing "strategic information."

When an entire group of companies is linked by an information network such as an SIS, with each sales company, final products manufacturer, and supplier interconnected as members of an integrated network, information on current market needs can reach the right people very quickly.

In other words, information concerning demand changes in the marketplace (such as changes in consumer preferences and sales trends for certain product types and quantities) can be passed swiftly along to the people in product development, sales, production, and parts procurement, who in turn can respond more quickly. This adds up to a more responsive company or corporate group.

At Toyota, much labor has gone into the development of a strategic information system called the Toyota Network System (TNS). Within TNS, Toyota has an in-house production information system called Assembly Line Control (ALC). ALC includes information used in Computer-aided Manufacturing (CAM) and Computer-aided Planning (CAP) systems, both of which fall under the general category of Computer-integrated Manufacturing (CIM). Another element in CIM is Computer-aided Design (CAD). We discussed CAD in Chapter 6 and will not study it again here.

To enable practical application of SIS and CIM at the factory level, Toyota has developed a production management infrastructure that is referred to as the Toyota production system or the just-in-time (JIT) production system. Its main elements include the *kanban* system, production leveling, and improvement activities.

This chapter briefly describes how production managers at Toyota have utilized SIS, CIM, and JIT in their production management organization.

### TOYOTA'S STRATEGIC INFORMATION SYSTEM

A SIS or CIM must include more than a computer-based communications network. One key element in the Toyota Group's SIS is the *order entry system* by which sales companies (dealers, etc.) pass along orders and other sales data to the parent company (Toyota Motors).

Another key element is the mechanism for converting the sales data received by Toyota into instructions for production scheduling. This conversion of data to production orders must be done not only for Toyota's own production operations but also for those of Toyota's many parts suppli-

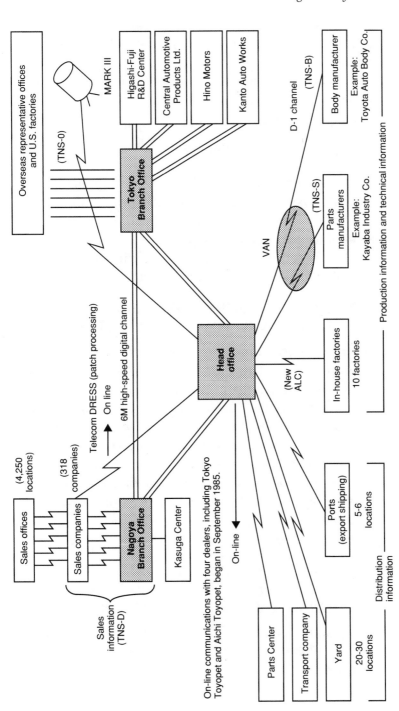

**Figure 7-1. TNS: Toyota's Strategic Information System**

ers. Figure 7-1 illustrates Toyota's TNS, its strategic information system.

The TNS shown in Figure 7-1 includes the following six subsystems:

1. TNS-D: a network linking Toyota with its dealers
2. TNS-B: a network linking Toyota with its body manufacturers
3. TNS-S: a network linking Toyota with its suppliers
4. New ALC system: New automobile production order system (for Toyota's in-house production)
5. Sales office information system
6. TNS-O: a network linking Toyota with its overseas assembly plants and representative offices

### TNS-D: ORDER ENTRY SYSTEM BETWEEN TOYOTA AND TOYOTA DEALERS

Toyota uses information from its dealers when planning production schedules. There are two main steps in this process. Step 1 determines the estimated production schedule for the following month. (This is mainly the master production schedule for finished products and the parts delivery table.) Step 2 determines daily production orders for implementing the daily production schedule. (This consists primarily of setting up a delivery timetable for finished products and an assembly line feed-in sequence of parts for various product models.)

Let us examine these two steps more closely.

### STEP 1: DETERMINE THE MONTHLY PRODUCTION SCHEDULE (MASTER PRODUCTION SCHEDULE AND PARTS DELIVERY TABLE)

This step starts with sales plans sent from the sales divisions. These plans relate to both domestic and overseas sales divisions.

Toyota dealers in Japan send the domestic sales division a monthly report forecasting demand for each product line over the next three months. These demand forecast figures are tallied up under product-line categories and major specification categories. Also monthly, the overseas sales division receives overseas orders for the next three months. These figures also are categorized in some detail concerning product specifications.

The production planning division coordinates these two sources of demand information into a single production plan for the next three months. The total volume of finished products (automobiles) to be produced during the first month is divided into daily output figures for each product line. This division is oriented toward *production leveling*, allowing an even work load during all regular working days. The resulting schedule is called the *master production schedule.*

The major specification categories include various combinations of body type, engine type (classified by piston displacement, fuel consumption, etc.), transmission type (gear shift method, etc.), and product grade (luxury car, etc.).

Next, a bill of materials is made up based on the master production schedule to establish a materials requirement plan (MRP). Whether they call it MRP or something else, all automakers have some plan by which they estimate the required parts and materials.

Once it has the data on required materials and parts, Toyota notifies its own assembly plants and its affiliated suppliers of its needs. These notices are called *parts delivery tables.*

However, as we will examine in more detail later on, the parts and materials suppliers are not expected to follow the parts delivery table to the letter. Instead, their daily production volumes are determined primarily by the more detailed and up-to-date instructions that circulate under the kanban system.

## STEP 2: DETERMINE THE DAILY PRODUCTION SCHEDULE (FEED-IN SEQUENCE)

At this step, the production planners must figure out exactly how many cars to produce in each model and specification category. The final assembly feed-in sequence is determined as follows, based on ten-day and single-day orders received from dealers. We will examine each of these steps.

*Step 1:* Dealers send in their ten-day orders to the Toyota sales division office in Nagoya.

*Step 2:* The Toyota sales division also receives daily orders (also called daily revisions) from dealers.

*Step 3:* The sales division sends the daily order information to the manufacturing division.

*Step 4:* The detailed data concerning daily feed-in schedules are sent to the relevant Toyota assembly plants and affiliated suppliers.

Step 1 involves dealers sending in their ten-day orders to the Toyota sales division. These ten-day orders must remain

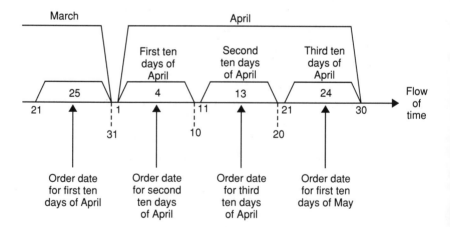

**Figure 7-2. Reception of Ten-day Orders from Dealers**

within the framework of total monthly volume set by the master production schedule. One week or eight days prior to production, the dealers send the Toyota sales division ten-day orders that indicate the selected options for each final specification category. (See Figure 7-2.) The final specifications combine the major specifications described earlier and the selected options and colors.

The production management divisions uses these ten-day orders to plan daily production volumes for each assembly line and each product line. This represents a revision of the master production plan.

Next, the production planners use the actual customer-specified orders to revise (within a range of plus or minus 10 percent) the production orders derived from the total orders sent to the sales division from dealers across the country. (See

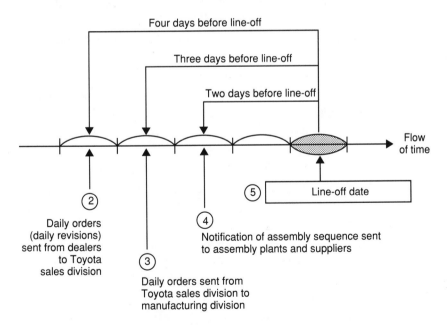

**Figure 7-3. Steps from Dealer Orders to Line-off**

Figure 7-3.) For example, to accommodate a customer-specified order, they might change the color of a car scheduled for shipment on June 1 from white to red. These *daily revisions* are made four days prior to the date when the finished car is scheduled to roll off the line.

Daily revisions are allowable within the framework of the number of vehicles scheduled for each dealer. Ten-day orders can be revised up to about 23 percent. The average revision is about 10 percent, which is why we used the figure of 10 percent in describing the daily revisions.

Next, the computers in the Toyota sales division sort out the dealer orders according to car model, body type, engine type, grade, transmission type, color, and so on.

Once sorted out, these data are sent to Toyota assembly plants three days before the line-off date for the ordered automobiles. There is no way to overemphasize the importance of these data — they are what tell the Toyota assembly plant managers exactly what they will be required to produce in three days time.

Finally, the manufacturing division uses daily revision data from the sales division to set up a feed-in sequence for the mixed assembly lines. Even without any delays, the assembly plant has only two days before the line-off date to prepare for the feed-in sequence.

Notice that the feed-in sequence schedules are made and issued on a daily basis. Figure 7-3 illustrates the ordering process from Steps 2 to 4. Thanks to this four-step ordering process, there is a period of only four days between the sales division's receipt of the dealer's order and the ordered automobile rolling off the assembly line. The actual manufacturing-line lead time, from the start of the body welding line to the end of the final assembly line, is only one day.

Naturally, the lead time for shipping the ordered cars to the dealers varies according to the distance and transport system between the assembly plant and the dealer.

## HOW THE ASSEMBLY LINE USES THE
## FEED-IN SEQUENCE DATA

On the assembly line, the only thing the line workers need to know is the type of automobile to be assembled next. The final assembly line has a computer terminal with a CRT display and printer to receive and display this information.

The data indicating the kind of automobile to assemble next are sent from the central computer, which calculates the data based on the feed-in sequence schedule. These data are sent to the display terminal via an on-line real-time communications link.

In addition to displaying various other information, this display terminal also prints out an adhesive label for each car to be assembled, stating its model and specifications. The assembly line workers read these labels to see exactly what kind of car they are to make. Toyota uses labels and feed-in sequence schedules at its assembly lines only. To control the production volume at almost all other processes from forging to machining and subassembly, Toyota uses the kanban system.

Labels and feed-in sequences are used frequently by suppliers who supply main assembly components to the final assembly line, such as transmissions and engines. This is based on the production concept of the *sequential pull method.* Feed-in sequences are used sometimes at body welding lines and painting lines.

The feed-in sequence for wide-variety, small-lot production of subassembly parts directs the operations of subassembly lines and parts supplier lines. As such, they are coordinated with the feed-in sequence schedules at the Toyota final assembly lines, which "pull" the required subassembled parts through the various upstream lines.

Apart from these lines, all other parts production processes and supplier lines are regulated by the kanban system. In other words, the kanban system functions as a "supply support" system for the sequential pull production system.

### DISTRIBUTION-LEVEL ON-LINE SYSTEM

After receiving a customer order, the dealer naturally would like the lead time to delivery to be as short as possible. This includes the time required for processing the order information. To help dealers respond more quickly to customer orders with shorter delivery periods, Toyota has built an on-line communications network to link the company with its dealers and to expedite daily order processing.

This on-line Toyota-dealer network uses the nationwide optical fiber cable route that recently has been put into operation by NTT, Japan's largest telephone company. This route is known as Japan's most extensive high-speed, high-capacity digital trunk route.

The network links central mainframe computers in the Toyota head office in Toyoda City and the branch office in Nagoya with computers and terminals at Toyota dealerships. Every day, the dealers send in their order data, which go immediately into the four-step ordering process described previously to minimize delivery lead time.

This network supports three main types of communication functions: real-time processing, file transfer, and electronic mail. In addition, Toyota has developed its own business protocol to enable linkage between various types of computers. This utilizes a basic element in the standard protocol referred to as open systems interconnection (OSI).

This OSI network has made various kinds of activities possible. First, it enables Toyota to keep close tabs on the product stock data maintained by each dealer. It also enables dealers to meet orders quickly by providing each other with ordered cars that are already in stock at a neighboring dealership. In addition, it allows Toyota to make last-minute changes, such as sending a certain car to Dealer B instead of Dealer A — if Dealer B needs it more urgently.

The network also enables Toyota to inform dealers of the latest trends regarding fast-selling and slow-selling car models and to provide dealers with advice on making orders. This is the same kind of information-sharing that occurs at department stores and supermarkets via POS (point-of-sale) communication systems.

These kinds of communications between Toyota and its dealers are centered in the Nagoya branch office (formerly the head office of the now-defunct Toyota Motor Sales Company).

### OVERSEAS INFORMATION NETWORK (TNS-O)

This is the basic communication network linking Toyota in Japan with Toyota America in the United States. These connections are made via ordinary public telephone lines and enable Toyota to stay in direct touch with its assembly plants and offices in various parts of North America. By keeping track of order data, shipping data, and parts distribution data in a timely manner, it helps Toyota provide better service to customers.

## INFORMATION SYSTEM BETWEEN TOYOTA AND ITS SUPPLIERS

### PARTS DELIVERY TABLE

As the finished product manufacturer, once a month Toyota sends its parts manufacturers an estimate of its production output for the next three months. This notification is made in the form of a *parts delivery table* as shown in Figure 7-4. The parts manufacturers use the contents of this table for the next month to estimate how many parts they will need to deliver each day. The figures for the subsequent two months are looser estimates that are subject to revision in the parts delivery table to be issued next month.

Sometimes, the production output is changed slightly even during the current month. These minor changes are the parts delivery adjustments made under the kanban system.

Under this system, the finished product manufacturers sends out a parts delivery table to each of its parts suppliers. This table specifies (using part numbers) the quantity of each type of part to be delivered. The following shows the total amounts to be delivered of one type of part (Part C, for example) during a three-month period.

The parts delivery table shows the following three-month estimates for Part C:

1. Parts to be delivered during the month of May 199X: 1,600
2. Estimated parts to be delivered during June: 1,600
3. Estimated parts to be delivered during July: 1,700

The total for (1) is a fairly accurate figure that is subject only to minor adjustment under the kanban system. The totals for (2) and (3) are more loosely estimated figures that are subject to change in the next monthly parts delivery table. To save space, Figure 7-4 shows only the information for (1).

The parts delivery table also specifies how many parts are in each case (10, in this example).

The table shows the daily and monthly totals for each type of part to be delivered. Since May in Japan contains several national and company holidays, we can see that zero parts were delivered on May 3, 4, 5, 11, 12, 18, 19, 25, or 26. During the twenty-two workdays in the month of May, the amount delivered has been leveled out to seven cases per day.

Actually, seven cases per day for twenty-two days equals $(7 \times 10 \times 22 =)$ 1,540 parts, which leaves a shortage of

| Delivery by: _____ | | | | | **Parts Delivery Table (May)** | | | | | | | | | Issue date: April 22 |
|---|---|---|---|---|---|---|---|---|---|---|---|---|---|---|

| | Delivery trips | | | Number of kanban | Difference from previous trip | Cases per day (1 case = 10 units) | | | | | | | Total part units for month of May |
|---|---|---|---|---|---|---|---|---|---|---|---|---|---|
| | | | | | | 1st | 2nd | 3rd | ~ | 29th | 30th | 31st | |
| Part A | 1 | 14 | 3 | 4 | –1 | 8 | 8 | 0 | | 8 | 8 | 8 | 1,718 |
| Part B | 1 | 14 | 3 | 3 | 0 | 6 | 5 | 0 | | 5 | 5 | 4 | 1,020 |
| Part C | 1 | 10 | 2 | 3 | –1 | 7 | 7 | 0 | | 7 | 7 | 7 | 1,600 |
| Part D | 1 | 14 | 2 | 19 | 3 | 44 | 44 | 0 | | 44 | 44 | 44 | 9,761 |
| Part E | 1 | 14 | 3 | 2 | –1 | 5 | 5 | 0 | | 5 | 5 | 5 | 1,141 |
| Part F | 1 | 10 | 2 | 1 | 0 | 1 | 0 | 0 | | 1 | 0 | 0 | 94 |

**Figure 7-4. Parts Delivery Table**

sixty parts. To deliver these missing sixty parts, we could add an extra case to the daily delivery total, but that would mean a surplus of 160 parts. Instead, we should make up the shortage by assigning six eight-case days and by spreading those days out during the month as every third or fourth workday.

## TOYOTA GROUP VAN

Toyota has made a number of developments in building an information system for communicating with suppliers.

Several years ago, Toyota established a value-added network (VAN) to provide an on-line link with major Toyota Group parts manufacturers such as Nippondenso, Toyoda Boshoku, and Toyoda Automatic Loom Works. More recently, Toyota established an on-line network with its major auto body contractors, which includes Toyota Auto Body, Kanto Auto Works, and Daihatsu Motor.

Companies that are linked to Toyota via these kinds of networks now receive parts delivery tables and exchange other data by computer communications instead of by hand delivery of documents or magnetic tape.

## NETWORK WITH AUTO BODY MANUFACTURERS (TNS-B)

There used to be situations in which a parts manufacturer would receive a parts delivery table from Toyota for a certain month's production much sooner than it received the parts delivery table for the same car from the Toyota-affiliated auto body manufacturer. Toyota's recently established TNS-B communication network has enabled the delivery of such tables and other information to be synchronized when desirable, as in this case. These kinds of data have been unified within the TNS-B network's central data base.

## PARTS TRANSPORT METHOD

The kanban system has led to more frequent delivery trips for parts suppliers. In response to rising transport costs, parts suppliers have decided to form a cooperative load-sharing system. Under this system, delivery trucks shared by two or more parts suppliers stop at several factories on their way to Toyota's delivery dock. This way, each supplier still makes frequent deliveries while making fewer trips of its own.

However, it is not always possible to work out a schedule for load-sharing because of Toyota's strict delivery time schedule for various parts. Consequently, the parts suppliers have organized a warehouse-type distribution center near the Toyota assembly plant that they can all deliver their parts to. A third-party transport company is responsible for delivering parts from the distribution center to the Toyota warehouse on an hourly basis in accordance with instructions written on the kanban cards.

The transport company's distribution center/warehouse holds one or two days of inventory. The transport company also passes on kanban to the parts suppliers.

The total number of delivery routes that would be required for all parts suppliers to deliver their goods directly to the Toyota assembly plant would number in the hundreds and result in unacceptably high transportation costs. The use of an intermediary warehouse, where parts are delivered and sorted before delivery to their destination assembly plants, has reduced the number of delivery routes to about ten. This third-party warehouse and delivery operation provides the additional benefit to parts manufacturers of serving as a distribution center for deliveries to clients other than Toyota.

## TOYOTA'S SIS DEVELOPMENTS

Toyota's Strategic Information System is the overall TNS, which as shown includes subsystems such as the TNS-D network linking Toyota with its dealers, the TNS-O network linking Toyota with its overseas assembly plants and representative offices, the TNS-S network linking Toyota with its suppliers, and the TNS-B network linking Toyota with its body manufacturers. These subsystems function beautifully. As of this writing, however, Toyota operates these subsystems independently and has yet to integrate them. Toyota manager Ei'ichi Sumibe remarked in 1990 that the TNS is not yet fully completed. They intend to establish mutual interconnections among subsystems, building an overall system that will enable product orders from sales outlets to be processed and sent directly to the relevant parts suppliers as parts orders.

Currently, system managers must take an active part in transferring information between TNS subsystems. To integrate all of the subsystems into a single Toyota Group TNS, Toyota must: (1) stay abreast of developments in Open System Interconnection (OSI) technology as a promising standard communications protocol, (2) unify and standardize the business protocol being used in the Toyota Group, and (3) devote further investment in TNS development as part of its mid- to long-term management strategy.

## MULTILAYERED, DECENTRALIZED FACTORY CONTROL SYSTEM

This section describes Toyota's version of computer-integrated manufacturing (CIM). At Toyota assembly plants, the system takes the form of a multilayered, decentralized factory control system. This long term simply means that each factory includes several autonomous subsystems that mutually adjust and control factory operations. The multilayered, decentralized factory control system also goes by the name compatible autonomous decentralized system.

Figure 7-5 illustrates the multilayered control system used by Toyota Group member Kanto Auto Works. The Kanto system was almost identical to the one used at Toyota assembly plants. Since then, however, a new system has been introduced at Toyota and will be described later.

1. The head office has a mainframe (host) computer for clerical data processing and each factory has a minicomputer connected to high-speed digital (optical fiber) communication channels.

2. At each factory, the minicomputers are linked via high-speed digital (optical fiber) communication channels to separate workstations for production control of various processes (such as the auto body processes, painting processes, and assembly processes).

3. The process-specific workstations are also called "line computers" since they are used to control the production lines. The line computers are connected as master computers to several smaller programmable controllers (PCs) that function as service units in performing tasks such as reading cards, printing out data, and controlling connected industrial robots and *andon* (alarm lamp) systems.

The functions of the line computers are described in more detail in Figure 7-6. (See Note 2 in the reference section.)

The minicomputer for each assembly plant is kept in an office called the assembly line control (ALC) room. Once a day, the host computer at the head office sends these ALC minicomputers feed-in sequence schedules and vehicle specifications files. The minicomputers then carry out daily distribution of files containing production schedule data to the process-specific line computers.

Once the process-specific line computers receive the production schedule data files, they control the processes

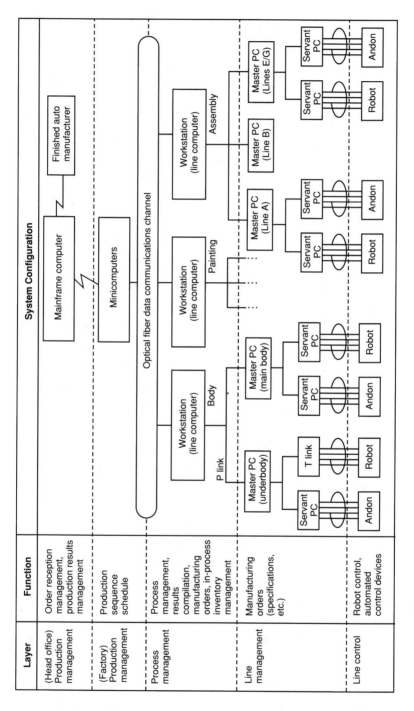

**Figure 7-5. Computer Control Functions in a Multilayered System**

independently and no longer rely upon the ALC room's minicomputer. Their only relationship with the minicomputer at this point is to send real-time progress report data to the ALC room.

Let us examine how process-specific control is carried out at the body assembly, painting, assembly, and inspection processes.

## CONTROL SYSTEM FOR THE BODY ASSEMBLY PROCESS

The workstation (line computer) at the body assembly process issues body assembly work instructions for each vehicle in accordance with the feed-in sequence schedule. This workstation includes a printer that prints out cards to indicate the vehicle body identification (ID) numbers. Each card is attached to the vehicle body it identifies and is read by card-reader devices at various points during the body assembly process. The specifications for each vehicle body are obtained via a file search of the line computer's file. Then the specifications are output as work instructions that are sent to the factory center where conditions in the body assembly process are monitored.

A magnetic card printer at the start of the shell body line prints out magnetic ID cards for each vehicle on the line. (See the magnetic card example in Figure 7-7.) The magnetic card printer operates according to instructions sent from the ALC room. The vehicle ID card shows the car's model number and is attached to the car at the start of the shell body line. This magnetic card is *not* a kanban. It has a magnetic strip across the bottom, much like the magnetic commuter train tickets now used in some urban subway systems. As the vehicle makes it way down the car body line, its magnetic card is read at various stages by card-readers, which send the magnetic card's data to the ALC room to update the display monitoring each vehicle's progress on the line.

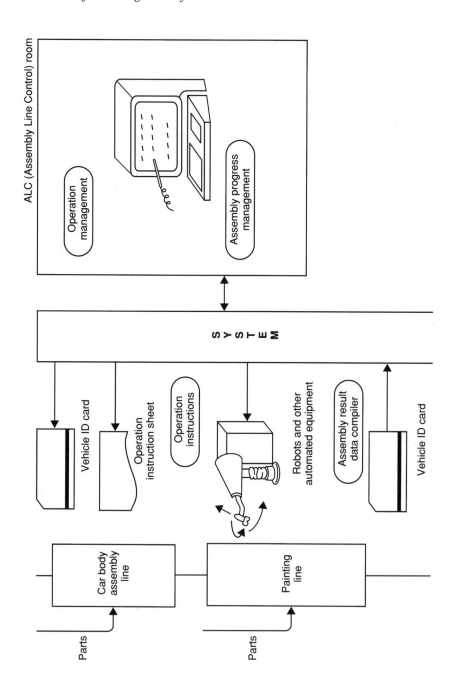

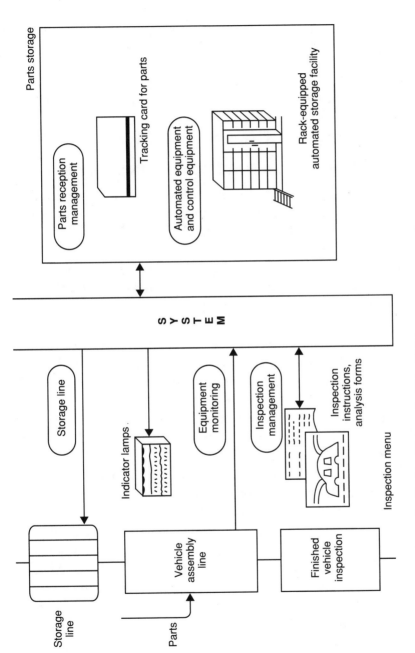

**Figure 7-6. Process-specific Line Computer Functions**

The line computer on the body line uses the factory line controller to issue vehicle ID cards and to control various equipment. For example, it selects the type of welding equipment needed according to the feed-in sequence and has that equipment brought to the side of the line in time to be used. It also manages the operation and changeover of automated body welding equipment that remains installed on the line.

## CONTROL SYSTEM FOR THE PAINTING PROCESS

The painting process also utilizes card readers connected to the process-specific line computer, which prints out work instructions for the line workers based on the magnetic card data.

More recently, Toyota has introduced another type of card-shaped ID device that contains an integrated circuit (IC chip) and can transmit wireless signals. These cards are used to indicate the progress of vehicles passing through the painting process. The IC-based ID cards (also known as ID tags) have a much larger data memory capacity than magnetic cards have and are used in various assembly lines in addition to the painting line.

The industrial robots and other automated equipment on the line read their work instructions from each ID card's specification data.

Each vehicle's ID number corresponds to its body number. The ID card continuously transmits signals as it moves through the painting process and thereby indicates exactly how far the vehicle has come and when the painting process is finished. The ID card is highly resistant to heat and is not damaged when it gets painted along with its vehicle. After the painting process is finished, a worker shuts off the transmitter switch on the ID card.

The painting line operates under the following two types of sequence control:

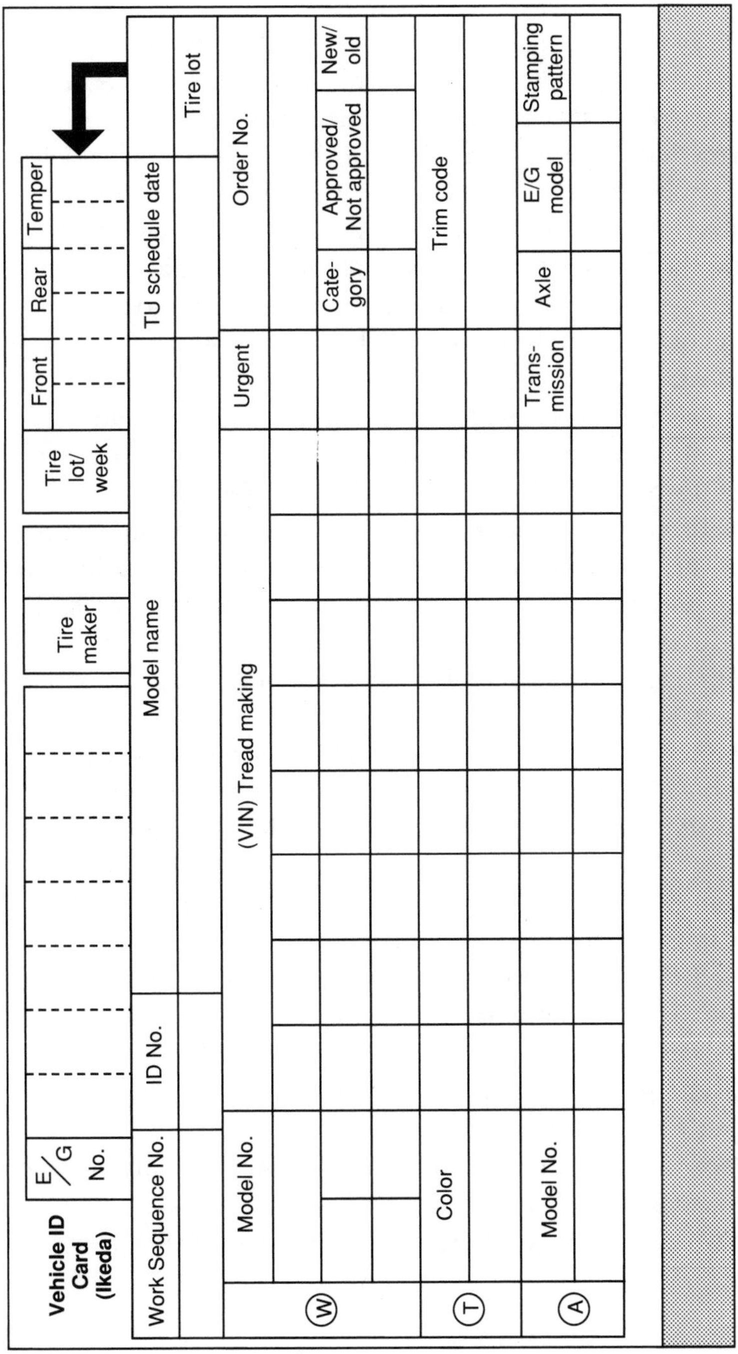

Vehicle ID Card (Ikeda)

E/G No.

Tire maker

Tire lot/week

| Front | Rear | Temper |
|-------|------|--------|

Tire lot

Work Sequence No.

ID No.

Model name

TU schedule date

Model No.

(VIN) Tread making

Urgent

Order No.

Cate-gory

Approved/Not approved

New/old

Trim code

Color

Color

Trans-mission

Axle

E/G model

Stamping pattern

Model No.

(W)

(T)

(A)

**Figure 7-7. Magnetic Card**

The first type controls the feed-in and feed-out of car bodies to the storage line that is attached between the intermediate and final stages in the painting process. After the intermediate painting stage when the sequence of vehicles needs to be changed to obtain the maximum number of consecutive same-color car bodies in the final-stage painting booth, the sequence change is done in this storage line. This effectively cuts down on the number of paint color changeovers, which reduces both paint waste and changeover loss.

The second type of sequence control is feed-in and feed-out control of the painted-body storage line that follows the painting process. This storage line is used to change the order of vehicles before they enter the final assembly process. This is in response to real-time feed-in scheduling to obtain an optimum work-load balance on the final assembly line. Toyota employs an *expert system*, which is a computer system using artificial intelligence technology, to execute this sequential control.

The sequence in the painting line is susceptible to disruption due to the sorting out and repainting of car bodies that are found to have defective paint jobs. Repainting is always necessary for two-tone car bodies, and this makes sequential control quite complicated. When the car bodies exit the final stage in the painting process, freshly painted and suspended for drying, they must be put into the correct order for the final assembly line. The painted car bodies that enter the assembly process come from the painted-body storage line, where several painted car bodies are kept and their sequence rearranged.

Once the sequence of vehicles in the painted-body storage line has been worked out, the sequence information is input to the ALC room. The ALC room then sends the factory the corresponding sequence data for supplying engines and parts to the final assembly line.

Let us consider the Daihatsu assembly plant in Kyoto as an example. The Fuji Seat Company's factory is thirty minutes away from the assembly plant. Daihatsu's Shiga engine plant is an hour and a half away. However, after each vehicle enters the final assembly line, it takes two and a half hours to reach the engine installation stage. This allows enough time to order engine and seat supplies once the final assembly sequence has been determined.

## CONTROL SYSTEM FOR THE FINAL ASSEMBLY LINE

As each vehicle is placed onto the final assembly line, a card reader reads its ID card and prints out a sticker with assembly work instructions.

The most recent type of work instructions used at Toyota and some other companies utilize symbols (such as pictures or single letters) instead of words to indicate the vehicle model and other assembly specifications. These symbols are stored as files in a data base. A different set of symbols is issued to each vehicle as it enters the assembly line. The use of such labels makes it easier for newer line workers to read and understand the work instructions quickly. Figure 7-8 illustrates some of the work instruction labels used at a Kubota tractor assembly plant.

The line workers at the start of the assembly line attach the label to the hood of the vehicle and the line workers downstream follow the label's instructions as they work.

The final assembly line includes nearly 100 stages and the variety of parts is mind-boggling — for example, there are thirty different types of speedometers. Since all of these options cannot be specified on a single label attached to the car's hood, additional labels are added downstream.

Working in parallel with this assembly line are various subassembly lines for engines, tires, seats, and other assembled parts. Work instructions for these subassembly lines are also read from the ID card and issued to their respective destinations.

In addition to the printing out of work instruction labels, a *multilayered electronic loop* operates a set of work instruction indicator lamps on the shelves where parts are stored. The electronic loop consists of a main workstation connected to several (from ten to 200) personal computers, all connected in a daisy-chain configuration via a twisted-pair cable. This loop operates sets of indicator lamps installed on parts storage shelves to show the line workers which parts to select. Sometimes, the loop is connected to devices that automatically select the indicated type and quantity of parts or materials and feed them to the assembly line. (See Figure 7-9.)

## TOYOTA'S NEW ALC SYSTEM

Toyota first introduced its ALC system in 1966 and established a new ALC system in 1989 at its Tahara Plant. Since then it has introduced this new system to all of its other plants. (See Note 6 in the reference section.)

The design concepts behind this new ALC system naturally are based on the Toyota production system. They are intended to provide information on production needs on a just-in-time basis via a control system that is versatile and expandable.

These two systems — the ALC system and the Toyota production system — fit in with the multilayered, decentralized factory control system described earlier in this chapter. Toyota puts a strong emphasis on implementing the "pull system" approach to ensure a just-in-time flow of information.

Toyota uses an IBM mainframe as the head office's host computer. This mainframe is equipped with data-bank func-

| Line | Serial No. | ID No. | Model Name | Model No. | Specs | Page Issue Date |
|---|---|---|---|---|---|---|
| 003030 | -3917 | 1070926 | 19202-00000 (110 ) | V1902 | OEM 15 15 - 47 47 | 0032 11 15 / 0001 12 05 |
| Engine slat | | | V1902B | 63779 | | N CEA0403E |

| | | | | | |
|---|---|---|---|---|---|
| Cylinder head | Head gasket | Water temperature flag | Injection pump | Sym | Speed adjustment plate |
| **Green** | **G3** | **Equipment** | **Blue** | **Thickness = 2**  **0.45 = 2** | **15** |
| Gear case | Stud for speed adjustment plate | Valve sheet | Water pump | Water flange | Steering |
| 3 | 6 x 22 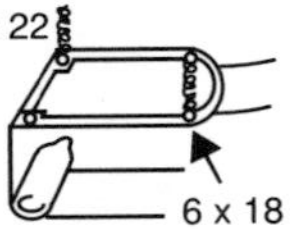   6 x 18 | **Carrier** | **Carrier** | Installation  Short Large Existing |  High idling |
| Fuel restrictions | Hour meter | Fuel pump | Engine hook | Jet cock | |
| | **Cover** | **Cover** 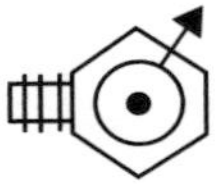 | | Long (exclusive) | **Blue** |
| Engine stop lever | Solenoid support | Fan-driven pulley | Oil gauge | Thermostat cover | Glow plug |
| | | | | Inlet hole   **19202** | Inlet manifold |
| | | | | Thermostat | Water drain |

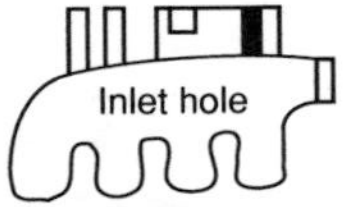

(Source: p. 37 of Takahashi, M. "Mixed Production of Truckter Factory," *Kojokanri*, Vol. 35. No. 1, Jan. 1989.)

**Figure 7-8. Work Instruction Label**

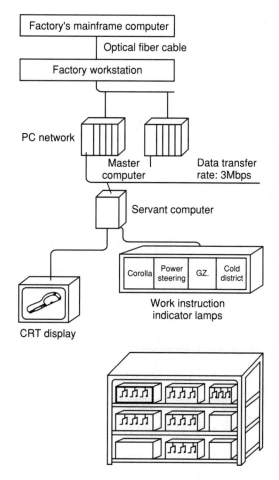

| | Work instruction indicator lamps | |
|---|---|---|
| | CRT display | Work instruction indicator lamps |
| Instructions | Screen display of color, shape, parts, etc. | Lamp display of model type, specifications, parts, symbols, etc. |
| | 1 location | 33 locations |

**Figure 7-9. Work Instruction with Specification Indicator Lamps**

tions for managing production information at all levels of the company.

Toyota establishes production sequence schedules that smooth out parts supply operations. All information regarding revisions and other changes to the schedule, as well as production results, are compiled and stored in the host computer's data banks. This system enables the head office to respond promptly to all information requests received from the company's factories and assembly plants.

The head office is also home to related information systems, such as for accounting (including cost calculation and budget management) and quality control. Toyota has made cross-referencing among these systems so easy that they are all virtually connected as one giant information system.

Please refer to Figure 7-10 as you read the following description of Toyota's new ALC system for issuing vehicle production work instructions.

The main computers at each Toyota plant are Fujitsu's FACOM-A-50 and FACOM-A-60. The FACOM-A-50 computer is connected via communication lines to the head office's IBM mainframe from which it receives data transmissions and performs communications protocol conversion. These functions make the FACOM-A-50 the plant's communications "gateway."

Data that have been converted by the gateway computer are input to the FACOM-A-60, which functions as a file server. Most of these data are parts of the production sequence schedule. The file server computer sends the head office mainframe requests for production information and manages the progress of vehicle production operations in its plant.

In Toyota's case, the process-specific line computers carry out various functions autonomously. Once a car body has received its ID tag, which is an ID unit that contains an IC card, the ID tag sends the file server a request for production

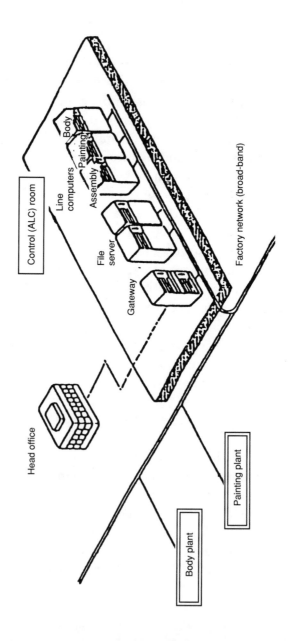

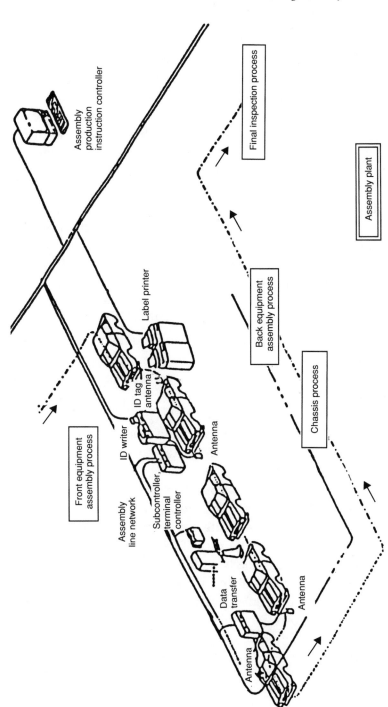

Assembly production instruction controller

Final inspection process

Assembly plant

Label printer

Back equipment assembly process

ID tag antenna

Chassis process

Front equipment assembly process

ID writer

Antenna

Assembly line network

Subcontroller, terminal controller

Data transfer

Antenna

Antenna

**Figure 7-10. Overall View of the New ALC System**

information. The file server sends the requested production information to the ID tag via the line's ID writer, which inputs the information into the ID tag. In this sense, the vehicle and the information are joined together in the line.

The most important characteristic of this new ALC system is that it works as a pull system in which each line and process in each plant requests, receives, and uses only the information it needs at the moment. As the vehicles make their way through the line, ID-tag antennas placed at strategic points on the line contact the ID tags and read information from them. This information is fed to the production work instruction controller, which controls the robots and other automated equipment on the line in accordance with the production work instructions.

## JIT'S GOALS AND FRAMEWORK

The ultimate goal of the just-in-time production system is to make the entire company a profit-making operation. Therefore, JIT's basic objective is to reduce costs to aid profitability.

The goal of cost reduction and the goal of productivity improvement are largely the same thing. The key to achieving both goals is to thoroughly eliminate waste in all its forms, including excess inventory and excess labor.

We have been speaking of costs in very broad terms. In real terms, costs are the sum of past, present, and future cash outlays, all of which must be subtracted from total sales to determine whether or not a true profit has been achieved. These costs are referred to casually as the overall production cost, which properly includes not only the manufacturing costs but also sales expenses, general management expenses, capital costs, and other costs.

Many people think of JIT production as being mostly a matter of reducing inventory. Reducing inventory costs ties in directly with cutting capital costs, but these costs are classified as non-operating expenses and not as part of the manufacturing costs. However, reducing inventory helps expose hidden problems in the factory and solving these problems via small-group improvement activities can greatly reduce waste-related costs. Therefore, reducing inventory does tie in indirectly with cutting manufacturing costs.

Another indispensable part of cutting manufacturing costs is reducing manpower needs. Therefore, it is especially important that we understand the manpower reduction techniques used in the JIT production system. In fact, it is no exaggeration to say that reducing manpower costs is a more important part of JIT production than reducing inventory.

Within the framework of cost reduction, three subgoals must be achieved to make the main goal attainable:

1. _Volume management._ The scheduling of production output volume must be flexible on both monthly and daily bases in order to be responsive to market demand fluctuations.
2. _Quality management._ A system must be established that ensures that each process sends only nondefective goods to the next process.
3. _Respect the humanity of employees._ It is not possible to achieve the goal of higher productivity (nor that of lower costs) unless the company effectively develops the talents and skills of employees, instills enthusiasm in them, and respects their humanity.

How do these goals relate to the various levels of the JIT production system? Figure 7-11 outlines the overall framework of JIT production. This system contains an output (results) section that includes costs, quality, volume, and humanity and an input section that includes the company's constituent elements. Without getting into too much detail,

Figure 7-11 outlines the relationships among the various sub-systems that make up the total system. We will discuss these subsystems one by one.

The first step is to eliminate inventory waste, manpower waste, and other waste in the factory to attain the goal of cost reduction. To do that, the management of production volume must be "flexibly responsive" to market demand fluctuations. This is a logical part of the JIT concept of making only the types and amounts of products that can be sold. When production line workers are also versatile enough in their skills to be able to switch from one line to the next as needed to meet fluctuating market demands, the result naturally will be a reduction in manpower-related waste.

## JIT AND THE KANBAN SYSTEM

The goal of flexible production volume management can be reached if the concept of just-in-time production is well implemented. The JIT concept is summarized as producing *just what is needed, just in the amount needed, and just at the time it is needed.*

Toyota has developed and employed the kanban system as a system of daily production indicators and instructions that effectively implement the concept of just-in-time production. At Toyota, the monthly production schedule described earlier in the chapter plays a central role as a fairly accurate estimate of the next month's production requirements. As such, the monthly schedule for each production process is issued to all relevant processes and parts suppliers. The production schedule for the entire company is set with the help of a number-crunching computer, which in itself is admittedly a push production approach. However, the actual production instructions that come to each production process are issued by the final assembly line. They make their way upstream to

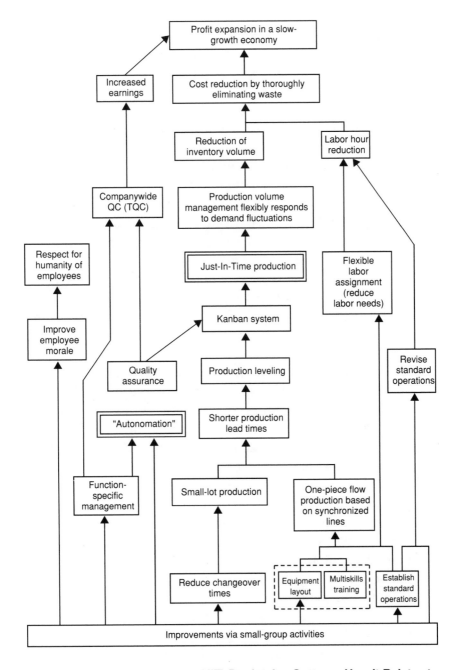

**Figure 7-11. Outline of Toyota (JIT) Production System: How It Relates to Costs, Volume, Quality, and Humanity**

earlier processes via kanban to ensure that only what is needed is sent downstream and only when it is needed. This is clearly a "pull production" approach.

Many people equate the Toyota production system with Toyota's famous *kanban* system. The two are not the same, however. The Toyota production system is group of practical methods for manufacturing products and the kanban system is a control method for ensuring just-in-time production. In other words, the kanban system is an information system that finely controls the volume and timing of production. Once all of the preconditions for the kanban system have been established (such as appropriate process design, standardized operations, and production leveling), some preliminary kanban are introduced to pave the way for full-fledged JIT production.

The Japanese word *kanban* means simply "signboard." This word was used for the system's kanban not because they are actual signboards but because they are indicators that, like signboards, require our attention.

Actually, kanban come in various shapes and sizes. Most are cards that slip into long plastic envelope-like holders. There are two main types of kanban: *withdrawal kanban* and *production kanban*. Withdrawal kanban indicate the amount of goods that the downstream process must withdraw from the previous (upstream) process. Production kanban indicate what kind of goods must be made at the previous process as well as their amounts. Kanban are cards that circulate within Toyota factories, between Toyota factories and their many parts suppliers, and also within the supplier factories. In this manner, kanban are the medium that carries information relating to the types and amounts of parts and products to be manufactured and supplied to achieve JIT production.

Let us imagine, for example, that an assembly line makes three product models A, B, and C. Parts a and b used to be manufactured on a machining line upstream as shown in Figure 7-12. Once machined, they are stored in an area behind the assembly line. Each lot of parts carries a production kanban from the assembly line.

A worker transports a set of withdrawal kanban from an assembly line geared up to assemble Model A to the machining line in order to withdraw the required number of part a's. At this point, the worker (1) exchanges the withdrawal kanban for boxes containing the exact number of part a's that the kanban indicate, (2) removes the production kanban attached to these boxes of parts, and (3) returns to the assembly line with this box of parts.

The production kanban that were removed are left at the kanban reception post at the parts store for the machining line. Because they represent a supply of parts that need to be resupplied, here they become production orders for the machining line. Remember — there is always one production kanban per box of parts.

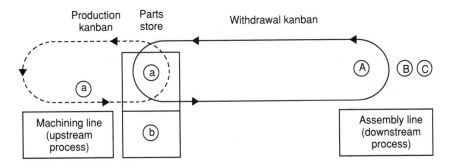

**Figure 7-12. Flow of Two Types of Kanban**

Actually, things are not quite this simple because the machining line in an actual factory constantly receive production-kanban resupply orders for both types of parts. However, this does not result in confusion. The machining line simply responds to the production kanban in the order they are received.

## CONDITIONS FOR IMPLEMENTING
## JIT PRODUCTION

To help the kanban system avoid sudden, impossible-to-meet demands for products from an upstream process or parts suppliers, factories must implement a technique called *production leveling* as a precondition for JIT production. In a nutshell, production leveling (or load smoothing) is the arrangement of mixed-flow production using several product models. This spreads out demand fluctuations among various types of parts, thereby dividing the impact of these fluctuations among several upstream sources. To implement this kind of mixed-flow production, a computer must be employed for the complicated task of figuring out the daily feed-in sequence for the final assembly line.

In turn, production leveling based on mixed-flow production can only work when there are short production lead times for all types of parts used in the products. (*Production lead time* is the time period between receiving a sales order for a product and shipping the finished product.)

The way to shorten production lead time is to produce all parts in small lots, if possible, using single-workpiece lots in a *one-piece flow production* and *one-piece conveyance* system. Although one-piece flow production is the ideal, it is more practical for some types of processes, such as press and forge processes, to handle small lots that do not exceed one day's output requirement for each part.

Small lot production rarely is achieved without reducing changeover times. Changeover operations are divided into (1) *external changeover,* or changeover that takes place while the process equipment is operating, and (2) *internal changeover,* or changeover that occurs while the process equipment is stopped. To shorten changeover time, we first turn as much internal changeover as possible into external changeover. We then find ways to shorten the times required for each type of changeover operations.

The key to achieving one-piece flow production lies in having production operations carried out by multiskilled workers who each handle a series of different processes, moving each workpiece through the series within a time period called the cycle time. Accordingly, we define *cycle time* as the amount of time needed to produce each product in order to meet the required daily output. To find the cycle time, we divide the operation time per day by the required daily output (the number of products needed per day). In JIT production, the required daily output is defined as the number of ordered products for that day. Consequently, cycle time is determined by the current market demands.

Another important precondition for one-piece flow production is what Toyota calls *standard operations*. At Toyota, standard operations includes the standardization of all operations that each of the line workers must perform in order to operate a series of processes within the cycle time. This combination of standardized worker operations is called *standard combinations*. Standard combinations make it possible to complete the manufacturing of each product within the cycle time.

*METHODS FOR REDUCING*
*LABOR-HOUR REQUIREMENTS*

Next, the company must seek to cut costs by reducing labor-hour needs. The best way to do this is to establish flexible work assignments that enable the factory to add and subtract workers from lines in accordance with the demand fluctuations shown in the monthly production schedules. At Toyota, the concept of manpower reduction revolves around whether or not operators can be removed readily from lines that experience sudden demand drops.

One precondition for labor-hour reduction capability is reforming the equipment layout into *U-shaped cells*. It is especially beneficial to have a series of linked U-shaped cells so that reductions in demand can be accommodated more easily by reducing the number of U-shaped cell operators. Each U-shaped cell operator should be a multiskilled worker who is able to handle several different types of machines in accordance with the standard operation combination chart. In so doing, the operator should be able to operate all of the processes within his or her cell, making a full circle back to the first process within the cycle time.

## *QUALITY ASSURANCE METHODS*

The kanban system is a key support for quality assurance. It clears away excess inventory and requires that the production line be stopped whenever defective goods appear one after another. In fact, the kanban system requires that only 100 percent defect-free goods be fed into and turned out of each stage of the production line.

One of Toyota's main quality control techniques is called *autonomation*, or "automation with a human touch." Autonomation is based on the development of mechanisms that can monitor production processes and detect abnormalities (defective goods or faulty production equipment). When these mechanisms detect an abnormality, they automatically stop the line and sound an alarm. Such devices help reduce manual labor and raise productivity.

After detecting an abnormality, the next step is to find and remove its root cause (usually, by making an improvement) so that the same abnormality does not recur. At Toyota, the improvements generally come from the company's suggestion system or from its small-group activities organization.

## COMPANYWIDE IMPROVEMENT ACTIVITIES

The activities of QC circles and other small improvement groups include not only developing autonomation improvements but also improving changeover methods, standard operations, and other aspects of company operations. It is safe to say that small-group improvement activities comprise the most fundamental layer of support underlying the Toyota production system. The kanban system plays a large part in giving rise to the themes pursued by these improvement groups. It does so by eliminating inventory. Inventory tends to hide various types of problems — and less inventory means that more latent problems become apparent and demand solution by small-group improvement activities.

At the same time, the improvements made by these small groups motivate group members, who are ordinary factory workers. Improvement activities not only boost worker morale but also reiterate the company's respect for the humanity of workers as creative problem-solvers.

The Toyota production system also includes companywide quality control and cost control programs that encompass everything from product planning and design to production engineering (such as equipment capacity planning and production operations) and sales activities. After all, the overall goal of the production system is not so much quality control within the narrow confines of individual company departments as it is across-the-board improvement in corporate performance and profitability. To achieve this goal, the Toyota production system targets specific functions such as quality assurance and cost reduction and calls for regular function-specific conferences that cut across departmental boundaries with a view toward improving the overall company's performance of the function in question. Toyota calls this function-specific management.

## CHAPTER 8

# International Production Strategies of Japanese Automakers

THE PAST DECADE has seen a conspicuous internationalization trend among Japan's automakers. The purpose of this chapter is to analyze the international production strategies taken thus far and to predict what course this internationalization trend is likely to take in the future.

First, let us clarify what we mean by internationalization. Some people think that merely exporting cars overseas is internationalization, while others draw the line at setting up sales companies and after-sales service centers overseas. One could even say that selling imported foreign cars is enough to make Japan's automotive industry "international." Here, however, our definition of internationalization is restricted to cases where Japanese automobile companies and automotive parts companies have set up production operations overseas, either to assemble and market finished automobiles or as suppliers of engines and other components to local automobile companies. In other words, we will focus on Japanese automotive companies that have shifted some of their production and parts procurement operations overseas as part of an international production and procurement strategy.

In the case of automakers, the costs and expertise required for overseas operations is enormous. The scope includes not only production operations *per se*, but also the construction of plants, the installation of equipment, the hiring of employees, and the development of supplier relationships. The various obstacles that lay in the path of setting up production overseas take a lot of time and effort to clear, and Japanese automakers cannot look upon overseas expansion of production as simply a matter of transplanting their domestic production systems overseas. Although they have built their success in Japan on home-grown practices such as the kanban system and affiliated supplier relationships, when moving such practices overseas these companies must be flexible and sensitive to the numerous issues related to international trade friction. Our discussion of international production strategy will also touch upon these trade issues.

The automotive industries in North America, Western Europe, and Japan are all mature industries that face a challenging future of limited growth amidst saturated domestic markets. Automakers in these countries must look to newer markets — such as in Eastern Europe and Asia — for growth potential. We will see how the international expansion strategies being employed by Japanese automakers in important markets such as North America, Korea, Taiwan, and other countries compare with the strategies of their U.S. and European competitors. We will study the goals that Japanese automobile companies have set for themselves in their overseas expansion of production and procurement. We will see what strategies they have adopted in pursuit of those goals and what their strategies are for the future. We will draw a relationship pattern describing the characteristics of various automakers in their international production and procurement strategies and study their direct production operations overseas.

## OVERVIEW OF INTERNATIONAL PRODUCTION AND PROCUREMENT

There are advantages and disadvantages to each automaker's internationalization strategy and some of the problems encountered. Six categories will be examined:

1. the acquisition of overseas companies
2. the establishment of joint-venture companies overseas
3. contracted production
4. technology transfer
5. Original Equipment Manufacturer (OEM) production
6. independent expansion

These categories all involve situations in which Japanese automakers are setting up shop in countries that already have well-developed automotive industries — such as Western Europe, North America, and South Korea. Our first case study concerns a company that independently has built and operated its own overseas production facilities. The second describes a company that formed a joint venture with a local automaker to build new production facilities. The third looks at a company that bought out a local company and used its existing production facilities. The fourth looks at indirect overseas production expansion through contracted production at a local company's facilities. The fifth looks at technology transfer between a Japanese and a local company. Finally, the sixth case study looks at a Japanese automaker that accepts supplies of finished and semifinished products from a local automaker. We will begin with the cases that show the strongest connections between Japanese and local automakers. The final case study involves the expansion of a Japanese automaker into a developing country.

## ACQUISITION

The acquisition strategy refers to a foreign automaker buying out a local automaker lock, stock, and barrel and then setting up production and procurement operations using that company's existing facilities.

Recent major examples of this strategy include the acquisition of the British automobile company Lotus by America's General Motors (1986), Italy's Maserati by America's Chrysler (1986), Spain's Seatto by Germany's Volkswagen (1986), Italy's Lamborghini by America's Chrysler (1987), and Britain's Jaguar by America's Ford (1989). There also have been acquisitions by same-country automakers, such as Alfa Romeo's acquisition by Fiat in Italy (1986) and American Motors by Chrysler in the United States (1987).

The buyers in these transactions have been America's "Big Three" (GM, Ford, and Chrysler) and some of Europe's biggest automobile companies (Volkswagen and Fiat). Note also that all of the acquired companies are small-scale manufacturers who boast a long tradition of excellent engineering in certain speciality fields, such as sports cars or four-wheel-drive vehicles. Recently, major automakers have been acquiring not only smaller automakers but also companies that specialize in various high-tech fields, such as computers or robotics.

With so many acquisitions occurring in recent years, we can assume that there must be some strong advantages in this strategy. Perhaps the greatest benefit is that acquisition is the fastest way to expand production to a new location. When one automaker buys out another, it acquires production facilities that have been operating for a long time, trained employees, production equipment, and a technological tradition that lives on in the engineering staff. These things are waiting and ready to go as soon as the acquisition deal is signed. In contrast to cases where one company uses another independent company's production facilities with little or no capital participation, a full-fledged acquisition enables the new owner to implement its own management strategy with complete freedom and maximum effectiveness.

Now, what is the downside? First, there is the question of financial risk. Needless to say, it takes a lot of money to buy out an automobile company, and the risk of not recovering the full investment rises dramatically if the buyer finds the actual benefits of the deal to be less than expected or has trouble implementing new management policies. In addition, even small automakers have considerable impact on local employment and local auto parts suppliers, and the local citizenry may be adverse to buy-outs. Generally, these factors alone have been enough to dissuade Japanese automakers from buying out overseas companies.

The following categories of overseas production strategies — namely, joint ventures, contracted production, original equipment manufacturer (OEM) production, and technology transfer — all involve some kind of tie-up with another automobile company. While tie-ups between automakers are nothing new, in recent years they have become increasingly subtle and complicated.

## *JOINT-VENTURE PRODUCTION*

This category includes cases where a foreign automaker joins with either a local automaker or with another foreign automaker from the same country to establish a joint-venture plant.

Looking at the "Japanese partner" column in Table 8-1, we can see that in most cases, the Japanese partner is one of Japan's smaller automakers, such as Isuzu, Subaru, Suzuki, and Mitsubishi. This makes sense in light of the fact that the chief advantage of joint-venture expansion is that its investment cost burden is roughly half that of direct expansion of production. In addition, the two partners share the investment risk. Another advantage is that the two partners get to share each other's production management skills and expertise. Looking at the joint-venture company, NUMMI, established by Toyota and General Motors, Toyota's strategy was to share the investment risk while testing the waters for possible further expansion of production in North America on its own in the future. NUMMI also provides Toyota with an invaluable opportunity to study firsthand how American automobile plants are managed and how labor-management relations are handled.

**Table 8-1. Major Joint-venture Production Between Japanese and Western Automakers**

| Japanese Partner(s) | Western Partner | Target Country | Production Start | Production Capacity | |
|---|---|---|---|---|---|
| Toyota | GM | U.S.A. | 1985 | 250,000 vehicles per year | Provides finished cars to both partners |
| Mitsubishi | Chrysler | U.S.A. | 1988 | 240,000 vehicles per year | Provides finished cars to both partners, scheduled to switch over to Chrysler engine production in the future |
| Suzuki Motors | GM | Canada | 1989 | 200,000 vehicles per year | About 80% of output goes to GM |
| Isuzu and Subaru | | U.S.A. | 1990 | 240,000 vehicles per year | Provides finished cars to both partners |
| Isuzu | GM | Britain | 1990 | 40,000 vehicles per year | Produces commercial vehicles only |
| Honda | British Rover | Britain | 1991 | 100,000 vehicles per year | Provides finished cars to both partners |

On the other hand, there are disadvantages in joint-venture production. First, there is the fact that the smaller the investment risk is, the smaller the potential for profit. Joint ownership also makes the prompt expansion of production output of popular automobile models more difficult. Also, even though investment costs are only about half of what they would be if the foreign company set up shop on its own, these costs are still much higher than for contracted production or other alternatives. Moreover, it takes longer to move from the planning stage to full-fledged production when there are two companies involved. This longer lead time boosts investment costs. Both companies must take the necessary time and effort to work together as partners. This is not only during the planning and construction phases, but also when dealing with the inevitable problems that arise during regular production operations — such as labor relations and local procurement policies.

### CONTRACTED PRODUCTION

Contracted production usually take the form of a foreign automaker providing capital and/or technology or joint research & development to a local automaker in exchange for producing cars to be sold under the foreign automaker's brand. This differs from OEM production in which one company's finished automobiles or components (such as engines) are used to fill a gap in another company's product line-up. The client company has no real input into the planning and production of those vehicles or components. By contrast, in contracted production, the client is always involved to some extent in developing the products it receives from the contracted company.

Let us look at some recent examples of contracted production. Our first example is a tie-up between Honda and Britain's Rover Group. In this case, Rover was contracted to produce 4,000 Honda Ballade models per year beginning in 1986. The next step concerned other models, such as the Honda Legend, which were jointly developed by Honda and Rover. The agreement was that Rover would produce all of these models destined for the European market at its own plants.

Another joint venture was made between Toyota and Volkswagen. Volkswagen was contracted to produce Toyota-brand small pickup trucks in then-West Germany for the European market. Meanwhile, in the United States, Nissan and Ford joined hands to develop several car models under both companies' brands to be produced at Ford plants for the U.S. market. Mazda also concluded a contract production deal with Ford to produce all of the Mazda-brand mini-pick-up models that previously had been exported from Japan to North America.

A common thread in all of these cases is that the Japanese partner provided technology and participated in joint product development that was restricted to certain specialized vehicle models and in relatively small volumes, with all vehicles to be marketed via the Japanese partner's sales channels. The advantages in this kind of contracted production deal are, first, that it eliminates the heavy cost and labor burden of building new production plants. Further, the small-scale production volume reduces the investment risks. Secondly, there is no need to enter sticky labor relations. The contracted automaker benefits from a boost in production and the introduction of new technology. In addition, these instances of contracted production help reduce trade friction.

The primary drawback is that these examples offer little potential for profit. However, when this disadvantage is weighed against such important considerations as the need to reduce trade friction and to cultivate better relations with overseas automakers, we can understand why Japanese automakers have made so many contracted production deals in a wide variety of specialized fields.

## TECHNOLOGY TRANSFER

Many technology transfer arrangements have been made between Japanese automakers and (1) those in developing or newly developed countries such as South Korea and Taiwan or (2) small-scale automakers in Europe and North America. In every case, the automaker who receives Japanese automotive technology or investment capital already has established a solid manufacturing base that possesses a certain level of technical sophistication and production capacity.

Such technology and/or capital is intended to help the recipient company expand production capacity and boost productivity and product quality. This kind of arrangement is currently the only one politically feasible in countries (such as South Korea and Taiwan) that are not receptive to the idea of direct production expansion by Japanese automakers. The Japanese regard technology transfer as a way to get their feet in the door for possible contracted production or other tie-ups in the future.

One way in which technology transfer differs from contracted production is that the vehicles produced as a result of a technology transfer agreement are sold by the local company under its own brand, and all sales revenue belongs to the local company. The only revenue the Japanese company who provided the technology receives is indirect revenue, such as technology licensing fees and profits from sales of exported parts. The main point of technology transfers is to help recipient companies raise their productivity, hold down costs, and improve quality to a level on par with that of Japanese, European, and U.S. automakers.

Even before receiving Japanese technology transfers, some companies in South Korea and Taiwan had developed their technology to a level where they established a niche for themselves in the subcompact sector of the North American automobile market. As they benefit from ongoing technology transfers from Japan, these companies can look forward to becoming better established as full-fledged manufacturers in their own market niches.

## OEM PRODUCTION

Original Equipment Manufacturer (OEM) production is defined as the production and delivery of entire finished vehicles or major components such as engines to another automaker that has not participated in the product's development or parts supply. The products are made completely by the supplier but are sold by the recipient under the latter's brand name. Usually, OEM production occurs when an automaker wants to market a type of vehicle that it is unable or unprepared to produce on its own. Recently, the most noteworthy examples of this have been cases in which one of America's Big Three automakers makes a deal with a Japanese, South Korean, or Taiwanese automaker to provide mass-market and subcompact models under an OEM arrangement. For instance, in the field of subcompact cars, GM has OEM deals with Japan's Isuzu and Suzuki and South Korea's Daewoo, Ford receives OEM cars from Japan's Mazda, South Korea's Kia, and Taiwan's Ford Ryuhua, and Chrysler has an OEM deal with Japan's Mitsubishi.

During the 1970s and 1980s, the Big Three responded to the fast-growing fuel-efficient subcompact and compact sectors of the U.S. market by launching programs to develop these types of cars. However, their lack of experience in these sectors, combined with high labor costs, has made success difficult. This prompted them to turn to a strategy of OEM production using Asia's low-cost subcompact automakers. In the 1980s, GM launched its Saturn project aimed at developing a new generation of compact car. By the time the first Saturn cars hit the market, however, GM had downscaled the project from half a million to 200,000 units and upgraded the Saturn's class ranking to the 2,000-cc level. (This is on par with the higher-ranked compact car class in Japan.)

In Japan, OEM production deals are not uncommon among domestic automakers. However, it is rare that an overseas automaker supplies OEM cars to a Japanese company. It is true that several Japanese car companies have purchased foreign-brand cars for sale in Japan, but these are not OEM deals — the Japanese merely are acting as import and marketing agents for the foreign-brand cars. Examples of this include the importation and sales of Germany's Opel cars by Isuzu, France's Peugeot cars by Suzuki, Sweden's Volvo cars by Subaru, and France's Citroen cars by Mazda. Nevertheless, it is possible that such arrangements may develop into OEM deals at some point in the future.

An advantage of OEM production is that the recipient company risks no investment in the production of the OEM cars and can remain flexible in renewing or canceling its OEM deals from year to year. OEM production also enables a car company to quickly introduce specialty models that it is not equipped to develop and produce on its own.

One drawback of OEM production is that OEM cars rarely fit in with the recipient company's overall design image.

Figure 8-1 illustrates the differences among the three strategies of contracted production, technology transfer, and OEM production.

## DIRECT PRODUCTION EXPANSION

Direct production expansion occurs when a company acts on its own to set up production facilities in a new location, in

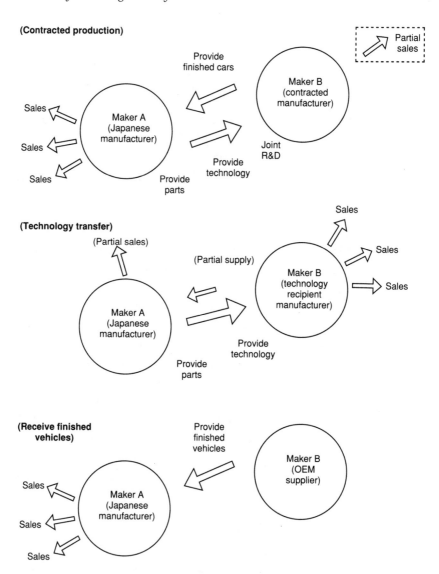

**Figure 8-1. Differences Between Contracted Production, Technology Transfer, and OEM Production**

this case overseas. Table 8-2 lists several cases in which Japanese automakers have directly expanded their production operations to North America and Europe during the 1980s to (1) reduce trade friction and (2) avoid higher domestic production costs resulting from a steep rise in the value of the yen.

The list of Japanese automakers that have directly expanded their production operations overseas is dominated by the bigger, more financially powerful companies — Toyota, Nissan, and Honda. The target countries, the United

**Table 8-2. Major Examples of Direct Production Expansion by Japanese Automakers in Europe and North America**

| Company | Target country | Factory site | Production start | Annual production capacity | |
|---------|---------------|--------------|------------------|---------------------------|---|
| Toyota | U.S.A. | Kentucky | 1988 | 200,000 vehicles | Full-fledged production of engines slated for 1991. |
| Nissan | U.S.A. | Tennessee | 1983 | 260,000 vehicles | In 1992, capacity will be raised to 400,000 vehicles and will start engine production. |
| Honda | U.S.A. | Ohio | 1982 | 360,000 vehicles | Soon will have second plant, raising capacity to 510,000 vehicles. Already has begun engine production. |
| Mazda | U.S.A. | Michigan | 1987 | 300,000 vehicles | Plans to produce engines also. |
| Toyota | Canada | Ontario | 1988 | 50,000 vehicles | |
| Honda | Canada | Ontario | 1986 | 80,000 vehicles | |
| Toyota | Britain | | 1992 | 200,000 vehicles | Plans to produce engines also. |
| Nissan | Britain | Tyne-and-Ware | 1986 | 100,000 vehicles | Already has begun engine production. |

States, Canada, and Britain, are major automobile markets that are most likely to support the large-scale local production of Japanese cars.

The advantages of this strategy are centered on the greater potential for profit that comes with such large-scale production and capital investment. The fact that these companies are going it alone in their expansion projects gives them the freedom to make rapid changes in production scale and planned vehicle models in response to changing conditions. Having local production facilities also has spin-off benefits such as improving the company's image in the local market.

As for the disadvantages, the huge investment required for large-scale direct overseas production creates a major financial risk for the company, which has a big impact on the company's management. The company must be prepared to spend many years in detailed planning and preparations before beginning production overseas. In addition, establishing large-scale production that does not include tie-ups with local automakers introduces a new major competitor on the local market, and this can create a new kind of trade friction.

## EXPANSION TO DEVELOPING COUNTRIES

Let us now consider cases in which automakers from major industrialized countries expand production to developing countries. When looking into this strategy, companies must consider the need to transfer manufacturing technology, some elements of the industrial infrastructure that may be missing in the target country, as well as the legal restrictions imposed by the target country on imported automotive products and direct investment. These factors, plus the fact that the typical developing country cannot offer a major market for automobiles, make it difficult for automakers to see any overall merit in this strategy.

Therefore, investing in developing countries, both large and small, has not been direct and independent. Instead it occurs within the framework of a consortium of companies, consisting perhaps of an automaker, a machinery manufacturer, and a financial institution, who together help build factories and provide financial assistance, install modern production equipment, and/or extend technical aid to a local automobile company. In any case, the amount of investment and scale of expansion are generally small, the project being shaped more by industrial and economic conditions in the target country than by the needs of the investors. There is no point in discussing the problems posed by different project formats.

Problems often encountered when attempting to operate these types of factories include inefficient production and low profitability due to the factories' small scale, unforeseen problems in parts procurement due to the underdeveloped state of local parts suppliers, a low level of education and skills among local workers, and restrictions imposed by the target country's government. Some countries also pose a large investment risk due to their political instability.

On the other hand, many developing countries receive preferential treatment in trade relations and other industry-boosting assistance. Any foreign automaker that helps such countries develop a stable, high-quality automotive industry can look forward eventually to enjoying a relatively low-cost production and procurement environment with potential for long-term growth.

## FUTURE DIRECTION OF INTERNATIONAL PRODUCTION AND PROCUREMENT STRATEGIES

Having examined several major examples of international production and procurement strategies undertaken by

Japanese automakers, let us look at which direction these strategies are likely to take for the future.

## THE OUTLOOK FOR INTERNATIONAL
## TIE-UPS BETWEEN AUTOMAKERS

We have already considered examples of Japanese automobile companies working with automobile companies in North America, Europe, South Korea, and Taiwan in three kinds of tie-ups: joint-venture production, contracted production, and OEM production. What directions might these strategies take in the future?

*DIRECTION 1* One direction is to make further progress in the international division of industry among companies. This means that manufacturers in various countries assume a greater share of operations for products or production processes in which they are especially competitive, such as in terms of their technological level in production, R&D, or their labor-cost advantage. The result is a global division of industry whose products are shipped to every market.

An example of the process-specific division of industry is when one country's automaker produces engines and other major components for various car models while a company in another country assembles the components into finished cars. An example of product-specific division of industry is when an automaker in one country sticks to its specialty of mass-market economy cars while one in another country turns out only luxury cars. This international division of industry has been pursued to some extent by Ford, General Motors, and Chrysler in the United States. It is a direction that involves some degree of capital participation among the member companies, and it is possible that the global auto industry will shift more in this direction as a way to ensure its survival amidst an increasingly competitive business environment.

The two categories of process-specific and product-specific division of industry are mixed in the current international industrial division as illustrated in Figure 8-2. The product-specific category can be seen in the case of subcompact cars being supplied to GM by Isuzu and Suzuki and to Chrysler by Mitsubishi. In this case, Japan is the country that currently shows the highest degree of competitiveness in the design, development, and manufacture of small economy cars. As for the process-specific category, this can be seen in the case of automotive components for certain car models in North America being supplied by South Korean manufacturers who have received technical guidance from their U.S. clients.

As a worldwide international division of industry is created, this trend may continue not only with regard to sub-compact cars and other economy cars but also in the field of luxury cars. We have already seen cases of luxury cars being made for other companies, such as in Ford's luxury-car export sales in Japan via Mazda, Opel's via Isuzu, and GM's via Suzuki. If profitable, these arrangements may develop into OEM deals in the future.

As automobile companies in South Korea and Taiwan continue to receive technology transfers, contracts for supply of parts and small cars suddenly may shift from Japan to these countries to take advantage of lower production costs. This shift already has begun at the most internationally diversified group centered on the Ford Group, as Mazda already imports and sells (in Japan) Ford cars manufactured in Taiwan. Meanwhile, South Korean automaker Hyundai is working hard to raise its technology level and already supplies parts to Mitsubishi.

*DIRECTION 2* Another strategic direction is the increasingly cut-and-dried, unsentimental nature of tie-ups among automakers. Automotive groups no longer stay so much

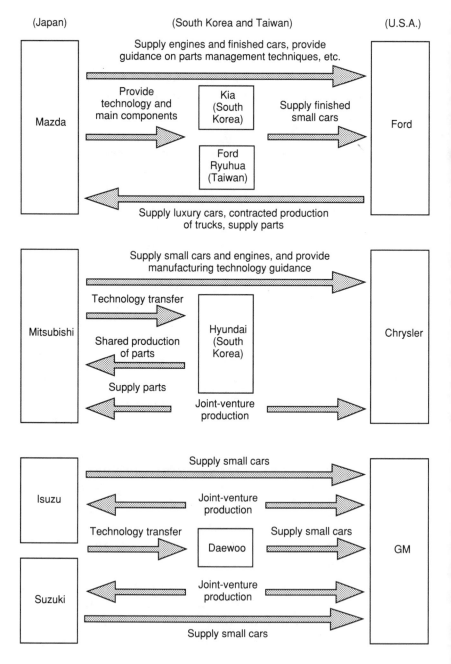

**Figure 8-2. Current International Industrial Division**

within the framework of their traditional supplier networks. Nowadays, they simply look for the best deal — even if it means joining forces with a domestic or overseas competitor.

It used to be that going outside the traditional supplier network was something only Western automakers would consider — Japanese companies remained firmly bound to their affiliated supplier system. However, Toyota was the first to break with tradition by entering into joint-venture production with GM in the United States. As the world's first and second largest automakers, they were the ultimate rivals in the automotive industry. But as explained earlier, Toyota recognized the joint-venture project as an opportunity to gain experience in U.S.-based production that could prove invaluable later on if Toyota decided to build production facilities on its own there.

GM also jumped at the opportunity to boost its small-car production while studying firsthand the legendary Toyota production system, noted for its excellence in production control, parts management, and quality control. In addition to its ties with Toyota, the GM Group has also made parts-supply arrangements with Nissan as well as commercial-vehicle production ties with Nissan via South Korea's Daewoo.

Consider also the case of Germany's Volkswagen, which has a tie-up with Toyota for commercial-vehicle production in Germany and with Toyota's main rival Nissan with regard to passenger cars. Such is the rational and completely unsentimental nature of today's global automotive industry. There are more examples: Nissan has an agreement with Ford concerning U.S.-based production of multipurpose vehicles while Ford continues to have a strong and wide-ranging relationship with Mazda in the areas of subcompact and mass-market economy cars.

Perhaps the most surprising break from the strongly group-oriented corporate tradition in Japan came when the small-scale automakers Isuzu and Subaru announced they were going to set up joint production facilities in the United States. After all, Isuzu already had been associated with the GM Group and Subaru with the Nissan Group. This did not prevent these two small companies from joining forces to improve their opportunities in the high-risk, mammoth-investment project of setting up a production plant in the United States. As one last example, we should note that broad-ranging tie-ups have been established in Australia between Toyota and GM and between Nissan and Ford.

As we can see, automakers in various countries have decided to transcend several boundaries, including corporate groupings and national borders, in a rational pursuit of tie-up arrangements that will help relieve trade friction and enable each company to concentrate on its strengths and compensate for its weaknesses in the global automotive market. We can expect similar tie-ups, based on certain car models, parts, or regional markets, to be even more common in the future.

### OUTLOOK FOR OVERSEAS PRODUCTION FACILITIES

In examining the role of the independent or joint-venture establishment of overseas production facilities in the international production and procurement strategies of Japanese automakers, we will focus on the size and strategic importance of overseas production facilities in Europe and North America.

### THE FIRST TREND

First, we can expect to see an increasing use of overseas plants to produce cars exported to a third country. For example, Japanese auto plants in Britain have been built to turn out cars not only for the British market but also for the European Community.

By contrast, Japanese auto plants in the United States and Canada have been intended to supply only the U.S. and

Canadian markets. A U.S.-Canadian automobile trade agreement has established standards for duty-free exportation and importation of automotive parts between the two countries. This bilateral agreement already has allowed a limited range of finished car import/export, a range that is expected to broaden in the future. However, considering that the Canadian market is dwarfed by the size of the U.S. market and has no automobile companies of its own, and in view of the two nations' geographical and cultural similarities, it is possible to treat the U.S. and Canadian automotive markets as one market. Although the Japanese auto plants in the U.S. and Canada began by serving only the U.S./Canadian market, some cars produced at these plants are now exported to third countries and it is likely that more will be exported to Europe or elsewhere in the future.

One case in point is NUMMI, the Toyota-GM joint venture in California that has begun exporting Corollas to Taiwan. The NUMMI Corollas exported to Taiwan are, in terms of technology and model class, ranked one step below the Corona models that are manufactured in Taiwan by Kouzei under a technology transfer agreement with Toyota. Another instance is Honda America, which now exports some of its Accord models to South Korea. In addition, Chrysler and Mitsubishi plan to export sports cars made at their American joint-venture plant to Europe. One factor that lies behind all of these third-country export strategies is the array of restrictions that various countries have placed on Japanese automotive imports in the wake of mounting trade friction. Japanese companies have used, and will continue to use, the pattern of third-country exports from U.S.-based production plants as one way to work within these restrictions. They still face various trade pressures, however, such as the call for a higher ratio of locally procured parts.

## A SECOND TREND

Other growing trends in overseas production include the "reverse import" phenomenon in which finished or semifinished vehicles are produced at Japanese auto plants overseas and then exported to Japan, while engine or other major component production is divided among two or more overseas plants. This strategy enjoys the double advantage of helping to alleviate trade friction while enabling more flexible responses to currency exchange fluctuations.

The first case of Japanese reverse imports came in 1987 when Honda began importing Accords from its Ohio plant. Mitsubishi followed suit in February 1990 when it began importing sports cars from the Chrysler/Mitsubishi joint-venture plant in the United States. The engines and some other major components in these cars were supplied previously from Japan. By the time the reverse imports began, however, the joint-venture plant had begun receiving the engines and components from other overseas plants. Also by 1987, the Nissan plant in Smyrna, Tennessee, had begun receiving engines from Nissan's plant in Mexico. This strategy helped ease trade tensions while avoiding the effects of the high yen and taking advantage of the two plants' relative proximity. More recently, the Japanese government began considering the idea of making it obligatory for Japanese automakers to establish overseas production to meet a minimum level defined as a percentage of their export volume.

As this trend continues, we will begin to see individual companies carry out their own international division of industry. It is even possible that Japanese automobile companies may assign all production for certain car models to overseas plants, from which they will be imported in reverse to Japan. Something approximating this has already occurred in the case of the sports cars that Mitsubishi imports to Japan from the Chrysler/Mitsubishi plant. Mitsubishi has never produced these cars in Japan. In addition, Mazda already has made plans to have certain sports car models produced only in America and to supply the Japanese market by reverse imports. Nissan is working out an international division of labor among its plants in Japan, the United States, and Britain for certain car models. Figure 8-3 compares the previous pattern of manufacturing and exporting with the pattern that is taking shape today.

## A THIRD TREND

A third trend worth noting is the shift toward greater independence for overseas plants. There has been a slow but steady transfer of authority from automobile company head offices in Japan to their overseas companies. This shift concerns not only decision-making authority but also the ratio of local managers to Japanese managers and the percentage of profits channeled back into the local company. Decision-making authority is being increased for overseas company managers in the area of production management as well as in other areas, such as management at subsidiaries and dealerships, marketing, and even research and development. We can expect such local independence to become even more prominent in the future.

As an example, in 1989 Toyota established its U.S. head office and transferred all of its equity in U.S.-based Toyota subsidiaries to that head office. It also gave its U.S. company the authority to manage and operate local Toyota factories, to plan marketing and sales strategies with local dealerships, and to coordinate and act as a liaison between Toyota-affiliated companies in the United States and Toyota in Japan.

Honda, the first Japanese automaker to establish production facilities in North America, has since created an independent

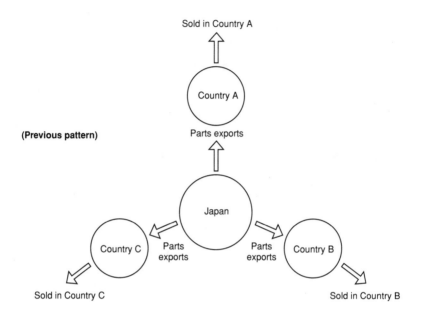

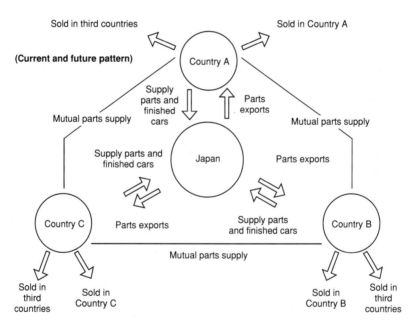

**Figure 8-3. Development of Manufacturing and Exporting Trends**

company, Honda North America, for both U.S. and Canadian markets. This company is now recognized widely both in Japan and North America as an independent local company. It has demonstrated this independence by moving on its own to build a second assembly plant. The Accords that are reverse-imported to Japan are advertised proudly as "Made in U.S.A." Honda North America makes every effort to demonstrate its success to North Americans as a successful local company. In this regard, Honda has moved beyond the strategy of an international division of labor to emphasize a strategy of making its overseas companies so strongly independent that they begin to compete with Honda in Japan.

Realizing that local developers are in closer touch with the preferences of local consumers, Japanese companies have begun to set up product development departments in their overseas companies. These overseas development departments are linked via a communications network with their counterparts in Japan to create a more efficient product development system.

## PROBLEMS AND ISSUES CONCERNING OVERSEAS PRODUCTION

This section looks at various problems and issues that have arisen as Japanese automakers carry out the overseas expansion strategies described in the previous section, including independent expansion and joint-venture expansion. We will focus mainly on examples of overseas expansion in the United States. The two issues that have been most critical in determining the success or failure of overseas production facilities are local content ratio (the percentage of parts procured from local companies) and labor relations. Other less critical issues include methods for training workers, social relations within the local community, and local perceptions regarding the Japanese staff. After describing these issues, we will see how Toyota has worked to solve them.

## PROBLEMS AND ISSUES CONCERNING THE ESTABLISHMENT OF OVERSEAS PRODUCTION FACILITIES

Local content is a pressing issue for Japanese companies that independently have set up production facilities overseas. Since beginning production operations, these companies have tried to raise the local content ratio in several ways. The growth in local production of Japanese cars and continued growth in imports have both contributed to the growing share Japanese-brand cars enjoy in the U.S. market. This share expansion has resulted in stronger demands for increasing the local content ratio.

In addition, a strong adverse reaction has been witnessed regarding the increasing numbers of Toyota and Nissan cars reaching European markets from production facilities in Britain. Toyota and Nissan face stiff opposition to this strategy of expanding their EC market shares via production bases in EC-member Britain, especially from France and other protectionist-prone European nations. The latter are seeking to impose a requirement that all cars must have a local content ratio of at least 80 percent to be recognized as EC-produced cars.

There are three ways to achieve such a high local content ratio. One way is to have the EC-based factories (in Britain, in this instance) get 70 or 80 percent of the parts from either in-house production or local suppliers. However, since most local suppliers have neither the technology nor the right equipment to provide major components such as engines and transmissions, the Japanese companies would have to manufacture these components in-house. However, in-house production would require huge investments of capital, and there probably would not be enough demand to make such investment profitable.

A second way is to buy parts from local manufacturers. After deciding that this would be the most effective approach since it would also help alleviate trade friction, Japanese companies began pursuing this policy. However, in so doing, they found that local parts manufacturers either were unable to meet their quality and delivery requirements or were unable to provide the needed parts. These problems, plus logistical and geographical ones, posed a major obstacle to recreating a Japanese-style production system that is based on the existence of top-quality parts suppliers. Rather than forcing the Japanese production system down the suppliers' throats, Japanese companies introduced technical guidance programs and recognized the need for flexibility in response to local conditions.

A third way to raise the local content ratio is to buy parts from Japanese suppliers who have also set up shop overseas. Recognizing the demand for their higher-quality and more technologically advanced auto parts, growing numbers of Japanese suppliers have set up overseas factories near their traditional clients. Naturally, a large influx of Japanese suppliers would not be welcomed by the local suppliers. To avert this kind of trade friction, many Japanese suppliers are establishing joint-venture factories with local companies.

In labor relations, there are big differences between Japanese and European/North American cultures with regard to racial identity, social customs, and attitudes toward work. These differences make it difficult to take a Japanese-style production system premised upon multiskilled workers, QC circle activities, and standard operations and apply it elsewhere. Japanese automakers setting up production facilities in the

West must work first to gain understanding from local managers and workers regarding the company's management methods and its Japanese-style production system and labor relations policies. In the United States in particular, the major stumbling block for Japanese companies in their labor relations has been reaching an understanding with the automotive industry's giant labor union — the United Auto Workers (UAW). Japanese managers realized that it was essential to reach an agreement with the UAW regarding Japanese-style labor relations.

Another important issue is personnel training. Efficient production operations depend upon a personnel training program that teaches local employees the multiple skills needed for their new jobs. Other important issues include the need for the company to contribute to the local community and to establish good social relations with people in the community. This ties in with another need, which is to establish good employer/employee relations with local workers, and to obtain their trust and encourage their loyalty and enthusiasm for the company. These human factors contribute much to the quality of products and to the efficiency of plant operations. It is important for overseas enterprises to approach these social and human factors carefully.

## HOW TOYOTA SET UP SHOP OVERSEAS

Let us examine how Toyota dealt with the kinds of issues just described when it established production facilities overseas.

First, how did Toyota establish its local parts supply network? Toyota had set a local content target of 60 percent when it started its new plant in Kentucky. One of the many reasons why Toyota chose Kentucky as the site for its plant was because it was close to Detroit, America's automotive capital. It was within sufficiently close range of not only the traditional Detroit parts manufacturers but also the manufacturers who were already supplying parts to other Japanese-run factories in the area. As part of its effort to use as many local parts suppliers as possible, Toyota contacted about 1,200 auto parts companies before opening its factory, selected sixty companies that appeared to have the needed levels of technology and product quality, and then began organizing its local parts procurement system.

In an attempt to recreate the kind of parts production and delivery system it has in Japan, Toyota sent engineers to help parts suppliers gear up for Toyota's needs such as developing new parts to meet Toyota's specifications. Toyota also planned meetings every six months, bringing representatives of all of its parts suppliers together to voice opinions, discuss problems, exchange ideas, and generally improve relations. Later, Toyota worked especially hard to develop supply contracts with local high-tech auto parts manufacturers.

These contracts enabled Toyota to add production facilities for engines and steering systems in 1987, which were slated to begin full-fledged production in 1991 with a local content ratio as high as 75 percent. In response to Toyota's difficulties in finding local auto parts companies to meet its needs, several of Toyota's main parts suppliers in Japan initiated plans to set up their own factories near Toyota's facilities in Kentucky. To avoid stirring up local resentment and trade friction, only three (Nippondenso, Toyoda Gosei, and Aisin Seiki) set up plants of their own, while other affiliated members set up facilities via joint-venture or technology-transfer deals with local auto parts companies.

How did Toyota deal with labor relations? First, Toyota chose to set up shop in Kentucky, a state with a very low UAW unionization rate. Next, Toyota built upon the relations it had developed with the UAW when establishing NUMMI. These two measures greatly reduced the number of labor relations problems to be dealt with. At NUMMI, Toyota had to accommodate GM's closed-shop union policy by agreeing to a hiring plan that made 800 of NUMMI's initial total of 1,200 employees former GM employees and that allowed 900 (75 percent) to be UAW members. This is why it took Toyota a full year of negotiations to get GM and the UAW to seriously consider introducing a Japanese-style production system.

Finally, an agreement was reached to depart from traditional union-oriented hiring practices and to adopt a Japanese-style labor agreement. This agreement reduced the number of job classifications to four. (Previously, GM had over thirty job classifications.) It also allowed the introduction of standard operations, multiple skills training, multiprocess handling, employee teams, and a suggestion system, while receiving a commitment from employees to avoid strikes. Toyota did not insist on a completely Japanese-style production system. For example, they agreed to do away with alternating day and night shifts and other practices that were seen as incompatible with U.S. lifestyles. Other compromises were negotiated and agreed upon.

How did Toyota approach the issues of personnel training? Toyota emphasizes demonstration and hands-on learning in its personnel training, and before starting production at the NUMMI plant Toyota hosted a "leaders class" in Japan for some 240 NUMMI employees. Toyota also worked out an agreement with the UAW that enabled training instructors to be sent to NUMMI from Japan. These instructors showed NUMMI employees the details of how the Toyota production system would work in their own plant.

Finally, Toyota took various measures to blend in harmoniously with the local community. Instead of following the

Japanese corporate tradition of sending employees from Japan to live near each other and without their families — a tradition that makes it too easy for Japanese employees to stick together as an insular expatriate group and does not encourage them to form friendships with local people — Toyota sent employees with their families and made sure they lived in places where their neighbors were Americans.

Toyota also established a hot line system by which local employees could make their suggestions and complaints heard. The hot line system itself is based on a suggestion made by a local employee. The system is composed of a network of hot line telephones, one at each factory or office, that employees can pick up anytime to voice suggestions or complaints. Messages are recorded on an answering machine and reviewed by the relevant managers. This system has been well received. Toyota also helps maintain good labor-management relations through traditional Japanese customs such as sending seasonal greeting cards to employees. In an American adaptation, the Christmas cards include turkey coupons.

# Notes

## Chapter 2

1. See Chapter 2 in Masaaki Imai's *Kaizen: The Key to Japan's Competitive Success* (New York: Random House Business Division, 1986). In the glossary he defines kaizen as continuing improvement in personal life, home life, social life, and working life. When applied to the workplace, kaizen means continuing improvement involving everyone — managers and workers alike. Further, he says, improvement can be defined as kaizen and innovation, where a kaizen strategy maintains and improves the working standard through small, gradual improvements, and innovation calls forth radical improvements as a result of large investments in technology.

2. See Yasuhiro Monden, *Applying Just-in-Time: The Japanese-American Experience* (Norcross, GA: Industrial Engineering and Management Press, 1986), p. 17. This is the first paper published in the United States to describe Japanese target costing and kaizen costing. (These terms literally were

translated from the Japanese terms "cost planning" and "cost improvement.")

In addition, see Y. Noboru and Y. Monden's chapter "Daihatsu Kogyo: Jidosha kigyo no genkakanri" (Daihatsu Motors: Cost management in an auto company) in Okamoto, Miyamoto, and Sakurai's text on high-tech accounting, *Haitekukaikei* (Tokyo: Doyuken, 1987). Some of this material is available in English in Yasuhiro Monden, *Applying Just-in-Time: The Japanese-American Experience* (Norcross, GA: Industrial Engineering and Management Press, 1986) and Y. Monden and M. Sakurai, eds., *Japanese Management Accounting: A World Class Approach to Profit Management* (Cambridge, MA: Productivity Press, 1989).

Also, in his article "Target Costing and How to Use It" (*Journal of Cost Management*, Summer 1989), Michiharu Sakurai covers target costing in many Japanese assembly-type industries and computer software companies.

3. See Takao Makido's chapter "Recent Trends in Japan's Cost Management Practices" in Monden and Sakurai, eds., *Japanese Management Accounting: A World Class Approach to Profit Management*, pp. 3-13.

4. See the following:

Monden and Sakurai, eds., *Japanese Management Accounting*, Chapter 2 ("Total Cost Management System in Japanese Automobile Corporations").

Yoshiteru Noboru and Y. Monden's chapter "Daihatsu Kogyo: Jidosha kigyo no genkakanri" (Daihatsu Motors: Cost management in an auto company), in Okamoto, Miyamoto, and Sakurai, *Haitekukaikei*.

5. For example, read about target development in Masayasu Tanaka's chapter "Cost Planning and Control Systems in the Design Phase of a New Product" in Monden and Sakurai, eds., *Japanese Management Accounting*.

6. Some companies distinguish VA from VE as described.
7. For example, see Takao Tanaka's "Toyota no kaizen yosan" (Toyota's kaizen budget), *Kigyokaikei*, Volume 42, Number 3, 1990.
8. For detail characteristics of Japanese-style MBO, see Y. Monden's chapter "Characteristics of Performance Control Systems in Japanese Corporations" in Monden and Sakurai, eds. *Japanese Management Accounting*, pp. 413-423.
9. Among Japanese automakers each process shown in Figure 2-7 constitutes the "process" in the process-costing system and each process is headed by a foreman.
10. Managers also have objectives of quality and productivity (efficiency or lead-time reduction) as well as a kaizen cost target.

*Chapter 4*

1. See the July 12, 1989 issue of *Seisansei Shimbun (Productivity newspaper)*, published by the Japan Productivity Center.
2. See the August 16, 1989 issue of *Seisansei Shimbun*.
3. See Kazuo Mizoguchi's *Nyumon rieki keikaku* (Introduction to profit planning). (Chuo Keizai-sha, 1980), pp. 202-205.
4. Mizoguchi, *Nyumon rieki keikaku*, pp. 208-215.
5. See Shoichi Terayama's article "Toyota jidosha: Genten jinji no daikigyo-byo o kokufuku dekiru ka?" ("Can Toyota overcome the large-company syndrome with its new streamlined personnel system?") in *Nikkei Business Magazine*, pp. 46-47.
6. See Note 1.
7. See the November 2, 1989 issue of *Nihon Keizai Shimbun* (also called Nikkei Shimbun or Japan Economic Newspaper).
8. See the November 11, 1989 issue of *Nihon Keizai Shimbun*.
9. See Note 8.

*Chapter 7*

1. See the following:

   Mitsuru Okano and Katsuo Yamamoto's "Kumitate-kako-kensa shisutemu no saishin gijutsu" (Latest technology for assembly/processing/inspection systems).

   Shigeru Watanabe and Yuzuru Akiyama, *Seisan shisutemu to saishin jidoka gijutsu* (Production systems and recent automation technologies), (1986), pp. 167- 190.

2. See Yoshinori Okada and Toshikazu Sasaki, "Matsuda in okeru seisan joho kanri no jissai" (Facts about production information management at Mazda), *Production Management* (Japan Management Association, July 1986), pp. 77-83.

3. See Kanto Information System Division, "Fukaura kojo ni okeru ALC shisutemu" (ALC system at the Fukaura plant), (Kanto Auto Works, November 1989).

4. See Eiichi Sumibe, "Sei-han ittaika o mezasu senryaku-teki joho shisutemu no tenkai" (Development of a strategic information system to integrate production and sales), *Nihon Keizai Shimbun*, September 24, 1990.

5. This material is excerpted from a presentation made by Hirotada Takahashi and Hiroyoshi Kubota, "ALC shisutemu ni tsuite" (About ALC systems), on December 12, 1990, at a seminar on the Toyota Production System held by the Tokyo Management Council.

6. This information comes from a paper by Yasuo Fukuoka, "Toyota jidosha KK ni okeru ALC shisutemu no kochiku" (Structure of the ALC system at Toyota), presented at the 1990 Fujitsu CIM Symposium in Osaka.

7. See Y. Monden, *Toyota Production System*. 2nd ed. (Norcross, GA: Industrial Engineering and Management Press, 1992).

# Bibliography

Aono, Toyosaku. Toyota hanbai senryaku (Toyota sales strategy). Tokyo: Diamond-sha, 1982.

Ban, S., and Kimura, O. "Toyota jidosha seisanbumon: Kihon nokettei to jyunansei no torikumi" (Toyota manufacturing division: Learning the fundamentals and incorporation of flexibility). *JMA Production Management* (October 1986): 13-22.

Furukawa, Eichi, et al. "Kokusai seisan seiko e no shishin o saguru" (Looking for the road to success in international production). *IE Review* (Vol. 30, No. 5, December 1989).

Honjo, Jiro. Toyota no hanbairyoku-tsuyosa no himitsu (The secret of Toyota's sales strength). Tokyo: Nisshin Hodo, 1988.

Ikari, Yoshiaki. Kaihatsu Nanbaa 179 A: Karoora no michi (Development No. 179A: The road to a new Corolla).Tokyo: Bungei Shunju, 1983.

Ikari, Yoshiaki. Toyota tai Nissan: Shinsha kaihatsu no saizen sen (Toyota versus Nissan: The leadership race in new car development). Tokyo: Diamond-sha, 1985.

Imai, Masaaki. Kaizen: The Key to Japan's Competitive Success. New York: Random House Business Division, 1986.

Japan Management Association (eds.). *Ajia NICS ni okeru kigyo senryaku* (Corporate strategies among the Asian NICs). Tokyo: 1987.

────. *Hokubei ni okeru kigyo senryaku* (Corporate strategies in North America). Tokyo: 1987.

Kaneko, Shozo. *Toyota vs. GM 21 seiki e no taiketsu* (Toyota versus GM: Showdown for the twenty-first century). Nippon Jitsugyo Shuppan-sha, 1986.

Kato, Y. "Genkakikaku-katsudo no shintenkai: Daihatsu kogyo no jirei" (New development of target costing activities: The case of Daihatsu). *Kaikei* (Vol. 138, No. 4, 1990): 46-62.

Kohno, Toyohiro. *Shin seihin kaihatsu senryaku* (New product development strategy). Tokyo: Diamond-sha, 1987.

Kusunoki, Kaneyoshi. "Kokusai jidai no seisan taio" (Production response to an international era). *IE Review* (Vol. 30, No. 5, December 1989).

Makido, Takao. "Recent Trends in Japan's Cost ManagemePractices." In Y. Monden and M. Sakurai, eds., *Japanese Management Accounting*. Cambridge: Productivity Press, 1989, 3-13.

Miles, Lawrence D. *Techniques of Value Analysis and Engineering*. New York: McGraw-Hill, 1961.

Monden, Yasuhiro. *Applying Just-In-Time: The American/Japanese Experience*. Norcross, GA: Industrial Engineering and Management Press, 1986.

────. "Characteristics of Performance Control Systems in Japanese Corporations." In Y. Monden and M. Sakurai, eds., *Japanese Management Accounting*, Cambridge: Productivity Press, 1989, 413-423.

────. "Cost Accounting and Control in the Just-in-Time Production System: The Daihatsu Kogyo Experience." In Y.

Monden and M. Sakurai, eds., *Japanese Management Accounting,* Cambridge: Productivity Press, 35-48.

———. *Cost Management in the New Manufacturing Age: Innovations in the Japanese Automobile Industry.* Cambridge: Productivity Press, 1992.

———. "Functional Management to Promote Company-Wide Quality Control and Cost Management," from *Toyota Production System.* Norcross, GA: Industrial Engineering and Management Press, 1993. Second edition.

———. "JIT seisan hoshiki to genkakeisan, genkakanri" (JIT production system, cost accounting, and cost management). *Kigyokaikei* (Vol. 40, No. 5, 1988): 24-32.

———. "Kanada ni okeru Nippon no jidosha meka to buhin meka no seisan senryaku" (Production strategies of Japanese automobile and auto parts manufacturers in Canada). *Kosei Torihiki* (Fair Trade). (No. 434, December 1986): 29-35.

———. "Seisan senryaku no kokusaika" (Internationaliz-ation of production strategies). *Corporate Management's International Strategies* by Shibakawa, Rinya, and Takayanagi, Akira. Tokyo: Dobunkan, 1987.

———. "Target Costing and Kaizen Costing in Japanese Automobile Companies," *Journal of Management Accounting Research.* (Vol. 3, Fall, 1991).

———. "Total Cost Management System in Japanese Automobile Corporations." In *Applying Just-In-Time* by Y. Monden, 171-184, and Y. Monden and M. Sakurai, eds., *Japanese Management Accounting,* Cambridge: Productivity Press, 1989, 15-33.

———. *Toyota Production System.* Norcross, GA: Industrial Engineering and Management Press, 1983.

Monden, Yasuhiro, and Sakurai, Michiharu, eds., *Japanese Management Accounting: A World Class Approach to Profit Management.* Cambridge: Productivity Press, 1989.

Morozumi, Takehiko. "Nyu moderu ga dekiru made: Serika keiretsu no baai" (The development story of the new line of Toyota Celica cars). *Motoru Fuan* (Motor Fan) (Vol. 33, No. 1, January 1990).

Nakata, Yoshinori, and Monden, Yasuhiro. "Jidosha kigyo no maaketeingu senryaku: Toyota no jirei no ronriteki bunse-ki" (Marketing strategy at an automobile company: Analysis of Toyota case studies). *Keiei Kodo* (Managerial Behavior) (Vol. 4, No. 3, 1989): 21-30.

Nissan Motor Co., Ltd. *Annual Securities Report: March 1990*. Ministry of Finance Printing Office, July 1991.

Noboru, Yoshiteru, and Monden, Yasuhiro. "Jidosha kogyo ni okeru sogoteki genkakanri system" (Total cost management system in Japanese automobile corporations) *Kigyokaikei* (Vol. 35, No. 2, 1983): 104-112.

────. "Daihatsu Kogyo: Jidosha kigyo no genka-kanri" (Daihatsu Motors: Cost management in an auto company). In *Haitekukaikei*. Okamoto, Miyamoto, and Sakurai, eds., Tokyo: Doyuken, 1987, 272-289.

Noguchi, Noboru. *Jidosha gyokai wa wndaka, shijo howa o do norikiru ka* (How will the Japanese auto industry survive yen appreciation and market saturation?). Tokyo: Nippon Jitsugyo Shuppan-sha, 1986.

Okamoto, M., Miyamoto, M., and Sakurai, M., eds., *Haitekukaikei* (High-Tech Accounting). Tokyo: Doyukan, 1987.

Roos, Daniel; Womack, James P.; and Jones, Daniel T. *The Machine that Changed the World*. New York: Macmillan, 1990.

Sakurai, Michiharu. "Target Costing and How to Use It." *Journal of Cost Management* (Summer 1989): 39-50.

Shibata, Koichiro; Omichi, Yasunori; and Ishiro, Masaharu. *Jidosha* (Automobiles). Tokyo: Nippon Keizai Shimbunsha, 1986.

Shiozawa, Shigeru. *Toyota Jidosha kaihatsu shusa seido* (Toyota Motor's development chief system). Tokyo: Kodansha, 1987.

Takeuchi, Toshio. *Jidosha hanbai* (Automobile sales). Tokyo: Nihon Keizai Shimbun-sha, 1986.

Tanaka, Masayasu. "Nihon kigyo no shinseihin-kaihatu ni okeru Genkakanri" (Cost management in the new product development of Japanese companies). *Kigyokaikei* (Vol. 41, No. 2, 1989): 19-25.

————. "Cost planning and control systems in the design-phase of a new product." In *Japanese Management Accounting*, Cambridge: Producitivity Press, 49-71.

Tanaka, Takao. "Toyota no kaizen yosan" (Kaizen budget of Toyota). *Kigyokaikei* (Vol. 42, No. 3, 1990a): 59-66.

————. "Jidosha-maker ni okeru shinseihin kaihatsu to mokuhyo-genka: Toyota no kenkakikaku" (New product development and target costs in an auto company: Target costing at Toyota). *Kigyokaikei* (Vol. 42, No. 10, 1990b): 46-62.

Toyota Motor Corporation, ed. *Annual Securities Report* (June 1982 to June 1988). Tokyo: Ministry of Finance Printing Office.

————. *Annual Securities Report* (June 1990). Tokyo: Ministry of Finance Printing Office, 1991.

————. *Sozo kagiri-naku: Toyota Jidosha 30 nen shi* (Unlimited creativity: A thirty-year history of Toyota). Toyota City: Toyota Motors, 1967.

————. *Sozo kagiri-naku: Toyota Jidosha 50 nen shi* (Unlimited creativity: A fifty-year history of Toyota). Toyota City: Toyota Motors, 1987.

# About the Author

Yasuhiro Monden is professor of managerial accounting and production management at the University of Tsukuba's Institute of Socio-Economic Planning. He received his doctorate from the University of Tsukuba, where he also served as dean of the Graduate Program of Management Sciences and Public Policy Studies.

Dr. Monden has gained valuable practical knowledge and experience from his research and related activities in the Japanese automobile industry. He was instrumental in introducing the just-in-time (JIT) production system to the United States. His English-language book *Toyota Production System* is recognized as a JIT classic and was awarded the 1984 Nikkei Prize by the *Nikkei Economic Journal*. Recent books include *Japanese Management Accounting: A World Class Approach to Profit Management* (1989) and *Cost Management in the New Manufacturing Age: Innovations in the Japanese Automobile Industry* (1992), published by Productivity Press.

Dr. Monden taught at California State University at Los Angeles in 1991 and 1992. Previously he was a visiting professor at the State University of New York at Buffalo in 1980 and

1981. He is an adviser for the Production and Operations Management Society (POMS) and has been an international director of the management accounting section of the American Accounting Association. He serves on the editorial board of the AAA's *Journal of Management Accounting Research*.

Professor Yasuhiro Monden, Institute of Socio-Economic Planning, University of Tsukuba, Tsukuba-shi, Ibaraki 305, Japan.

# Index

# BOOKS FROM PRODUCTIVITY PRESS

Productivity Press publishes and distributes materials on continuous improvement in productivity, quality, and the creative involvement of all employees. Many of our products are direct source materials from Japan that have been translated into English for the first time and are available exclusively from Productivity. Supplemental products and services include membership groups, conferences, seminars, in-house training and consulting, audio-visual training programs, and industrial study missions. Call toll-free 1-800-394-6868 for our free catalog.

### A Study of the Toyota Production System from an Industrial Engineering Viewpoint
*Shigeo Shingo*

Here is Dr. Shingo's classic industrial engineering rationale for the priority of process-based over operational improvements for manufacturing. He explains the basic mechanisms of the Toyota production system in a practical and simple way so that you can apply them in your own plant. This book clarifies the fundamental principles of JIT including levelling, standard work procedures, multi-machine handling, and more.
ISBN 0-915299-17-8 / 291 pages / $44.95 / Order STREV-B229

### Toyota Production System
**Beyond Large-Scale Production**
*Taiichi Ohno*

Here's the first information ever published in Japan on the Toyota production system (known as Just-In-Time manufacturing). Here Ohno, who created JIT for Toyota, reveals the origins, daring innovations, and ceaseless evolution of the Toyota system into a full management system. You'll learn how to manage JIT from the man who invented it, and to create a winning JIT environment in your own manufacturing operation.
ISBN 0-915299-14-3 / 162 pages / $44.95 / Order OTPS-B229

### 40 Years, 20 Million Ideas
**The Toyota Suggestion System**
*Yuzo Yasuda*

This fascinating book describes how Toyota generated tremendous employee involvement in their creative idea suggestion system. It reviews the program's origins, Toyota's internal promotion of the system, and examples of actual suggestions and how they were used. Personal accounts and anecdotes flavor the text and address problems encountered and their resolutions.
ISBN 0-915299-74-7 / 208 pages / $39.95 / Order 4020-B229

PRODUCTIVITY PRESS, INC., DEPT. BK, P.O. BOX 13390, PORTLAND, OR 97213-0390
**Telephone: 1-800-394-6868   Fax: 1-800-394-6286**

## Japanese Management Accounting
### A World Class Approach to Profit Management
*Yasuhiro Monden and Michiharu Sakurai (eds.)*

In response to innovations in manufacturing, Japanese companies have developed new management accounting techniques. Here, in 33 articles, dozens of experts reveal proven accounting practices with case studies, surveys, and the latest research. The book shows how to transform existing accounting structures into companywide cost management programs.
ISBN 0-915299-50-X / 568 pages / $65.00 / Order JMACT-B229

**TO ORDER:** Write, phone, or fax Productivity Press, Dept. BK, 541 NE 20th Ave., Portland, OR 97232, phone 1-800-394-6868, fax 1-800-394-6286. Send check or charge to your credit card (American Express, Visa, MasterCard accepted).

**U.S. ORDERS:** Add $5 shipping for first book, $2 each additional for UPS surface delivery. Add $5 for each AV program containing 1 or 2 tapes; add $12 for each AV program containing 3 or more tapes. We offer attractive quantity discounts for bulk purchases of individual titles; call for more information.

**INTERNATIONAL ORDERS:** Write, phone, or fax for quote and indicate shipping method desired. For international callers, telephone number is 503-235-0600 and fax number is 503-235-0909. Prepayment in U.S. dollars must accompany your order (checks must be drawn on U.S. banks). When quote is returned with payment, your order will be shipped promptly by the method requested.

**NOTE:** Prices are in U.S. dollars and are subject to change without notice.

PRODUCTIVITY PRESS, INC., DEPT. BK, P.O. BOX 13390, PORTLAND, OR 97213-0390
**Telephone: 1-800-394-6868   Fax: 1-800-394-6286**